**Resources**

re

D1587568

THE ROOTS OF REASON

The Roots of Reason

*Philosophical Essays on Rationality,
Evolution, and Probability*

DAVID PAPINEAU

CLARENDON PRESS • OXFORD

OXFORD

UNIVERSITY PRESS

Great Clarendon Street, Oxford OX2 6DP

Oxford University Press is a department of the University of Oxford.
It furthers the University's objective of excellence in research, scholarship,
and education by publishing worldwide in

Oxford New York

Auckland Bangkok Buenos Aires Cape Town Chennai
Dar es Salaam Delhi Hong Kong Istanbul Karachi Kolkata
Kuala Lumpur Madrid Melbourne Mexico City Mumbai Nairobi
São Paulo Shanghai Singapore Taipei Tokyo Toronto

Oxford is a registered trade mark of Oxford University Press
in the UK and in certain other countries

Published in the United States
by Oxford University Press Inc., New York

British Library Cataloguing in Publication Data

Papineau, David, 1947–
The roots of reason: philosophical essays on rationality, evolution, and probability /
David Papineau.
p. cm.
Includes index.
Contents: Normativity and judgement—The evolution of knowledge—The evolution
of means–end reasoning—Probability as a guide to life—Causation as a guide to life—
Uncertain decisions and many-minds interpretation of quantum mechanics.
1. Philosophy of mind.   2. Naturalism.   3. Reason.   I. Title.
BD418.3 P35 2003   128′.33—dc21   2002035584

ISBN 0–19–924384–0

Library of Congress Cataloging in Publication Data

Data available

ISBN 0–19–924384–0 (hbk.)

1 3 5 7 9 10 8 6 4 2

Typeset in Dante by
Cambrian Typesetters, Frimley, Surrey

Printed in Great Britain
on acid-free paper by
Biddles Ltd.
Guildford & King's Lynn

To Brit and the memory of Peter

PREFACE

This volume contains six recent papers on interconnected topics. They are reprinted here in more or less their originally published form, with the exception of 'Causation as a Guide to Life' which is a significantly expanded version of 'Evidentialism Reconsidered', first published in *Nous*, 2001.

Although I have not made any substantial revisions, I have taken the opportunity to improve what now seem to me muddy or overly cryptic passages. I have also removed repetitions of similar material appearing in more than one of the published pieces. In a couple of places I have explicitly added second thoughts in footnotes.

The original provenance of the articles is as follows.

'Normativity and Judgement', 1999, *Aristotelian Society Supplementary Volume*, 73, 16–43.

'The Evolution of Knowledge', 2000, in *Evolution and the Human Mind*, edited by Peter Carruthers and Andrew Chamberlain, Cambridge: Cambridge University Press, 170–206.

'The Evolution of Means–End Reasoning', 2001, in *Naturalism, Evolution and Mind*, edited by Denis Walsh, Oxford: Oxford University Press, 145–79.

'Probability as a Guide to Life' (written with Helen Beebee), 1997, *Journal of Philosophy*, 94, 217–43.

'Evidentialism Reconsidered', 2001, *Nous*, 35, 239–59.

'Uncertain Decisions and the Many-Minds Interpretation of Quantum Mechanics', 1997, *Monist*, 80, 97–117.

Thanks are due to the original publishers for their permission to reprint the articles in this collection, and to Helen Beebee for agreeing to the inclusion of the co-authored fourth paper. I would also like to thank the Leverhulme Foundation for the award of a Research Fellowship for the academic year 1999–2000, during which much of this material was written.

In addition, I am very grateful to the many philosophical colleagues who have helped to shape the ideas explored in these pieces. Many specific debts are acknowledged in the relevant papers. But I would like here to record a more general gratitude to the philosophical community in London. Since I first came to work here more than a decade ago, I have found London a marvellous place to do philosophy. There are many professional philosophers here, working on a wide range of subjects, but they are united by a strong collegial spirit and a willingness to collaborate intellectually. My philosophical work has benefited enormously from the constant and generous intellectual interchange I have enjoyed in London.

In particular, I would like to mention the King's College Department's Staff Seminar, which suffered early versions, of all these papers. I know that on occasion departmental colleagues have found some of my views odd, not to say cranky. But this has not stopped them all making the effort to grasp the issues I am concerned with, and invariably showing me how to understand them better.

David Papineau
February 2002

CONTENTS

Introduction

This volume contains six essays on rationality. The first two are about theoretical rationality, the rationality of beliefs, while the other four are about practical rationality, the rationality of actions.

Beyond this shared concern with rationality there is no single overarching thesis. There is, however, a methodological unity. The essays share a generally naturalist perspective—by which I mean both a readiness to attend to empirical considerations where relevant, and a disinclination to suppose that there is anything metaphysically unique about human minds.

Two particular empirical theories play a particularly prominent role in what follows. These are Darwin's theory of natural selection and quantum mechanics. Darwin's theory crops up in a number of places in what follows, if for no other reason than that it is often illuminating to note that many of the capacities underlying human rationality have been selected for their biological advantages. Moreover, Darwin's theory takes explicit centre stage in the second and third essays, which are concerned specifically with the evolutionary histories of theoretical and practical rationality.

The theory of quantum mechanics becomes relevant in the last three essays, all of which are concerned in different ways with the connection between decisions and objective probabilities. This topic in itself implicates quantum mechanics, given that any modern conception of objective probability must derive from an understanding of quantum mechanics. But quantum mechanics becomes even more directly involved in the final essay, when I argue that a satisfactory understanding of the connection between decision and probability is only possible if we adopt a specific interpretation of quantum mechanics—namely, the no-collapse theory pioneered by Hugh Everett.

Even if there is no single substantial theme running through all the essays, beyond the general concern with rationality and my commitment to methodological naturalism, there are a number of more specific threads joining some essays to others. The first two essays both hinge on a reliabilist consequentialism about theoretical rationality. The second and third, as I said, share a concern with the evolutionary provenance of theoretical and practical rationality respectively. The last three essays all pursue the issue of practical rationality against a decision-theoretic background: the fourth essay (written with Helen Beebee) defends a specific conception of the connection between objective probability and decision, the fifth then generalizes this story to cover decisions which hinge on causal information, and the sixth locates the story within the metaphysics of no-collapse interpretations of quantum mechanics.

Let me elaborate by briefly describing the contents of each essay. The first essay, 'Normativity and Judgement', disputes the widespread assumption that the normativity of judgement poses a problem for naturalism. My overall strategy in this essay is to argue that, while there are indeed norms of judgement, these are best understood in terms of reliabilist consequentialism, that is, as specifying appropriate means to the end of truth, an end which may in turn be valued for either moral or personal reasons. As I observe, this reliabilist approach assumes that truth itself can be understood naturalistically, that is, without presupposing any *sui generis* norms of judgement. While I do not in this essay directly defend the possibility of a naturalist understanding of truth, I do point out that such a naturalist approach to truth, together with the resulting reliabilist approach to theoretical rationality, avoids a number of intractable problems facing the non-naturalist alternatives which portray truth as constitutively dependent on prior norms of judgement.

The second essay, 'The Evolution of Knowledge', starts with the 'rationality debate' in contemporary psychology. This debate arises from experimental data showing that normal human beings are surprisingly prone to theoretical irrationality in many situations where we might expect them to do better. I explain how these data raise both an *evaluative* problem, about the status of our standards of theoretical rationality, and an *explanatory* problem, about the ability of humans to adhere to such standards. I then apply the perspective of reliabilist consequentialism to both these problems. In response to the evaluative question, I suggest that modes of reasoning should be counted as theoretically rational to the extent that they reliably deliver beliefs with worthwhile properties, including truth—an account which makes theoretical rationality quite independent of the possibly defective practices of ordinary humans. In response to the explanatory question, I point out that human beings are capable of reflection on their own belief-forming practices, and so in many contexts deliberately improve themselves by ensuring they get beliefs only from processes which reliably deliver true beliefs. This answer to the explanatory question is then set within an evolutionary context. I point out that this answer implicitly views high levels of theoretical rationality as a by-product of two abilities which we have good independent reason to regard as evolutionarily explicable, namely, understanding of mind and means–end reasoning. But at the end of the essay I add a further twist, and explore the possibility that natural selection may also have fostered theoretical rationality directly, and inclined us to seek out true beliefs as such.

The third essay, 'The Evolution of Means–End Reasoning', explores the possibility that there is a species of means–end reasoning which arrived relatively late in evolutionary terms, and is perhaps peculiar to human beings. The project here is partly definitional, aiming to identify an interesting sense of such higher 'means–end reasoning', and partly empirical, concerned with which abilities are present in which animals. I proceed by first considering how simpler organisms adapt their behaviour to circumstances, paying specific attention to data from associationist and ethological research, and I attempt thereby to isolate a category of means–end reasoning which is beyond the power of simple organisms. The hypothesis I develop is that non-human animals cannot piece together certain kinds of objective causal information to figure out that some novel action is a means to a desired end. The essay concludes by speculating on possible evolutionary histories by which this special power of means–end reasoning may have emerged in humans.

The subject of the fourth essay, 'Probability as a Guide to Life', is the connection between means–end reasoning and probability. The appropriateness of a choice of means clearly depends on the probability with which it will lead to desired results. But what kind of probability should matter here? One natural answer is *chance*, or objective single-case probability: on this view, an ideally rational agent should pick that action which maximizes the objective single-case probability of desired results. Helen Beebee and I agree that some notion of objective probability is needed here, but argue that the crucial notion is not chance, but knowledge-relative probability, by which we mean the objective probability of results relative to those circumstances that the agent knows about. At first this answer might seem highly counter-intuitive. But we show that it has great theoretical advantages over the alternative chance principle, in that it allows a uniform account of matters which would otherwise require separate explanation.

According to causal decision theorists, a chosen means should be apt to *cause* desired results, and not just be probabilistically correlated with them. Evidential decision theorists, by contrast, argue that there is no need to bring in the notion of causation here, and that correlations are enough, provided appropriate attention is paid to agents' knowledge of their circumstances. Given that Beebee's and my essay focuses on probabilities relative to agents' knowledge, it might seem as if I would favour the evidential view here. However, in 'Causation as a Guide to Life' I show that the issues are independent, and that a satisfactory account of rational action cannot ignore causation. There is great scope for confusion here. The evidential view may seem to be favoured over the causal alternative both by the view that causal facts can be reduced to probabilistic facts, and by the view that causation should be explicated in terms of the recently popular technical notion of 'intervention'. However, I show that these appearances are illusory, and that you should adhere to causal decision theory, whatever views you hold on these further matters.

The final essay starts with an old conundrum. Why choose the action that will *probably* lead to success, when what you want is *actual* success, rather than probable success? I show at some length both (*a*) that there is no non-question-begging answer to this question, and (*b*) that it is very curious that this should be so. I then describe the 'many-minds' interpretation of quantum mechanics, and show that the puzzle simply disappears if we accept the many-minds view. I draw no explicit moral. The many-minds theory is so counter-intuitive that it is difficult to take seriously. But it does have independent motivation in the philosophy of physics. Given this, it is at least noteworthy that it also dissolves one of the most deep-seated and difficult conundrums in the philosophy of probability and action.

I

Normativity and Judgement

1 Introduction

It is widely assumed that the normativity of conceptual judgement poses problems for naturalism. Thus John McDowell urges that 'The structure of the space of reasons stubbornly resists being appropriated within a naturalism that conceives nature as the realm of law' (1994: 73). Similar sentiments have been expressed by many other writers, for example Robert Brandom (1994: p. xiii) and Paul Boghossian (1989: 548).

In this essay I want to dispute this widespread view. I am not going to deny that there are norms of judgement. My thesis will only be that such norms raise no special problems for naturalism. The normativity of judgement can as easily be accommodated by naturalists as by anybody else.

Let me begin by fixing an agreed subject-matter. By norms of judgement I mean true statements about the way judgements *ought* to be made.[1] I take it to be uncontentious that there are many truths like this.

[1] And by judgements I mean beliefs and their linguistic expression

However, while I accept that there are many such truths, I do not accept that there is a species of normativity peculiar to judgement. My general strategy in this essay will be to argue that all norms of judgement are derived from moral or personal values, and do not involve any *sui generis* species of judgemental normativity.

A central role here will be played by the end of truth. I shall contend that the most significant[2] norms of judgement can be viewed as prescriptions to the effect that, in order to achieve the truth, you ought to judge in such-and-such ways. In my view, there is nothing constitutively normative about the end of truth itself. So I take the force of these prescriptions to derive from independent moral or personal reasons for attaching value to truth.

Thus truth may in some (or possibly all) contexts have a *moral* value. Alternatively, people may sometimes simply *want* the truth, for whatever reason. In either case, these evaluations will imply truths of the form 'you ought to judge in such-and-such ways'. In the former case, these will be derived moral oughts, about how to achieve the morally valuable end of truth; in the latter case, they will be derived hypothetical imperatives, about how to achieve the personally desired end of truth.

Of course, both these 'oughts' raise further questions for the naturalist. Most obviously, in the moral case the naturalist needs to explain how moral value itself is possible. There is also a less obvious difficulty about the second case, namely, to explain the status of the 'you *ought* to *Y*' that seems to follow from 'you want *X*' and 'action *Y* is necessary for *X*'.[3]

(though until Section 7 I shall use 'judgement' to refer specifically to beliefs). In this essay I shall stay silent on the issue of exactly which mental attitudes qualify as beliefs, and in particular on whether moral attitudes do.

[2] At the end of Section 5 I shall say something about norms which relate to truth-independent aspects of judgement.

[3] When I first started working on this essay I assumed that these hypothetical 'oughts' at least could be taken for granted by naturalism. More

However, neither of these difficulties is peculiar to the context of conceptual thought. The issue of moral value arises generally, not just in connection with norms of judgement, as does the more subtle problem of understanding hypothetical 'oughts', as in 'you ought to tune your car well, if you want it to go fast'. So, if there are problems facing the naturalist here, they are not problems occasioned by the special nature of conceptual judgement.

Moreover, both these problems arise for philosophers of all kinds, and not only for naturalists. The nature of moral values presents a puzzle to all philosophers, as does the problem of understanding the 'oughts' in hypothetical imperatives. So naturalists will have no more problems than any other philosophers, if they can reduce the normativity of judgement to derived moral or hypothetical prescriptions.

specifically, I assumed that there is a sense in which (i) '*A* ought to *X*' is an analytic consequence of (ii) '*A* wants *Y*' and (iii) '*X* is necessary to *Y*'. Given that there is nothing naturalistically problematic about facts of kinds (ii) and (iii), I therefore took it that there can be nothing naturalistically problematic about claims of kind (i): maybe such claims don't feature a *moral* 'ought' (maybe they involve a kind of pun on 'ought'), but even so they are analytic consequences of (ii) and (iii). More recently, however, I have been persuaded by a paper by John Broome (forthcoming) that this doesn't work. Broome shows that there is no special non-moral 'ought' that can be analytically derived from (ii) and (iii), because no 'ought' of any kind can be so derived. The only prescription in play is 'You ought, if you want *Y* (and *X* is a means), to perform *X*'. The non-conditional prescription 'You ought to *X*' cannot be detached. Broome draws an analogy. 'Necessarily, if John is married, he has a wife.' We ordinarily then say, knowing that John is married, that 'John must have a wife'. But this obviously doesn't mean that 'John *necessarily* has a wife'. It is simply an elliptical statement of the necessary conditional. No non-conditional modal claim can be detached. Similarly, Broome shows, 'You ought to *X*' is often elliptical for 'You ought, if you want *Y* (and *X* is a means), to perform *X*', and not itself detachable. This thus leaves us with the task of explaining the unreduced 'ought' which governs this prescriptive conditional.

For both these reasons, I will be content if I can persuade you that norms of judgement are derived prescriptions orientated to moral or personal values. I accept that there are philosophical problems attached to both these kinds of derived prescriptions. But these problems arise across the board, and for all philosophers.

The plan of this essay is as follows. In the next section I shall explain how my approach to the normativity of judgement presupposes a naturalist view of content. In Sections 3 to 5 I shall argue that my approach avoids three problems facing alternative views. Section 6 elaborates some of these points within the context of specific theories of content. Section 7 then asks whether the linguistic embodiment of judgements raises further problems for the naturalist.

Questions relating to linguistic norms will be postponed to this final section. Until then I shall assume that judgements are mental items, and moreover that their normativity is independent of any norms of language. This is a matter of expository strategy, not of any metaphysical commitment to a realm of pre-linguistic thought. As the final section will make clear, I am happy to allow that some judgements are in part constituted by norms of language. However, it will be helpful to proceed in stages, first showing how naturalism might account for non-linguistic norms of judgement, and then adding in the complexities that arise with language.

2 Norms and the Theory of Content

The approach I have just outlined assumes there is nothing essentially evaluative about truth itself. Truth is in the first instance a descriptive property, like car-speed or celibacy. Like car-speed or celibacy, it may be personally desired or morally valuable, in given contexts, but that is additional to its nature.

Here I am taking an implicit stand on the analysis of truth-conditional content. In particular, I am taking a stand against those approaches to content which place normativity *inside* the analysis of content, in the sense that they presuppose *sui generis* norms governing judgement in explaining truth-conditional content, and hence truth.[4] Let us call theories of this kind 'non-naturalist' theories of content. Neo-verificationist and Dummettian approaches to content are of this kind, since they take content to depend on the conditions in which you are *entitled to assert* a claim. So also are Davidsonian theories of content, which take content to depend *inter alia* on facts about when it is *reasonable to form* a belief.

From the point of view of such non-naturalist theories of content, the approach to normativity outlined in the last section will seem deficient, for that approach takes truth-conditional content and truth as given, prior to any issues of normativity, and then analyses norms of judgement as arising only when moral or personal value is attached to truth. Non-naturalist theories will regard this approach as necessarily ignoring the prior norms which play a role in constituting truth. Instead of explaining truth in terms of normativity, non-naturalists will complain, I am trying to explain normativity in terms of truth.

Still, this charge does not worry me, given the availability of a number of accounts of truth-conditional content which do not assume normativity in explaining truth-conditional content. I shall call theories of this kind 'naturalist' theories of content, and have

---

[4] Let us agree, against the deflationists (cf. n. 6 below), that a substantial account of truth-conditional content is presupposed by the notion of truth. We can also agree that, once we have such a substantial account of truth-conditional content, then truth itself falls out without further ado. Thus those who are prepared to reify truth conditions can simply say that a judgement is true just in case its truth condition obtains. And those who would rather not reify truth conditions, like myself, can note instead that a substantial account of truth-conditional content will imply, together with further facts, claims of the form 'this judgement is true iff *p*', for any given judgement, and will therewith specify what is required for any given judgement to be true. (Cf. Papineau, 1993: 83–6.)

in mind here such theories as indicator semantics (Stampe, 1977; Dretske, 1981), success semantics (Whyte, 1990, 1991), teleosemantics (Millikan, 1984, 1993; Papineau, 1984, 1993),[5] and Fodor's 'asymmetric dependence' theory of content (Fodor, 1987, 1990). All of these theories offer to explain truth-conditional content without any commitment to prior norms governing judgement.[6]

[5] Some readers may be wondering why I have classified teleosemantics as a theory that analyses content independently of norms. For many teleosemanticists take the view that their theory does indeed trade in norms, in particular 'biological norms', and that for this reason teleosemantics offers an immediate solution to the apparent conflict between naturalism and normativity (cf. Millikan, 1990; McGinn, 1989). However, I find this implausible. Although I myself uphold the teleosemantic theory of content, and so regard it as the right source for the sort of naturalist content I need for my own approach to normativity, I don't think that the teleosemantics itself says anything about norms, nor therefore anything about how to reconcile normativity with naturalism. Whatever norms are, I take it that they must involve some kind of *prescription*, some kind of implication about what *ought* to be done. This simply isn't true of the biological facts on which the teleosemantic theory rests. There is nothing wrong, I suppose, in talk of 'biological norms', if by this you mean simply that we have been designed by natural selection to operate in a certain way. But these biological 'norms' aren't norms in any prescriptive sense. It is a vulgar, and indeed dangerous, error to infer, from the premise that X has been biologically designed to Y, that in some sense X *ought* to Y. My knuckles have arguably been biologically designed to hit people with, but it doesn't in any sense follow that I ought so to use them. Again, a number of human male traits have undoubtedly been designed to foster sexual predatoriness, but it doesn't follow that men ought to be sexually predatory. Similarly with teleosemantics and judgement. As a teleosemanticist I hold that our beliefs have been biologically designed to track their truth conditions. But I don't think that this does anything to show they *ought* to do this.

[6] What about 'deflationary theories', by which I mean theories which combine the thought that truth falls out of content (cf. n. 4 above), with the suggestion that the device of disquotation (plus the idea of meaning as use) removes any need for a substantial account of truth-conditional

Given that views about normativity interact with general questions about content in this way, an obvious dialectical problem faces this essay. It seems that I won't be able to say anything useful about normativity without first establishing the right overall theory of content. Yet clearly there is no question of adjudicating fully on the right theory of content in this relatively short essay. Because of this, my primary thesis will perforce be conditional: *if* you have a naturalist theory of content, *then* you can explain norms of judgement as derived prescriptions orientated to the end of truth. Still, having said this, I do think that the line developed in this essay gives us some purchase at least on the larger issue of which approach to the theory of content is correct.

Most obviously, my line directly blocks the argument that naturalist theories of content are inadequate because they cannot account for the normativity of judgement. From the perspective of this essay, this argument begs the question. I am happy to agree that *non*-naturalist theories of content imply the existence of prior judgemental norms that resist appropriation 'within a naturalism that conceives of nature as the realm of law', in that non-naturalist theories postulate a peculiar species of content-constituting norms which appear mysterious from a naturalist perspective. But naturalist theories of content don't accept the existence of such special content-constituting norms, since naturalist theories explain content without any reference to such prior norms. They place the norms of judgement *outside* the theory of content, and hold that content and truth are constituted independently of facts of the form 'you ought to judge in such-and-such ways'. Given this, they can then account for such norms of judgement straightforwardly, holding that all the 'oughts' involved are derived oughts,

content? (Cf. Horwich, 1990.) I doubt that such theories will work (Papineau, 1993: 84–5), but as far as I can see there is no reason why deflationists should not agree with me on all the issues in this essay. After all, they don't assume anything in explaining content, so *a fortiori* don't assume prior norms.

arising when moral or personal value is attached to the independently constituted aim of truth.[7]

So the line defended in this essay directly blocks an argument *against* naturalist theories of content, namely, that they cannot account for the normativity of judgement. However, I also feel that it provides some positive support *for* such theories. This is because the naturalist approach dissolves a number of awkward problems about normativity facing non-naturalist theories of content. This isn't of course a conclusive argument. There may be further overriding considerations in favour of non-naturalist theories of content, in which case we will simply need to face up to the problems of normativity they generate. But it surely counts against non-naturalist theories of content that they generate difficult problems that do not arise for their naturalistic rivals.

In the next three sections I shall identify three such problems. The first relates to the *universality* of the requirement to seek the truth. The second relates to the *status* of norms of judgement. The third relates to animals, children, and other *unrefined beings*.

In this section I have explained how my naturalist approach to normativity stands opposed to non-naturalist theories of content, theories which explain content and truth in terms of norms of judgement, and so cannot in turn explain those norms in terms of truth. However, my approach to normativity will also be opposed by some philosophers who do not embrace such non-naturalist theories of content. I have in mind here those epistemologists who defend 'internalism', in the sense of upholding normative

[7] To avoid terminological confusion, let me make it clear that this is meant as an explanation of how naturalists *ought* to deal with normativity, not of what they actually say about the issue. I don't want to count a writer like Millikan as a non-naturalist, just because she adopts what I take to be the mistaken view that judgemental norms are present *inside* their theory of content (cf. n. 5 above). In my terminology, then, a theory of content is naturalist if it doesn't in fact commit us to prescriptive norms, whatever its proponents may say about this.

requirements on knowledge or justification that cannot be explained in terms of the pursuit of the external aim of truth. Such philosophers need not suppose that these 'internal' norms play any part in constituting content and truth (indeed they could embrace one of the naturalist theories of content listed above). But they would still deny my claim that the normativity of judgement can be fully explicated in terms of the pursuit of truth.

My main target in this essay is the resistance to naturalism arising from non-natural theories of content. In the space available I cannot also seriously address the motivations for epistemological internalism, and I shall not refer explicitly to such internalist views in what follows. Even so, some of the problems I shall pose seem to me to raise difficulties for epistemological internalists as well as for non-naturalists about content. In particular, the next two sections seem to me to raise such difficulties, even though the third problem, of unrefined beings, does not.

3 Is There a Universal Requirement to Seek the Truth?

I have contrasted naturalist theories, which place normativity *outside* the theory of content, with non-naturalist theories, which place it *inside*. In this section I want to point to a prima-facie reason for thinking that the naturalists are putting normativity in the right place.

Consider people who aim deliberately to mislead themselves. Suppose an elderly man realizes that he is likely to be upset if he learns about the real probability of his developing cancer, and so arranges to avoid any evidence that might undermine his sanguine belief that this probability is low. Or suppose an adolescent youth learns that people with an inflated view of their own worth are generally happier and more successful, and so deliberately seeks out evidence which will make him think overly well of himself. Of course, there are familiar psychological difficulties about deliberately arranging to have false beliefs, but examples like this suggest they are not insuperable.[8]

Are these people acting wrongly? Of course, they aren't doing what they need to, *if* they want their beliefs to be true. But by hypothesis they don't want their beliefs to be true. So is there any other sense in which they are proceeding improperly?

It is not obvious to me that there is. I would say that it can sometimes be quite proper, as in the above examples, not to be moved by the aim of truth. However, if this is right, then there is a problem for those non-naturalist theories of content that explain content in terms of normativity, and so place the norms governing judgement inside the theory of content. For such theories make it constitutive of your possessing a belief with a certain truth condition that you be subject to norms which are apt to guide you to the truth.[9] In particular, if you believe that you have a low chance of cancer, or that you are are blessed with above-average attributes, then the norms which constitute these beliefs will apply to you, and so you won't be thinking as you ought to, if you have formed those beliefs with due regard to normatively authorized evidence.

Let me be clear about the difficulty I am raising here. The complaint is not that non-naturalist theories of content suppose an *indefeasible* requirement to seek the truth at all costs. Prescriptions can compete, and there is no reason why the prescriptions required by non-naturalist theories of content should not be overridden by

[8] Note that these examples involve the manipulation of belief by the deliberate avoidance or pursuit of evidence, not any deliberate refusal to tailor your beliefs to the evidence you already have. I agree that cases of this latter kind are of doubtful psychological possibility. It is intriguing to consider exactly why this should be so.

[9] Here I assume that the non-naturalists' putative content-constituting norms will include truth-conducive norms. Some possible non-naturalist theories of content might lack this feature, as I shall observe in Section 6. But it is common to all actual non-naturalist theories, and in particular to theories in the Dummettian and Davidsonian traditions.

other considerations, such as the desirability of not upsetting your-self unnecessarily. My objection is to the weaker claim, to which non-naturalist theories of content do seem to be committed, that there is always *some* reason to seek the truth, even if it can be over-ridden. For even this weak claim seems to me implausible. Why should we suppose that the elderly man, or the adolescent youth, are in any sense obliged to comport their beliefs to the evidence? It doesn't seem to me that they are violating any prescriptions at all by adopting their entirely sensible strategies.

Note how there is no difficulty here if you adopt the naturalist view that all 'oughts' relating to judgements are derived oughts, arising because personal or moral value is attached to truth. For there is no obvious reason to suppose that derived 'oughts' of either of these kinds apply to cases like the elderly man or the youth. They don't want the truth, and it is not obvious that they are transgressing any moral boundaries in avoiding it. The natu-ralist view thus makes space for the possibility that people who aim to avoid the truth may nevertheless be acting entirely properly.

Perhaps some readers will wonder whether it is as easy as I am suggesting to lack personal or moral reasons for seeking the truth. Isn't there always at least some personal or moral reason for want-ing the truth? I am doubtful about this, but note that, even if I am wrong here, this won't really help non-naturalism. For non-natu-ralists are committed to the view that the elderly man and adoles-cent youth are proceeding improperly, *whether or not* there are moral or personal reasons for them to seek the truth. After all, non-naturalists believe in *sui generis* norms of judgement, which prescribe the pursuit of truth independently of moral or personal considerations. It is this underlying commitment to *sui generis* norms that I am objecting to, not the idea that there may always be reasons of some kind for pursuing the truth.

Still, even though it is not directly relevant to my line of argu-ment, it will be instructive to digress briefly, and consider whether it is indeed possible to lack any moral and personal reasons for seeking the truth. On the question of personal reasons, it might seem that there is at least one sense in which everybody has a personal reason to pursue the truth (even if they themselves suppose, like the elderly man or adolescent youth, that they will be better off without it). For doesn't it remain the case that everybody will be better able to satisfy their desires, whatever they may be, if their beliefs are true? Well, I agree that *if* you act appropriately on true beliefs, then your actions are guaranteed to satisfy your desires, and indeed I take this pragmatic connection to be a crucial component in the analysis of truth-conditional content (Papineau, 1993: ch. 3.6–3.7). And this pragmatic connection does mean that there is always a species of derived personal value to having true beliefs that are relevant to action, for such truth will always help you to find a way of satisfying whatever desires you have.

However, this prescription only applies to those beliefs that *are* relevant to your actions, and so provides no reason at all for your wanting truth in beliefs which are not so relevant.[10] For example, if the elderly man cannot do anything about cancer, then his belief about his chance of developing it is unlikely to influence any of his actions, and it won't therefore matter to his success in satisfying his desires whether this belief is true or not. More generally, while we can agree that everybody has an interest in seeking the truth on action-relevant matters, such pragmatic considerations do nothing to show that people cannot quite sensibly avoid the truth on other issues.

So our personal desires need not always give us reason to pursue the truth. What about morality? Might it not be that the truth is always to be morally valued? Well, while it is uncon-

---

[10] Note also that the pragmatic connection with successful action is by no means the only possible reason for personally wanting truth. You could want the truth for any number of reasons, or indeed for none. (In Section 7 below I shall explain how the institution of language in particular provides one specific reason for wanting true beliefs.)

tentious that the truth is morally valuable in some contexts (it is clearly morally valuable that we should have true beliefs about the dangers of smoking, for example), it is by no means obvious that it is *always* morally valuable. Does it matter *morally* if musicologists are mistaken about the drummer on Elvis's first Sun session? Or again, does it matter morally if the elderly man remains hopeful that he won't get cancer, or that the youth thinks he is more estimable than he is?

Of course this issue deserves further discussion. It may well be that reflection on the overall role of truth in human life, its importance for social institutions, and so on, might show us that we always have a moral duty to respect the truth. Still, as I said earlier, even if this is so, it won't really help my non-naturalist opponents. For they are committed to truth having a value independently of any such considerations. They put the value of truth inside the theory of content, not outside with moral values. And this seems wrong. If further reflection were to show us that truth is *not* always of moral value, then in what sense would the elderly man or adolescent youth necessarily be acting wrongly in ignoring it?

4 The Status of Judgemental Norms

I am aware that the points made in the last section will carry little dialectical force against non-naturalists. For clear-headed non-naturalists can simply repeat that their putative 'oughts' of judgement are special, quite different in kind from moral or personal 'oughts'. So, whether or not the elderly man and adolescent youth are not doing anything wrong by ordinary moral or personal standards, they will still be acting wrongly in a further sense, by violating the *sui generis* norms of judgement.

Even so, it has been worth rehearsing these issues, for they serve to highlight the peculiar status of the non-naturalists' putative norms of judgement. If these norms are quite distinct from moral or personal 'oughts', then where do they come from? What kind of fact is it that we categorically 'ought' to reason in certain ways? And whence does the guiding force of these 'oughts' derive—why *should* we reason in these ways? I know that I should do what is morally required. And there is an obvious sense in which I should do what will get me what I want. But I find myself in difficulty understanding why I should be moved by the non-naturalists' putative *sui generis* norms of judgement.

Thinkers in the non-naturalist tradition have in effect addressed this issue, but it cannot be said that they have arrived at any canonical answers. I have in mind here the discussion surrounding Wittgenstein's 'rule-following considerations'. This is not the place to unravel all the different strands of that discussion, many of which are to do with issues of language. But I take it that one central issue which remains, after we put issues of language to one side (cf. Boghossian, 1989: 514), is the question of why we ought to judge so-and-so on specific occasions. Why ought we to judge that *these* things are *green*? Why ought we to judge that *1,002* is the result of adding 2 to 1,000?

When we focus on this issue, non-naturalist theories seem to have little room to manoeuvre. It doesn't seem right to explain these 'oughts' in terms of individual dispositions. The fact that I am typically disposed to judge that certain things are green, say, doesn't make these judgements right, for I may be systematically prone to error. Nor does it help to widen the issue to some larger community, for whole communities too can be prone to error. In the end there seems to be little alternative for the non-naturalist except to hold that the norms of judgement are primitive and not to be further explained (McDowell, 1984). This seems unsatisfactory. Even if we can't reduce judgemental norms to other kinds of facts, it is surely desirable that we should have some kind of understanding of the peculiar force that judgemental norms are supposed to exert on us.

Once more, none of these difficulties about the status of judgemental norms arises on the naturalist line I am advocating. On my view, what makes it the case that you ought to judge in certain ways on specific occasions is that this will be a means to your judging *truly*. There is nothing circular about this analysis, provided truth itself can be analysed without appealing to norms of judgement, and the adoption of truth as an aim in turn explained by reference to moral or personal value attached to truth.

From my perspective, then, difficulties about rule-following are peculiar to non-natural theories of content. If you want to explain truth-conditional content in terms of norms governing judgement, as non-natural theories of content do, then you need to explain the source of these norms before you explain content, and it is not obvious there is any good way of doing this. But this problem simply does not arise for naturalist theories of content. They can explain content without mentioning norms. And then, given this, they can happily place norms of judgement outside the theory of content, as prescriptions which follow once moral or personal value is placed on truth.

Some readers may be wondering whether the naturalists' norms can suitably *guide* thinkers. We need norms of judgement not just to set a standard, but also to show thinkers how to conform to this standard. But bare prescriptions such as 'you should judge truly', or even such more specific imperatives as 'you should judge *green* of green objects', 'you should judge *n plus 2* when asked to add 2 to *n*', would seem not to fit this bill. They may articulate the aim of judging truly, either generally or on more specific matters, but they are not going to help thinkers who need guidance on how to achieve this aim.

This query calls for much detailed analysis, some of which will be sketched in Section 6 below. But at this stage let me merely observe that the adoption of a given end will standardly generate derivative norms about appropriate means to that end. Just as the adoption of car-speed as an end generates the prescription 'you ought to tune your car well', so will adoption of truth as an end generate prescriptions about means of arriving at truth. The reliabilist tradition in epistemology becomes relevant at this point. This tradition is concerned to identify belief-forming methods that generally produce true beliefs as output. These are just the kind of methods that you *ought* to use, if value is attached to truth. I would argue that inductive logic, deductive logic, standard observational procedures, and many other modes of reasoning are reliable methods in this sense. So, by derivatively prescribing these methods as means, the naturalist approach to normativity does not just assume truth as an aim, but also generates advice about how to achieve it.

At this point it is worth observing that reliability for truth is not the only desideratum that can be placed on belief-forming methods. At least two others offer themselves. It will normally also be desirable that our belief-forming methods are *important*, in the sense of delivering informative beliefs on matters of concern, and *economical*, in the sense of not using large amounts of time or other resources. Both these desiderata will generally pull against the requirement that belief-forming methods should deliver only true conclusions. Moreover, any moral or personal considerations that call for reliability are likely also to call for importance and economy, so that some joint optimization of these mutually conflicting desiderata will usually be required.

For naturalists, then, reliability for truth is simply one potentially valuable feature of belief-forming processes, alongside importance, economy, and possibly others. This marks a further contrast between the naturalists and their opponents, a further sense in which those norms of judgement which relate to the aim of truth are not *sui generis* for naturalists. For naturalists, truth-conducive norms of judgement constitute just one dimension among a number of possible ways of evaluating belief-forming methods. These norms have no special status which distinguishes them from evaluations orientated to further desiderata like importance and economy. This might seem odd to philosophers brought up to focus on truth-related issues, but it seems to me just the right attitude. There seems no good reason to privilege the desideratum of reliability for truth over others when we evaluate methods of belief-formation. True, an economical method that generates lots of important falsehoods is not generally worth much. But neither is a reliable method that consumes costly resources in generating trivialities.

Having said this, naturalists will do well to concede a significant terminological point to their opponents. When we consider whether a belief is 'justified', or constitutes 'knowledge', we evaluate the methods behind it purely from the perspective of reliability for truth, and in abstraction from such issues as importance and economy. Imagine a man who spends a month counting the individual blades of grass in his garden. We will no doubt feel this is a complete waste of time, and that the conclusion is of no possible interest to anyone, yet we will not say on this account that he does not *know* how many blades of grass there are, nor that his belief in their number is not *justified*.

It is striking how these central epistemological notions are exclusively truth-focused in this way. I am inclined to think that this tells us something about the central importance of truth-seeking for human society (cf. Essay 2, Section 10). Still, we can recognize this importance, and the epistemological terminology it carries in train, without supposing that there is some special type of normativity attaching to the aim of truth.

5 Unrefined Thinkers

Let me turn now to another respect in which naturalist theories of content fare better than non-naturalist ones. On the face of it, many beings who do not observe truth-conducive norms of judgement nevertheless seem to have contentful beliefs. The most obvious examples are higher mammals and very young children, who often act in ways that seem to call for the attribution of beliefs, but seem in no obvious sense to be observing norms of judgement. This poses a prima-facie problem for those non-naturalist theories which make sensitivity to such norms a precondition of the possession of contentful beliefs.

In addition, some grown-up human beings pose a similar problem for non-naturalist theories of content. I am thinking here of the large body of psychological literature which suggests that normal humans characteristically violate principles of logic, elementary probability theory, and so on (cf. Cherniak, 1986; Stein, 1996). In this case it is not just that the believers lack the sophisticated abilities required to observe norms. They have the intellectual wherewithal, yet simply fail to apply it to the pursuit of truth. If this is right, then again we have a prima-facie problem for those theories which make sensitivity to truth-conducive norms constitutive of the possession of contentful beliefs.

Once more, non-natural theories of content seem to have little room to manoeuvre. Some philosophers, it is true, have argued that the psychological research just alluded to should not be taken at face value, and that, when the matter is looked into fully, the supposed violations of rational norms can be explained away (Cohen, 1981). I myself doubt that anybody without philosophical preconceptions would find this line plausible, but, even if it is right, the non-naturalist still has the infants and animals to deal with.

Here the non-naturalist has two options. Either infants and animals are guided by norms, or they lack beliefs. Neither option seems attractive. It is hard to see how animals and pre-linguistic children could in any sense be said to be observing norms. So non-naturalists have tended to go for the other option, suggesting that animals and infants do not really have beliefs. ('Dumb animals are natural beings and no more.' McDowell, 1994: 70.) There seems little to recommend this move. It is one thing to recognize that there are significant differences between the beliefs of non-linguistic creatures and those of normal adult humans. It is another to inflate this into a fundamental division, with genuine thought on one side of the line, and nothing but mechanical response on the other.

Again, note how none of this is a problem for the naturalist. Naturalist theories of content regard judgement as prior to norms, and so have plenty of conceptual space for beings who have beliefs yet do not observe norms. Of course, specific naturalist theories of content will have specific views about the nature of judgement, and it will depend on the details exactly whom they recognize as believers. But by definition no naturalist theories will make sensitivity to norms itself a requirement for believing. (Moreover, for what it is worth, the specific naturalist theory I favour, teleosemantics, has no difficulty allowing that animals, infants, and systematically irrational adults all have beliefs.)

From the naturalist point of view, sensitivity to norms of judgement is an addendum to the possession of beliefs itself. Such sensitivity can arise in beings with beliefs, but does not have to. More specifically, given what I have said so far, it will arise in beings who adopt the end of true beliefs, for whatever reason, and consider what steps they need to take to achieve this end.

As it happens, I think adult human beings do this a great deal, and indeed that this plays a crucial role in human culture (cf. Essay 2, Section 5). But note that the deliberate pursuit of true beliefs involves a sophisticated meta-representational concern *about* beliefs, and is therefore not something that we should expect to be present in all beings who *have* beliefs. Since young infants, and probably all animals, lack the notion of true belief, they will be incapable of sensitivity to such norms. And even adult human beings, who do have the notion of true belief,[11] don't always take

---

[11] Footnote 4 implies that I am here taking ordinary adults to have a 'substantial account of truth-conditional content'. However, this needn't mean a sophisticated philosophical theory of content, like a teleosemantic

pains to ensure that they are getting their beliefs from reliable sources, and often simply take them as they come.

These points now allow a better understanding of the psychological literature on widespread human irrationality. In particular, they suggest an answer to one obvious query about this literature, namely, that it seems to be belied by the success of human enterprises which call for high levels of doxastic accuracy ('If we're so dumb, how come we sent a man to the moon?'). The answer is that humans normally reason badly, but can set themselves to do better. We can suppose that humans normally get their beliefs from 'quick and dirty' processes, which no doubt worked well enough in our evolutionary history, but all too often lead us astray in the modern world, and in particular in the experimental circumstances studied by psychologists. On the other hand, this is only part of the story. For humans can also deliberately set themselves to use reliable methods instead of the 'quick and dirty' tricks. Even if humans don't always follow norms that offer reliable routes to the truth, they are perfectly capable of this, and characteristically set themselves to do so when it matters.

According to the naturalist position, then, infant and animal believers lack the intellectual wherewithal to follow truth-conducive norms of judgement, and even adult human believers, who are intellectually capable of observing such norms, don't always do so. This position may be philosophically unfamiliar, but it has the virtue of plausibility. The usual condition, even for adult humans, is surely to think and act without worrying about what you are doing. Sometimes, I agree, we adults do make an effort to observe truth-conducive norms of judgement, and it is important that we be able to do this. But it overintellectualizes ordinary mental life to suppose that this kind of effort accompanies all judgement.

theory, say, or a Davidsonian analysis, but only some way of telling which people have which beliefs with which contents.

6 Some Specific Theories of Content

My remarks so far have contrasted 'naturalist' and 'non-naturalist' theories of content. In this section I want to attend to some different species within these broader genera, and note briefly how the details affect some of the points made so far. I think these refinements are of some intrinsic interest, but they will not affect my overall line of argument, so those who have been comfortable with the level of abstraction adopted so far may wish to skip to the next section.

The distinction between natural and non-natural theories of content interacts with that between 'output-based' and 'input-based' theories. By 'output-based' I mean those theories, like success semantics and teleosemantics, which analyse the content of beliefs in terms of the *actions they prompt*; and by 'input-based' I mean those theories, like verificationism and Dummettian theories, which analyse the content of beliefs in terms of the *conditions that produce them*. In more detail, output-based theories aim to equate the truth conditions of beliefs with those conditions that guarantee that resulting actions will satisfy desires (with success semantics then differing from teleosemantics in its account of desire satisfaction),[12] while input-based theories aim to equate truth (or assertibility) conditions with the circumstances that typically give rise to beliefs.

When I first started thinking about these matters, I saw the conflict as primarily between 'output-based' naturalistic theories and 'input-based' non-naturalistic ones. This was because the naturalist theories I favour are in fact output-based, while the most familiar non-naturalist theories are in fact input-based. However,

[12] See Whyte (1991), Papineau (1993: ch. 3.8). In this essay I am ignoring philosophical questions about satisfaction conditions for desires. There are non-naturalist as well as naturalist answers to these questions, as there are about the truth conditions of beliefs.

further reflection showed me that I was running two issues together here. The input versus output issue is orthogonal to the natural versus non-natural issue. After all, there are also naturalistic input-based theories, like indicator semantics and Fodor's asymmetric dependence theory. And, even if there is no clear-cut example of a non-natural output-based theory, there are elements of this position in Davidsonian approaches to content.

These distinctions complicate what I have said so far. Take first the division of *naturalist* theories of content into output-based (teleosemantics, success semantics) and input-based (indicator semantics, asymmetric dependence). I have suggested that naturalist theories of content can regard truth-conducive rules guiding belief-formation as specifications of means appropriate to the valued end of truth. But this comes out somewhat differently for output-based and input-based naturalist theories. For output-based theories, all such means will be *contingently* connected to the end of truth: since what makes a belief true are circumstances picked out by the belief's relation to action, it will be an independent further fact that any given way of arriving at the belief should track the truth. With input-based theories it works differently. Since the circumstances that make a belief true will now be equated with some subset of the possible causes of that belief, any recommendation that this belief should issue only from those causes, while still construable as a derived imperative orientated to the valued end of truth, will now be recommending a course that is *constitutively* connected with the end of truth.

Given this, we might expect a related contrast on the output side. That is, we might expect output-based naturalist theories to view some aspect of output as constitutively related to truth, which input-based natural theories regard as only contingently connected. There is indeed such a contrast. To see this, note first how input- and output-based naturalist theories are a kind of mirror image of each other. Just as an input-based theory needs to distinguish, among all the circumstances which can actually cause beliefs, those canonical conditions which constitute their truth conditions (this is why Fodor's asymmetric dependence, or something similar, is needed), so also does an output-based theory need to distinguish, among all the behavioural choices which can actually be occasioned by beliefs, those canonical behavioural consequences that play a role in constituting truth conditions: for it is the specific circumstances in which *those* canonical choices lead to successful actions that constitute the truth conditions. (The point is that we need to winnow out choices occasioned by rushes of blood, acting in haste, and so on, or we will get the truth conditions wrong. It is a challenge for a naturalistic output-based theory to make this distinction naturalistically, a challenge which I think is best met by teleological considerations. Cf. Papineau, 1993: ch. 3.7.7.)

Now consider the recommendation that people with true beliefs *ought* to choose in those canonical ways, *if* they are to satisfy their desires, first from the perspective of an output-based naturalist theory, and then from the point of view of a input-based one. From the output-based perspective, this hypothetical imperative falls constitutively out of the nature of truth: if your belief is true, and you so choose, then, by the nature of truth, you will satisfy your desires. For, on the output-based theory, true beliefs are in effect identified as those which lead to desire satisfaction specifically when they combine with such canonical choices. On an input-based theory, by contrast, this hypothetical imperative (that you *ought* to choose in the canonical ways, *if* you are to satisfy desires) will depend on contingent facts. For there is nothing in an input-based analysis of content (truth conditions = canonical *sources*) to ensure that if you have true beliefs, and choose in the canonical ways, your desires will be satisfied. This may be true, even for an input-based theorist, but if so it will be because of contingent facts about the world, and not because of the nature of truth.

Let me now quickly consider these matters from the point of view of non-naturalist theories of content. On input-based non-naturalist theories, like verificationism or Dummettian theories, recommendations about appropriate sources for beliefs will be taken to be primitive norms which fix truth (or assertibility) conditions for those beliefs. These theories are thus akin to input-based naturalist theories like Fodor's, in fixing truth conditions by reference to appropriate sources, except that they hold that there is an essential normativity involved in the reference to 'appropriate'. Moreover, they seem to come out exactly like Fodor-style theories on the output side. When it comes to recommendations that people with true beliefs *ought* to choose in such-and-such canonical ways, if they are to satisfy their desires, an input-based normative account offers no constitutive rationale. Just as with Fodor, they can still say that these choices are sensible because they will ensure satisfaction of desires, if your beliefs are true. But there is no constitutive tie here, and this claim will be true, if it is, because of contingent facts about the world.

What about output-based normative theories? Nobody seems actually to hold such a theory, but it is easy enough to imagine one. It would be like success semantics or teleosemantics in fixing truth conditions as those circumstances in which appropriate choices will succeed, except in holding, again, that 'appropriate' here is primitively normative. So on the input side this theory wouldn't disagree with its output-based naturalist counterpart: it would view belief-forming recommendations as derived imperatives specifying that certain sources are an effective means, as a matter of contingent fact, when value is attached to the end of truth.

Even if there are no exclusively output-based non-natural theories of content, the Davidsonian approach to content can be viewed, as I said, as embodying elements of this approach. For we can view Davidson as in effect upholding a non-naturalist theory of content which is *both* output-based and input-based, in that he identifies beliefs as states which ought primitively to arise from such-and-such epistemological inputs *and* which ought primitively to lead to such-and-such choices.

Won't a Janus-faced theory like Davidson's at some point face an embarrassing doubling of primitive and derived norms? In its initial identification of beliefs, the theory invokes both primitive input and output norms. But there seems no barrier to a Davidsonian also recognizing derived norms: derived input norms arising whenever moral or personal value is attached to the end of truth, and derived output norms about which choices you ought to make, if you are to satisfy your desires. This seems like an over-abundance of norms. Surely we do not want to allow *both* primitive *and* derived norms prescribing effectively the same strategies for forming beliefs and making choices.

I think this is indeed a genuine problem, but it is not peculiar to Davidson's theory. Rather it is a problem that arises for all non-naturalist theories, and indeed is simply a special case of the problem I raised in Section 3. We can put the point like this. Naturalists (whether input- or output-based) want to construe all norms relating to beliefs as derived imperatives: input norms are orientated to moral or personal values placed on truth, while output norms are orientated to the satisfaction of desires. Non-naturalists, by contrast, hold that at least some norms (input, or output, or both) are prior, *sui generis* and non-derived, and moreover that these prior norms underpin the constitution of content for beliefs. But this means that non-naturalists of any kind are going to be threatened with some doubling of norms. For there will be always be room for corresponding derived norms, orientated to the value of truth, or to the satisfaction of desires, alongside whichever norms non-naturalists take to be primitive and content-constituting. (Of course non-naturalists, by definition, will suppose that these primitive norms come first, so to speak, in that they are needed to constitute truth-conditional content; but the trouble is that, once content has been so constituted, non-naturalists won't be able to stop extra derived norms arising, because certain ways of reasoning are additionally valued as a means to the end of truth, or because certain ways of choosing are additionally valued as a means to the satisfaction of desires.)

In Section 3 I pressed the implausibility of there being primitive norms for truth-seeking, as required by input-based non-naturalist theories, in addition to derived norms which arise when value is attached to truth. We can now see that the point generalizes. An output-based non-naturalist theory would have primitive output norms (you ought to choose in certain canonical ways) *and* the hypothetical recommendation that you ought to so choose, if you are to satisfy your desires. And a Davidsonian Janus-faced theory will have primitive norms for both outputs and inputs, *and* in addition both derived input and output norms.

I take this generalized point to argue against non-naturalist theories of any kind, just as the special case in Section 3 argued against non-naturalist theories with primitive input norms. Primitive norms are an embarrassment, given the extent to which derived prescriptions are available anyway.

7 *Norms of Language*

In this final section I want briefly to consider the linguistic dimension of judgement. Obviously, in the space available, much will have to be taken for granted. Let me cut through a number of issues by adopting the following simple two-part model for an assertoric language L. (1) *Knowledge of truth conditions.* For all sentences s in L, speakers agree on a claim of the form: s is true if and only if p.[13] (2) *A rule of truth.* Utterances are governed by the prescription, 'You should utter s only if (you know that) p'.[14]

Given anything like this model, linguistic judgements will

---

[13] Perhaps they need also to know that such claims are derived canonically from facts about the semantic roles of s's parts, if this is to constitute knowledge of truth conditions. Alternatively, they may derive such claims from claims of the form that *s means that p*, or *s expresses the belief that p*, or *s would be true iff p*. I shall skip these refinements.

[14] See Williamson (1996) for arguments in favour of inserting the knowledge requirement here.

uncontroversially be constituted in part by a normative rule of truth. I have argued that content for non-linguistic judgements is not constituted by norms. By contrast, assertoric utterances would clearly not have their contents without a rule of truth. If it were not the rule that *s* is only to be asserted when *p*, then utterances of *s* would not have the significance they do. (Maybe *s* would still in some sense be *true* if and only if *p*, given its agreed truth condition, but it is only in virtue of the rule of truth that we can regard those who utter *s* as *committed* to *p*, as offering the judgement that *p*—as opposed to conjecturing that *p*, say, or denying that *p*, or whatever.)

So I accept that linguistic judgements are in this sense normatively constituted, if anything like the simple model above is right. However, I do not accept that there is anything in this to trouble naturalism. To start with, note that the issue of normativity arises rather differently in the present context from the way it did in earlier sections of this essay. In earlier sections I was concerned to explain how naturalists can *uphold* claims of the form 'you ought to judge in such-and-such ways'. That is, I wanted to show how naturalism can accommodate the *truth* of such normative claims. But there is no need for me, as a naturalist theorist, to *uphold* the norm which I take to constitute linguistic assertions. What matters is that the speakers of the relevant language accept the rule of truth for assertions, not that this rule is true. It doesn't matter whether they *really* ought only to say what is true. Their assertoric practice will still contain a rule of truth, which will constitute certain utterances as assertions, as long as they *think* they ought only to say what is true.

In sociological parlance, what matters is that the rule of truth is a *social fact* in the linguistic community in question, not that it is in fact a good rule. As such, it is akin to social facts proscribing theft, extra-marital sex, broken promises, driving on the right, or splitting infinitives. Such social facts are constituted by the evaluative attitudes of the members of the relevant community, quite independently of the normative truth. Even if extra-marital sex is in fact quite proper in many circumstances, it would still be true that in many societies there is a social norm prohibiting it, in the sense that the members of those societies disapprove of it and will exert pressure to prevent it.

Now, there are many interesting philosophical questions about the constitution of social facts. For example, there seems reason to distinguish social facts which depend on the community's moral attitudes (to sex, theft, promises), from those which rest on feelings about etiquette or style (splitting infinitives), and again from those which derive from a common interest in coordination (driving on the left). And it is by no means clear in which of these three categories the rule of truth ought to be placed. But, wherever we put it, there seems nothing to trouble the naturalist. Social facts of all kinds are constituted by the psychological attitudes of the members of the relevant society. In the earlier sections of this essay I have sought to rebut the most common argument for thinking that naturalism cannot accommodate psychological attitudes. If I am right, and naturalism can accommodate psychological attitudes, then it should be able to accommodate social facts in general, and the rule of truth in particular.

I have argued that the constitution of languages presupposes only that the relevant rule of truth is a social fact, and not that is true. But it is worth observing that, if a rule of truth is indeed a social fact, then members of linguistic communities will generally have some kind of pro-attitude towards saying only what is true, and this in itself will imply hypothetical imperatives about what they ought to do to to get the truths they want. Moreover, if it is morally valuable that languages exist, as it arguably is, then this in turn will imply that people ought morally to avoid false utterances.

It is also worth observing that any such prescriptive truths about *utterances* will also generate prescriptions about the avoidance of false *belief*. If there is moral or personal value in speaking truly, then there will be derived moral or personal value in believing truly, since aiming to believe truly is a presupposition of aiming to speak truly. In preceding sections of this essay I have considered what follows if true beliefs have moral or personal value. We now see how the institution of language can add to the reasons for which true beliefs might have such value.

Let me finish by briefly addressing the issue of the relation between thought and language. My overall expository strategy may have seemed to commit me to the priority of thought over language. After all, I have explained representation, in the first instance, by applying naturalist theories of content to beliefs, without attending to any possible dependence beliefs may have on language. And, more specifically, when I have turned to language, I may seem to have credited speakers with language-independent abilities to *think* that *p*, in explaining their understanding of sentences in terms of beliefs of the form *sentence s is true iff p*.

However, I don't think there is in fact anything worrisome here. Despite any initial appearances to the contrary, I am happy to concede that thought depends on language in ways I have yet to address. But I do not accept that this dependence invalidates my overall analysis. More specifically, it does not preclude the application of naturalist theories of content to beliefs, nor does it preclude the explanation of assertoric language in terms of speakers' beliefs about truth conditions.

It is worth distinguishing two ways in which belief depends on language: psychodevelopmentally and constitutively. To start with, linguistic training obviously exerts a developmental influence on psychological abilities. Many thoughts are clearly too complex for humans whose perceptual sensitivities and inferential associations have not been shaped by a relevant linguistic upbringing. In addition, there is also a more fundamental, constitutive dependence of thought on language. I am thinking here of those now familiar cases where my possession of a concept does not depend on individual factors like my perceptual sensitivities and inferential associations, but rather on the structure of my linguistic community. Names of people (*Aristotle*) or kinds (*arthritis*) provide obvious examples. Here it is not that my linguistic upbringing has caused me to develop new internal states. Rather, my possessing such concepts is *constituted* by my being embedded in a linguistic community. If you change the community, while leaving me the same, my concept changes.

I deny that there is anything in either of these kinds of dependence that is inconsistent with the overall story I have told in this paper. The first point to address is my use of naturalist theories to analyse the representational contents of beliefs. Now, such theories need clearly have no difficulty with the fact that linguistic training affects psychological sensitivities and abilities. For they can simply embrace these linguistically developed abilities as part of what fixes the representational contents of beliefs. Moreover, they can make just the same move with respect to the social constitution of content. Again, they can simply embrace this, and agree that certain of your states represent such-and-such, not just because of intrinsic facts about you, but also because of your relationships to other people, and in particular because of your embedding within a lingusitic community. Of course, exactly how these points might work will depend on the specifics of different naturalist theories of content. But it is not hard to see in outline how your development of special psychological abilities, or your membership of a linguistic community, might affect the informational significance of your states, or their teleological purposes, or their success conditions. All in all, there seems no obvious reason why naturalist theories of belief content should not simply accept that beliefs depend on language in the two ways I have indicated.

The other point where I might seem to be committed to the priority of thought over language is where I assume that assertoric language depends on speakers' beliefs that sentences *s* are true iff *p*. The worry here is that I apparently need to assume that speakers can think *p* *before* they learn sentences which mean that *p*.

However, I do not in fact need any such assumption of temporal priority. I need only claim that once the linguistic institution is up and running, as it were, and speakers are capable of thinking that p, then the different parts of the institution, thinking and speaking, are coordinated by beliefs of the form: s is true iff p.

True, this will leave us with an interesting kind of circularity in some cases. Speakers have concepts like *arthritis* because they belong to a linguistic community. This community exists in part because speakers follow rules for the linguistic expression of these concepts (they aim to assert 'arthritis' sentences only when certain arthritis facts obtain). But speakers will only be able to follow these rules if they already have the concepts (they won't be able to grasp the rules for 'arthritis' sentences unless they are capable of *arthritis* thoughts). So the concepts are constituted by the rules which are constituted by the concepts.[15]

However, while I accept there is a circle here, I do not think it vicious. It is just a special case of certain phenomena (here, mastery of concepts) being constitued by rules which in turn presuppose those phenomena. Many familiar social phenomena display this feature. There wouldn't be soccer matches unless there were rules about who wins soccer matches. There wouldn't be bank balances were there not regulations about who has access to bank balances. Certain concepts wouldn't exist were there not norms governing the linguistic expression of those concepts. This kind of circularity is certainly interesting, but it does not present any more of a special philosphical problem than soccer matches or bank balances do.[16]

[15] It is specifically the constitutional, not psychodevelopmental, dependence of thought on language that generates this interesting circularity. It is scarcely noteworthy that a new generation's concepts should causally depend on the linguistic practices of older people with those concepts.

[16] Earlier versions (some very early) of this essay were read at the Scottish Postgraduate Philosophy Society, King's College London, University of Nottingham, University of St Andrew's, and the Cambridge

REFERENCES

Boghossian, P. (1989), 'The Rule-Following Considerations', *Mind*, 98.

Brandom, R. (1994), *Making it Explicit* (Cambridge, Mass.: Harvard University Press).

Broome, J. (forthcoming), 'Relative Rationality'.

Cherniak, C. (1986), *Minimal Rationality* (Cambridge, Mass.: MIT Press).

Cohen, L. J. (1981), 'Can Human Irrationality be Experimentally Demonstrated?' *Behavioural and Brain Sciences*, 4.

Dretske, F. (1981), *Knowledge and the Flow of Information* (Oxford: Basil Blackwell).

Fodor, J. (1987), *Psychosemantics* (Cambridge, Mass.: MIT Press).

—— (1990), *A Theory of Content* (Cambridge, Mass.: MIT Press).

Horwich, P. 1990. *Truth* (Oxford: Basil Blackwell).

McDowell, J. (1984), 'Wittgenstein on Following a Rule', *Synthese*, 63.

—— (1994), *Mind and World* (Cambridge, Mass.: Harvard University Press).

McGinn, C. (1989), *Mental Content* (Oxford: Basil Blackwell).

Millikan, R. (1984), *Language, Thought, and other Biological Categories* (Cambridge, Mass: MIT Press).

—— (1990), 'Truth Rules, Hoverflies and the Kripke–Wittgenstein Paradox', *Philosophical Review*, 99.

—— (1993), *White Queen Psychology and other Essays for Alice* (Cambridge, Mass.: MIT Press).

Papineau, D. (1984), 'Representation and Explanation', *Philosophy of Science*, 51.

—— (1993), *Philosophical Naturalism* (Oxford: Basil Blackwell).

—— (2000), 'The Evolution of Knowledge', in P. Carruthers (ed.), *The Evolution of Mind* (Cambridge: Cambridge University Press).

Stampe, D. (1977), 'Towards a Causal Theory of Linguistic

Moral Science Club. Thanks are due to all who contributed on these and other occasions, in particular to Robert Black, John Broome, Edward Craig, Peter Goldie, Christopher Hill, Paul Horwich, Alan Millar, Gabriel Segal, Scott Sturgeon, Julia Tanney, Timothy Williamson, and especially Neil Manson.

Representation', in P. French, T. Ueling, and H. Wettstein (eds.), *Midwest Studies in Philosophy*, ii.

Stein, E. (1996), *Without Good Reason* (Oxford: Clarendon Press).

Whyte, J. (1990), 'Success Semantics', *Analysis*, 50.

—— 1991), 'The Normal Rewards of Success', *Analysis*, 51.

Williamson, T. (1996), 'Knowing and Asserting', *Philosophical Review*, 105.

2

The Evolution of Knowledge

1 **Introduction**

Human beings are one of the great success stories of evolution. They have spread over the globe and refashioned much of it to their own convenience. What has made this possible? Perhaps there is no one key which alone explains why humans have come to dominate nature. But a crucial part has surely been played by our high potential for theoretical rationality. Human beings far surpass other animals in their ability to form accurate beliefs across a wide range of topics, and many aspects of human civilization rest on this accomplishment. My aim in this essay will be to explain this ability from an evolutionary perspective. I want to understand how beings with our biological history came to be so good at theoretical rationality.

The claim that humans are good at theoretical rationality is not entirely uncontroversial. Much recent psychological research suggests that humans are far less good at forming accurate beliefs than you might initially suppose. I shall discuss this research at some length below. It raises many interesting issues, and will force me to be more specific about the precise sense in which humans possess a high level of theoretical rationality. But this research does not in the end undermine the claim that humans do have a high degree of theoretical rationality, nor that this has played an important role in human development.

Evolutionary explanations do not always account for traits in terms of selective advantages they provide. Some biological traits have not been selected because of their effects. Rather they are by-products of other traits which have been so selected. They do not serve any function themselves, but have been carried along by different traits that do yield advantages. Such evolutionary side-effects are 'spandrels', in the sense made familiar by Stephen Jay Gould (Gould and Lewontin, 1979).

My explanation of human theoretical rationality will in the first instance be spandrel-like. I shall not explain theoretical rationality directly. Instead I shall argue that it piggy-backs on other traits. In particular, I shall argue that it piggy-backs on the evolution of cognitive abilities for 'understanding of mind' and for means–end thinking. I shall argue that once these other abilities are in place, then nothing more is needed for humans to achieve high levels of theoretical rationality.

However, at the end I shall add a twist. Even if theoretical rationality didn't initially arise because of its biological advantages, there seems little doubt that it does provide such advantages. Given this, we would expect it to be encouraged by natural selection, even if it wasn't natural selection that made it available in the first place. So maybe there have been biological adaptations for acquiring knowledge, so to speak, alongside the other cognitive adaptations bequeathed to us by natural selection. I shall explore this thought at the end of this essay, not only for the light it throws on theoretical rationality itself, but because it seems to me to point to some general morals about the evolution of human cognition.

I shall approach these issues via a discussion of the 'rationality debate' in contemporary psychology. As I said, the claim that human beings display high levels of theoretical rationality is not as straightforward as it may seem, since there is now a good deal of evidence that human beings are in fact suprisingly prone to theoretical *irrationality*. Subjects in a well-known series of psychological experiments tend to produce highly inaccurate answers in many situations where we might expect them to do better.

In the next section I shall point out that these experimental data raise two immediate problems. First, there is an *evaluative* problem about the status of our standards of rationality: what makes these standards the correct ones, given that the intuitive practice of many normal humans does not respect them? Secondly, there is the *explanatory* problem of how humans are capable of adherence to such standards: how do people sometimes manage to perform to high standards of theoretical rationality, if divergence from those standards is the norm? (Or, as the question is sometimes posed, 'If we're so dumb, how come we sent a man to the moon?')

The following two sections, 3 and 4, will be devoted to the evaluative problem. In the end there is nothing terribly deep here, but a lot of confusing undergrowth needs to be cleared away. Once this has been done, then an obvious answer to the explanatory issue will become apparent, and accordingly in Section 5 I shall account for the ability of humans to achieve high levels of theoretical rationality, the experimental data notwithstanding.

In Sections 6 to 9 I shall place this answer to the explanatory problem in an evolutionary context. I shall show how my answer assumes that theoretical rationality is a by-product of two other intellectual abilities which we have independent reason to regard as evolutionarily explicable, namely, understanding of mind and means–end thinking. The final Section 10 will then explore the possibility that natural selection may also have fostered theoretical rationality directly, and given us certain inborn inclinations to seek out true beliefs as such.

A terminological simplification. Theoretical rationality, the rationality of the beliefs you adopt, contrasts with practical rationality, the rationality of the choices you subsequently make. Since I shall be focusing on theoretical rationality for the next few sections, it will be helpful to drop the 'theoretical' for now, and refer to 'rationality' *simpliciter*. When I do discuss practical rationality later in the essay, I shall make the distinction explicit.

2 Widespread Irrationality

Consider these three famous puzzles.

(1) Linda studied sociology at the London School of Economics. She reads the *Guardian*, is a member of the Labour Party, and enjoys experimental theatre. Which of these is more probable? (*A*) Linda is a bank teller. (*B*) Linda is a bank teller and an active feminist.

(2) You are worried that you have a not uncommon form of cancer. (It is present in 1 per cent of people like you.) There is a simple and effective test, which identifies the cancer in everyone who has it, and only gives a false positive result in 10 per cent of people without it. You take the test, and get a positive result. What is now the probability you have the cancer? (*A*) 90 per cent (*B*) 9 per cent (*C*) 50 per cent (*D*) 89 per cent.

(3) A pack of cards each has a letter on one side and a number on the other. The following four are dealt one side up. Which cards should you turn over to test whether *every vowel has an even number on the other side*?

$$|t| \quad |4| \quad |3| \quad |e|$$

Most people are terrible at these problems. There is now a huge amount of experimental data showing that only a small minority give the appropriate answers in tests of these kinds. (The appropriate answer in (1) is (*A*): a conjunction cannot be more probable than its conjuncts. In (2) it is (B). In (3) it is $|e|$ and $|3|$.[1] For two useful surveys of such studies, see Evans and Over, 1996, and Stein, 1996.)

Of course, many questions can be raised about the interpretation of experiments like these, and we shall raise some of them below. However, let us assume for the moment that these experiments do point to widespread deficiencies in human theoretical rationality. Two obvious questions then arise.

(A) The Evaluative Question. What is the status of the normative *standards* according to which some judgements and inferences are rational, and others not? One natural answer would be that these normative standards are a distillation of our best intuitions about rationality. On this view, a set of normative principles about rationality should be viewed as a kind of theory, a theory whose job is to accommodate as many as possible of our basic intuitions about rationality. However, this answer seems to be in tension with the experimental data, since these data suggest that the intuitions of ordinary people diverge markedly from orthodox standards of normative rationality. So, if we take the experimental data at face value, then we will need a different account of the source of these orthodox standards of normative rationality, an account which will make room for everyday intuitions to diverge from those standards.

(B) The Explanatory Question. A further puzzle is that many human activities seem to improve on the dismal performances in the psychological experiments. As I put it above, 'If

---

[1] Why isn't $|4|$, which many subjects choose, another appropriate answer? This answer mightn't be capable of falsifying the hypothesis, as $|3|$ is, but it does at least promise to add support by instantiating it. This is a reasonable point, but the fact remains that most subjects choose $|4|$ *instead* of $|3|$. It may be appropriate to view $|4|$ as an answer, but it is not appropriate to think that $|3|$ isn't one.

we're so dumb, how come we sent a man to the moon?' The experimental data suggest that most people are irrational much of the time. But if this is right, then we need some further account of how these limitations are transcended in those many modern human institutions that seem to rely on a high degree of accuracy and precision.

3 The Evaluative Question

Let me begin with the evaluative question. One possible line of attack is to argue that the experimental data should not be taken at face value. Perhaps the intuitive judgements of ordinary people do not stray as far from orthodox assumptions about normative rationality as the experiments at first suggest. If so, then perhaps we can equate standards of rationality with the intuitions of ordinary people after all.

L. Jonathan Cohen, for example, has argued that, if we pay due attention to the distinction between intellectual *competence* and *performance*, then the apparent gap between ordinary practice and real standards can be made to disappear. 'Competence' here refers to underlying capacities, to basic reasoning procedures. 'Performance' refers to actual behaviour, which might not reflect competence for any number of reasons, such as momentary inattention, forgetfulness, drunkenness, or indeed the distractions of undergoing a psychological experiment. Once we make this distinction, then it is possible to argue, as Cohen indeed does, that, while the *performance* of ordinary people often deviates from normative standards of rationality, the match between ordinary intuitions and normative standards is restored at the level of *competence* (Cohen, 1981).

Indeed, argues Cohen, how could it be otherwise, given that our normative theory must in the end answer to our best intuitions about the right way to judge and reason? Since our judgemental behaviour will also be guided by these intuitions (when inattention, drink, or strange experimental settings do not intrude), there is no real room for a mismatch. Our underlying competence cannot fail to conform to our normative theory.

Cohen's position might seem plausible, but it has some odd consequences. Imagine that human beings really were incompetent in the ways sugested by the above experiments. That is, suppose that their underlying intellectual capacities, and not just failures of performance, made them take some conjunctions to be more probable than their conjuncts; and similarly to commit the 'base rate fallacy' of ignoring the prior probability of some event when considering the relevance of new information; and, again, to fail to see that counter-examples will normally be more informative about putative generalizations than positive instances. Now, if humans really were like this, would different standards of rationality then hold, would it then be rational to judge conjunctions more probable than their conjuncts, and so on? Surely not. Standards of rationality are not relative in this way. It is an objective matter whether or not a given intellectual move is rational, quite independent of whether people intuitively take it to be rational. Yet is difficult to see how Cohen can avoid making rationality such a relative matter. If people did think as just hypothesized, then the theory that their thinking was rational would fit their intuitions about rationality perfectly, and so, by Cohen's argument, be fully vindicated.

This thought experiment (adapted from Stich, 1990) bears on the interpretation of the actual experimental data. If it is *possible* for the underlying intellectual competence of human beings to incline them to irrationality, then surely the best explanation of the *actual* performance of human beings is that they have just such an irrational intellectual competence.[2] The experimental data indi-

---

[2] Is such a community really possible? Some philosophers might argue on a priori grounds that such irrationality would be inconsistent with the

cate that human beings behave like the community in the thought experiment. So, in the absence of special arguments to the contrary, the obvious conclusion is that the basic intellectual inclinations of ordinary humans are indeed irrational.[3]

This now returns us to the evaluative problem. If the ordinary intuitions of ordinary people don't support objective standards of rationality, then what is the status of those standards? What makes it right to reason in certain ways, even when reasoning in those ways seems unnatural to most people?

I would like to explore a very simple answer to this question. Suppose we say that a method of reasoning is rational to the extent it issues in true beliefs.[4] If we adopt this view, then there is no difficulty at all in understanding how the normal practice and intuitions of most people can be irrational. It is just a matter of their reasoning in ways which characteristically give rise to false beliefs (such as judging probabilities by reference to stereotypes, as in the Linda experiment, or ignoring base rates, as in the probability-of-cancer experiment, or failing to seek out possible counterexamples, as in the card-selection experiment).

This move is related to the 'reliabilist' strategy in epistemology. 'Reliable' in this context means 'a reliable source of true beliefs', and reliabilists in epistemology argue that the notion of *knowledge*

supposition that the community have beliefs. However, while some minimal degree of rationality is no doubt required to qualify as a believer, it seems very doubtful whether this standard is high enough to rule out the postulated community. (Cf. Cherniak, 1986.)

[3] Perhaps a match between orthodox notions of rationality and actual human practice can be restored by focusing on '*experts*', rather than the general run of humans. The difficulty here, however, is to identify the experts in a non-question-begging way. (Cf. Nisbett and Stich, 1980.)

[4] Note that for inferential methods the relevant notion is *conditional* reliability. Rational inferential methods needn't always deliver true conclusions, but they should deliver true conclusions *if* their premises are true.

is best analysed as 'true belief issuing from some reliable method'. Some, but not all, reliabilists go further, and also analyse the notions of *justified* belief, and of a *rational* mode of thought, in terms of belief-forming methods which are reliable-for-truth. Now, there is a widespread debate about whether this reliabilist approach fully captures all aspects of the notion of knowledge, and *a fortiori* whether it is adequate to the further notions of justification and rationality. However, I shall not enter into these debates here, though many of the points made below will be relevant to them. Rather, my aim will merely be to show that *if* we adopt a reliabilist approach to rationality, *then* we can easily deal with the evaluative and explanatory problems generated by the experimental data on irrational human performance. I certainly think this lends support to a reliabilist approach to rationality (and to justification and knowledge). Whether other objections undermine the reliabilist programme in epistemology lies beyond the scope of this essay.

A common first worry about my reliabilist suggestion is that it cannot really help. For what does it *mean* to say that a belief is 'true', so this worry goes, other than that it is reachable by methods of rational thought? Given this, my reliabilist suggestion would seem to collapse into the empty claim that a method of thought is rational if it yields answers which are reachable by methods of rational thought.

I agree this would follow if 'true' means something like 'rationally assertible'. However, I think this is the wrong analysis of truth. I take it that truth can be analysed independently of any such notion as 'rational' (and thus can be used to analyse rationality in turn, as in my suggested reliabilist account). These are of course matters of active controversy. My view, that truth can be analysed first, before we come to questions of rational assertibility, would certainly be resisted, *inter alia*, by neo-pragmatists like Hilary Putnam, by neo-verificationists influenced by Michael Dummett, and by the followers of Donald Davidson. There is no question of entering into this debate in this essay. I have written about the issue elsewhere (Papineau, 1987; 1993: ch. 3; Essay 1 in this volume). Here I can only invite readers to take my attitude to truth on trust, and note how naturally it allows us to deal with the irrationality debate.[5]

4 More on the Evaluative Question

4.1 Further Desiderata on Modes of Thought

I have suggested that we should equate the theoretical rationality of modes of thought with their reliability-for-truth. In effect this is to treat 'theoretical rationality' as a consequentialist notion. We deem a mode of thought to be rational to the extent that it is an effective means to the consequence of true beliefs.

Given this, however, an obvious further objection suggests itself. Why privilege truth as the only consequence that is relevant

---

[5] Even if 'true' doesn't *mean* 'rationally assertible', won't the suggested reliabilist strategy for assessing rationality still lack practical teeth? For, when we assess the reliability of our belief-forming methods, how else can we check their outputs except by using those selfsame belief-forming methods? So won't we inevitably end up concluding our methods are reliable? Not necessarily. For one thing, there is plenty of room for some belief-forming methods to be discredited because their outputs do not tally with those of other methods. And, in any case, assessments of belief-forming methods don't always proceed by directly assessing the *outputs* of those methods, but often appeal to theoretical considerations instead, which creates even more room for us to figure out that our standard methods of belief-assessment are unreliable. (For example, when I judge that newspaper astrology columns are unreliable sources of truth, I don't draw this conclusion inductively from some survey showing that astrological predictions normally turn out false, but from general assumptions about causal influences. For more on this, see Papineau, 1987: ch. 8.)

to the evaluation of belief-forming processes? There are a number of other consequences that might also be thought to matter. Most obviously, it will normally also be desirable that our belief-forming methods are *significant*, in the sense of delivering informative beliefs on matters of concern, and *frugal*, in the sense of not using large amounts of time or other resources. And we can imagine other dimensions of possible consequentialist evaluation of belief-forming methods, to do with whether they deliver beliefs that will make you rich, say, or are consistent with traditional values, or indeed pretty much anything, depending on who is doing the evaluating. To equate rationality specifically with reliability-for-truth would thus seem arbitrarily to privilege one dimension of theoretical rationality over others.

I don't think there is any substantial issue here. I agree that methods of belief-formation can be evaluated in all kinds of consequentialist ways. Moreover, I am happy to concede that reliability-for-truth is just one among these possibilities. While I think that truth is generally important for human beings, for various reasons, to be discussed in my final section, I certainly do not want to argue that it is the *only* consequence of belief-forming methods which can be given evaluative significance. Indeed it is hard to imagine a realistic human perspective which ignores all other dimensions of possible evaluation in favour of truth. In particular, it is hard to imagine a realistic perspective that ignores significance and frugality. While we indeed normally want to avoid error by having methods which are highly reliable-for-truth, we won't want to do this by restricting our beliefs to trivial and easily decidable matters, or by always spending inordinate amounts of time making sure our answers are correct. From any pragmatically realistic point of view, there wouldn't be much point in high levels of reliability, if this meant that we never got information on matters that mattered to our plans, or only received it after the time for action was past.

Given these points, it will be helpful to refine our notion of theoretical rationality. Let us distinguish 'epistemic rationality' from 'wide theoretical rationality'. I shall say that a belief-forming method is 'epistemically rational' to the extent it is specifically reliable-for-truth, and that it has 'wide theoretical rationality' to the extent it produces an optimal mix of all the different desiderata imposed on it. I have no views about what this wide range of desiderata should be, and am happy to allow that different people with different interests may properly be concerned with different desiderata. In particular, therefore, I make no assumption that epistemic rationality is always more important than other aspects of wide theoretical rationality, nor that it should always be given any special weight in constructing an 'optimal mix' of different desiderata.

Having said all this, however, it is worth noting that 'epistemically rational' is not simply a term of art of my own construction, but is a component in such everyday notions as 'knowledge' and 'justified belief'. These everyday notions do focus exclusively on reliability-for-truth to the exclusion of other desiderata. In particular, while frugality and significance are unquestionably significant aspects of our belief-forming methods, by anybody's standards, they are ignored by everyday epistemological notions like 'knowledge' and 'justified belief'.

To see that these everyday notions concern themselves only with reliability, and abstract from further considerations of economy and importance, imagine a man who spends a month counting the individual blades of grass in his garden. We will no doubt feel this is a complete waste of time, and that the conclusion is of no possible interest to anyone, yet we will not say on this account that he does not *know* how many blades of grass there are, not that his belief in their number is not *justified*.

For the moment I offer this as no more than an anthropological observation. It is simply a fact about our intellectual repertoire that we have prominent concepts ('knowledge', 'justified') which we use to assess the sources of our beliefs purely from the perspective of reliability-for-truth, and in abstraction from such issues as significance and frugality. This anthropological fact does nothing to show that reliability-for-truth is somehow more basic or significant than these other desiderata, nor indeed is this something I believe. But I do take this fact to point to something interesting about our cognitive economy, and I shall return to the point in my final section.

4.2 *Perhaps Humans are (Widely) Rational After All*

In Section 3 I suggested that the data from psychological experiments do indeed show that ordinary people are 'irrational'. But perhaps we should reconsider this judgement, now that we have recognized that there are further desiderata on belief-forming methods in addition to reliability-for-truth. Perhaps the allegedly poor performance of ordinary subjects in the psychological experiments is due to their using methods of belief-formation that *sacrifice* some degree of reliability-for-truth for further desiderata like significance and frugality. It is obvious enough that these further desiderata are in some tension with reliability, and indeed with each other, and that sensible belief-forming strategies will therefore aim to achieve some optimal balance between them. In particular they will generally trade in some degree of reliability-for-truth in the hope of gaining significant information while remaining frugal.

Given that such a trade-off is clearly a sensible strategy for dealing with the world in general, it would seem unreasonable immediately to condemn ordinary thinkers as 'irrational' just because they are using methods whose less-than-ideal reliability-for-truth is highlighted by the psychological experiments. Maybe their methods of thought characteristically give false answers in these settings, but this doesn't show that they don't embody an optimal mix of reliability, significance, economy, and other desiderata. In the terms introduced above, maybe ordinary people are 'widely theoretically rational', even if not 'epistemically rational'.

This is a reasonable suggestion, yet even so I have my doubts about whether ordinary methods of thought are 'rational' even in this 'wide' sense of yielding an optimal mix of reliability with other desiderata. It does not seem hard to imagine modes of thought which would get the right answers to the experimental puzzles, without sacrificing anything of frugality or significance across the board. However, I shall not press this point here, since there seems no principled basis for deciding how to weigh the ingredients in the optimal mix of reliability and other desiderata on belief-forming methods. Moreover, the issue of whether ordinary people qualify as 'rational' does not matter to either the *evaluative* or the *explanatory* questions we set ourselves earlier.

To see why the performance of ordinary people does not matter to the *evaluative* question, we need only remember that I am now treating 'rationality' as a *consequentialist* matter. On Cohen's non-consequentialist view that evaluative standards of rationality must somehow be distilled from the normal practice of ordinary people, there is no real room for the possibility that the majority of ordinary people may fail to be 'rational'. But, from the consequentialist point of view I have developed here, the *evaluation* of belief-forming methods is quite independent of whether actual human practice conforms to these evaluations. The notions of 'epistemic rationality' and 'wide theoretical rationality' distinguished above are both consequentialist notions, in that they both evaluate belief-forming methods in terms of whether they *actually* deliver certain results, be this truth alone, or some mixture of truth and and other requirements. So whether a method is rational, in either of these consequentialist senses, is quite independent of whether ordinary people intuitively conform to that method.[6]

[6] This shows why, even given the complications introduced by different possible desiderata, my position on the evaluative question remains different from Cohen's. Where Cohen ties rationality to intuitions about rational thinking, I tie it to facts about which methods actually deliver

To see why the performance of ordinary people does not matter to the *explanatory* problem, note that this will remain a problem even if (which I am inclined to doubt) the practice of ordinary people is indeed 'rational' in the wide sense that it optimizes a mix of reliability, frugality, significance, and so on. For the psychological experiments certainly show that most people are bad in the specific dimension of reliability-for-truth, in that they characteristically give incorrect answers to the experimental puzzles. Maybe it is true that their high error rate in achieving truth in these situations is a necessary by-product of their modes of thought satisfying other sensible desiderata. But it is still a high error rate for truth. So there is still a puzzle about how these imperfections in reliability-for-truth are transcended in certain contexts, such as sending a man to the moon, where it is crucial that the kind of failures of truth displayed in the psychological experiments should be avoided.

4.3 Human Thought is Suited to the Environment of Evolutionary Adaptation

There is a yet further dimension to assessments of rationality. As some of my last remarks may already have suggested, assessments of rationality are crucially sensitive to the *range of environments* against which modes of thought are assessed. A mode of thought

which consequences. True, I have now in a sense admitted an element of relativism into judgements of 'wide rationality', in that I have allowed that it can be an evaluator-relative matter which desiderata are to count. But this is not the kind of relativism for which I earlier criticized Cohen's position. I allow that people and communities can have good reasons for differing on which desiderata they want belief-forming methods to satisfy. But it does not follow, as Cohen's position seems to imply, that whatever methods they practise will be rational for them if they *take* them to be so rational. For there will remain the question of whether those methods *actually* deliver the desired consequences, and nobody's merely thinking this will make it so.

that scores badly within one range of contexts may do well within another.

Note that this means that there is another way in which the performance of ordinary people can be defended against aspersions cast on their 'rationality'. In addition to the point that they may be sacrificing reliability-for-truth in favour of increased significance, frugality, and so on, there is also the defence that they may score much better, on both epistemic and wide theoretical rationality, if they are evaluated against a range of environments to which their abilities are well suited. Maybe ordinary people can be made to look stupid in the specific setting of the psychological laboratory. But it does not follow that their intellectual performance will be poor across a different range of enivironments, and in particular across the range of environments in which they normally find themselves.

This point had been stressed by those writing within the tradition of recent 'evolutionary psychology'. These evolutionary writers have set themselves against the standard psychological understanding of the experimental data on irrationality. This standard psychological understanding has come to be known as the 'heuristics and biases' approach, and explains the data by arguing that humans adopt certain *heuristic* strategies in solving theoretical problems, strategies which often provide useful short-cuts to reasonably accurate answers, but can be experimentally demonstrated to *bias* subjects irrationally towards certain kinds of mistakes (Kahneman *et al.*, 1982).

Against this, the evolutionary psychologists (see Barkow *et al.*, 1992) argue that our characteristic modes of thought must necessarily be well suited to the range of environments in which they were originally selected. In this sense, they argue, our modes of thought cannot help but be 'rational', even if they go astray when forced to work in unnatural contemporary environments, including those of contemporary psychological experiments. This thought is normally presented in tandem with the evolutionary psychologists' picture of the human mind as a 'Swiss Army Knife', containing a number of self-contained and hard-wired *'modules'* each designed for a specific cognitive task, such as visually identifying physical objects, thinking about other minds, selecting suitable mates, enforcing social contracts, and so on. Since these modules have been developed by natural selection over the last five million years, argue the evolutionary psychologists, we should expect them to be good at satisfying the important desiderata, not across all imaginable contexts, it is true, but specifically in the 'environment of evolutionary adaptation', in the range of contexts in which they evolved by natural selection.[7]

An initial reservation about this evolutionary argument is that it assumes that natural selection always delivers optimal designs. This is simply not true, if for no other reason than that natural selection never designs things from scratch, but must build on structures already in place. (Thus, for example, the involvement of the emotions in cognition arguably derives from their role in the reptilian brain, and could well have constrained modern cognition in distinctly sub-optimal directions.)

But suppose we let this point pass. A more significant observation is that there is far less distance between the evolutionary psychologists and their opponents in the 'heuristics and biases' tradition than might at first appear (cf. Samuels *et al.*, 2001). After all, both sides agree that the apparently poor performances in the psychological experiments are due to people using 'quick and dirty' cognitive techniques, which may work pretty well in some

---

[7] The classic example of this approach is Cosmides and Tooby's account of the Wason selection test (that is, puzzle (3) in Section 2 above). They offer experimental evidence which indicates that people are much better at this test when it is framed as a question about which individuals might be violating some social agreement; and they argue on this basis that the underlying abilities must be adaptations which are well-designed to detect social cheats. (See Cosmides and Tooby, 1992.)

ranges of contexts, but which fail in the experiments.[8] And there seems no reason why those in the 'heuristics and biases' tradition should not accept the suggestion that these 'fast and frugal' techniques are in fact evolved modules, the neural underpinnings for whch have been fostered by natural selection in environments of evolutionary adaptation.

The only remaining issue is then whether all this shows that humans are 'irrational' or not. And here too there seems no substantial matter for disagreement. Both sides can agree that our modes of thought must have worked reasonably well in the range of environments where they were originally developed by natural selection. Maybe they aren't the best of all possible modes of thought, even in those environments, given that natural selection is often hampered by the blueprints it inherits from earlier stages of evolution. But they must have produced the goods often enough when it mattered, otherwise they wouldn't have been favoured by natural selection at all.

Similarly, on the other side, both sides can agree that our modes of thought fail in a wide range of modern environments. This is the inference that is normally drawn from the psychological experiments by those in the 'heuristics and biases' tradition. Sometimes it seems as if the evolutionary psychologists wish to deny this inference, in so far as they aim to defend 'human rationality' against the doubts widely thought to be cast on it by the experimental data. But on closer examination this impression dissolves. For, after all, the evolutionary psychologists defend human modes of thought by insisting that they must at least have worked well *in the environment of evolutionary adaptation*, even if they break down in modern environments. This shift of evaluative context, from

---

[8] Except that the evolutionary psychologists prefer the phrase 'fast and frugal' on the grounds that it suggests more rationality than 'quick and dirty'. Since I think there is no issue here, I shall use the two phrases interchangeably.

the modern environment to the evolutionary one, would not be necessary if our modes of thought worked equally well in both, and so implicitly concedes that our biologically natural modes of thought do not work optimally in a wide range of modern situations.

5 The Explanatory Question

This now brings us back to the explanatory question. If it is agreed on all sides that human thinking depends on 'quick and dirty' problem-solving strategies which often go astray in modern environments, then how are we humans able to succeed in enterprises that demand a high level of accuracy across just such modern contexts? Or, as I put it before, 'If we're so dumb, how come we sent a man to the moon?'

The discussion so far suggests a natural answer to the explanatory question. As a preliminary to this answer, note that some people are better at the puzzles in the psychological experiments than others. In particular, I would expect those of my readers who had met versions of these puzzles before, and who understand their workings, to have had no great difficulty in avoiding the wrong answers.

My thought here is *not* that some people are innately smarter than others. On the contrary, it is that nearly all humans are quite capable of *improving* their performance in such puzzles, if they prepare themselves appropriately. And the appropriate preparation is obvious enough. We can simply set ourselves to be more reliable sources of true belief. That is, we can identify and analyse different kinds of problem situation, figure out which methods of belief-formation will actually deliver true answers in those situations, and then set ourselves to practise these reliable methods. In this way we can 'transcend' the 'fast and frugal' modes of thought bequeathed to us by evolution. These 'heuristics' or 'modules' may work fine in a certain range of situations, or when speed is of the essence, but we can do much better when we want to make sure that we get the right answers, and are prepared to expend a significant amount of intellectual time and energy in finding them.

Thus some of us have learned to deal with the puzzles given above by applying the principles of the probability calculus and propositional logic. We 'calculate' the answers in accord with such principles, rather than relying on our intuitive sense of the right answer, precisely because we have learned that our intuitive judgements are an unreliable guide to the truth, and because we know that reasoning in line with the probability calculus and propositional logic is guaranteed to track the truth.[9]

[9] Jonathan Evans and David Over distinguish 'personal rationality' ('rationality$_1$') from 'impersonal rationality' ('rationality$_2$'). They characterize the former as 'thinking . . . or acting in a way that is generally reliable and efficient for achieving one's goals', and the latter as 'thinking . . . or acting when . . . sanctioned by a normative theory' (1996: 8). It has been suggested to me, in various discussions, that this is similar to my distinction, between 'quick and dirty' methods hard-wired by evolution, and sophisticated methods deliberately designed to achieve the truth. I disagree. Even if we restrict Evans and Over's definitions to the subject area I am interested in, namely theoretical rationality, there remain crucial differences. Focus first on their 'personal rationality', picked out as good for achieving personal goals. Some thinkers, especially those influenced by evolutionary psychology, may think this coincides with 'quick and dirty' thinking, but I don't, since I believe that 'quick and dirty' thinking often *prevents* us from achieving our personal goals in the modern world. Conversely, my sophisticated methods are themselves orientated to what will normally be a particular personal goal, namely, the goal of true beliefs. So Evans and Over's 'personal rationality' excludes some of my 'quick and dirty' methods, but normally includes my 'sophisticated' methods. Consider now their 'impersonal rationality', picked out as 'sanctioned by a normative theory'. I have no place for such a notion, if a 'normative theory' is some a priori non-consequentialist construction. I explain any 'normativity' attaching to sophisticated methods in terms of

I would be prepared to argue that this ability, to identify and deliberately adopt reliable methods of belief-formation, has played a huge part in the development of human civilization. Of course, it is not the only factor that separates us from other apes, and indeed I shall argue below that this deliberate pursuit of reliability rests on a number of further abilities which may also be peculiar to humans. But at the same time it is clear that a wide range of advances in civilization are simply special cases of the strategy of deliberately adopting methods designed to increase knowledge and eliminate error. Those ancient astronomers who first kept accurate records did so because they could see that this would enable them to avoid false beliefs about past events, and the same goes for every other kind of system of written records. Voyages of exploration, by their nature, are explicitly designed to gather accurate information that would otherwise be unavailable. The elaborate procedures adopted in courts of law and similar formal investigations have the overt function of minimizing any chance of false verdicts. Arithmetic, geometry, double-entry bookkeeping, mechanical calculating devices, and so on, are all at bottom simply elaborate instruments invented in order to allow us to reach accurate conclusions on matters which would otherwise be left to guesswork.[10]

Not everybody whose belief-forming strategies are improved by

their being good routes to the goal of truth, and not in terms of some independent sense of normative correctness. (Cf. Essay 1 above.)

[10] To guard against one possible source of confusion, let us distinguish between *modern science*, in the sense of the institution that has developed in Western Europe since the beginning of the seventeenth century, and the general enterprise of deliberately seeking true beliefs, which I take to have been part of human life since before the beginning of recorded history. While deliberately seeking true beliefs is certainly part of science, the distinctively modern institution clearly rests on the confluence of a number of other factors, including distrust of authority, the use of mathematics, and the expectation that simplicity lies behind the appearances.

human civilization need themselves have reflected on the advantages of these improvements. Once a certain technique, such as long division, or logarithms, or indeed the use of mechanical calculators, has been designed by innovative individuals, in the interests of improved reliability-for-truth, then others can be *trained* to adopt these techniques as routines. We humans have widespread institutions designed in large part for just this purpose—namely, schools and universities. Of course, it is to be hoped that many students will not only master the techniques, but also come in time to understand *why* they are good routes to the right answers. But this ideal is not always achieved (there are plenty of people who can use calculators, and indeed logarithms, without understanding how they work), and even when it is, it is normally only after at least some techniques have first been instilled by rote.

6 Transcending Nature: The End of Truth and the Means to Achieve It

From a biological perspective, the argument of the last section may seem only to have pushed the explanatory problem back. The explanatory problem was to understand how we can do such clever things as send a man to the moon, given the limitations of our biologically natural 'quick and dirty' modes of thought. My answer has been, in effect, that we can do another clever thing, namely, deliberately identify ways of thinking that are reliable for truth and set ourselves to practise them. But now it could reasonably be complained that I owe a further explanation, of how we can do this further clever thing, given our biological limitations. ('If we're so dumb, how come we can deliberately choose ways of thinking that are reliable for truth?')

This is an entirely reasonable challenge. So far I have not questioned the evolutionary psychologists' picture of the human mind as a Swiss Army knife, comprising an array of 'fast and frugal' modules each designed to solve some specific problem quickly. But now I am talking as if we can transcend this biological nature at will, and simply set ourselves to cognize differently. But what enables us to do this? Am I supposing that we have some non-biological 'higher mind', with which we can transform our baser biological selves?

Not at all. I certainly don't wish to suggest that our ability deliberately to seek out the truth somehow requires us to transcend our biological natures. Fortunately, no such transcendence is needed. We can indeed transcend the limitations of our innate 'fast and frugal' methods. But this doesn't depend on some non-biological part of our beings. Instead we use other abilities bequeathed to us by biological evolution to correct any failings in our innate belief-forming routines.

At first pass, two simple abilities would seem to suffice for the enterprise of deliberately seeking out reliable belief-forming methods. First, humans need to be able to identify the end of truth. Secondly, they need to figure out how to achieve it. After all, what are reliable belief-forming methods, except an effective means to the end of truth?

It may initially seem that the first of these sub-abilities—namely, identifying the end of truth—will present the bigger hurdle from a biological-evolutionary perspective. Surely, you may feel, it would beg all the interesting evolutionary questions simply to credit our ancestors with a grasp of a *sophisticated notion like truth*. On the other hand, if only our ancestors had been able to identify the end of truth, then wouldn't it be easy to explain how they figured out how to achieve it? For couldn't they simply have used general *means–end reasoning* to work out which means are an effective route to the aim of truth?

However, it is arguable that this may have things the wrong way round. Recent work on cognitive evolution suggests that acquiring a notion of truth may have been the easy part for our ancestors, by comparison with their identifying the best means to this end. This is because the notion of truth falls out of 'understanding of mind', and there is plenty of independent reason to suppose that our ancestors evolved such an understanding of mind. By contrast, the issue of means–end thinking is not at all straightforward, and it is not clear when, and in what sense, our ancestors acquired a general ability to identify effective means to given ends.

I shall consider these two topics in turn. First, in the next section, I shall make some remarks about theory of mind. Then, in Section 8 I shall turn to means–end reasoning. On this topic I shall not go into details, as means–end reasoning is the subject of the next essay in this book. But I shall make some general points. In particular, I shall say enough to deal with an issue which may have been worrying some readers: namely, how exactly is the deliberate pursuit of truth, as guided by means–end reasoning, supposed to *supplant* the older 'quick and dirty' belief-forming routines bequeathed to us by natural selection? After all, it is not as if we can simply slough off our biologial heritage. So won't we be stuck with the older methods, however much we might like to have better ones? I shall address these questions in Section 9. The final Section 10 then considers the possibility that the deliberate pursuit of truth may not only be a spin-off from understanding of mind and means–end reasoning, but may itself also be a biological adaptation.

7 *Understanding of Mind*

The striking ability of humans to attribute a wide range of mental states to each other, and to use this to predict and explain behaviour, has been intensively discussed in recent years by philosophers and psychologists (Davies and Stone, 1995*a* and 1995*b*; Carruthers and Smith, 1996). However, the right analysis of this 'understanding of mind' is still a controversial matter, and it would be foolhardy for me to try and defend any agreed position here.

One popular contemporary view goes as follows. Normal adult humans have a *'theory* of mind', which allows them to reason about beliefs, desires, and other 'common-sense' mental states, and moreover this theory resides in a *genetically based* 'module' which has been selected in the course of human evolution because of the specific advantages which derived from facility with psychological reasoning.

However, some dissenters doubt whether human understanding of mind consists in anything like a 'theory'; instead, they argue, it derives largely from our ability to *simulate* other human beings by running certain mental processes 'off-line'. A further question is whether understanding of mind is acquired during individual development via some more *general learning ability*, rather than from genes selected specifically to facilitate understanding of mind.

Fortunately, these intricacies are orthogonal to my concerns here. All that matters for present purposes is that at some point in evolutionary history all normal humans came to have an ability to think about each other's mental states. We can ignore such further questions as whether this understanding was itself a genetically based adaptation, or derived from some more general learning ability, or whether it required a 'theory', as opposed to simulation.

The important point here is that any being who has an understanding of mind, in any of these senses, will inevitably have a working grasp of the difference between true and false belief. To see this, recall that the diagnostic evidence for full possession of understanding of mind is the ability to pass the 'false belief test'. In this test, the experimenter tells a subject the following story. 'Sally puts her sweets in the basket. While Sally is out of the room her mother puts them in the drawer.' The experimenter then asks the subject, 'When Sally comes back, where will Sally look for her sweets?' If the subject has full-fledged understanding of mind, the subject will be able to answer that Sally will look in the basket. Even though the sweets are really in the drawer, subjects with an understanding of mind will know that Sally's actions are guided by her *beliefs* about the world, not by the world itself, and moreover that beliefs can represent the world as other than it is, as with Sally's belief about where the sweets are. There is now fairly clear-cut evidence that all normal human children acquire the ability to pass the false belief test between the ages of 3 and 4, but not before. By comparison, animals other than apes seem incapable of passing the false belief test, while the situation with chimpanzees and other apes is obscure, not least because the experiment is very difficult to conduct if you can't talk to the subjects, and the results obtained with apes are therefore open to different interpretations.

Let us leave the chimpanzees and other apes to one side, and concentrate on the fact that, at some stage in evolutionary history, normal humans became cognitively sophisticated enough to pass the false belief test. Once humans could pass the false belief test, they would willy-nilly have been able to distinguish between true and false belief. They would have been able to think that *Sally believes the sweets are in the basket, when they are not*, and contrast that with the situation where *she believes them to be in the basket, and they are*. This would seem enough for them to be able to identify the end of true belief ('I don't want to be like Sally') and to start thinking about ways of achieving it.

Perhaps I am glossing over some different levels of sophistication here. It is one thing to note that Sally believes that the sweets are in the drawer, when they are, and to note that that Ugh-Ugh believes the tiger is in the cave, when it is, and so on, and similarly to note that Jane believes the cake is in the cupboard, when it isn't, and that Kargh believes the snake is in the hole, when it isn't, and so on. It is perhaps a further step to classify all the former beliefs together, as true, and all the latter together, as false.

Maybe so. Still, it doesn't seem all that big a step. In the rest of this essay, after this section, I shall accordingly assume that our ancestors were able to take this generalizing step, and think of truth and falsity as such. After all, human beings clearly came to grasp these notions at some stage, even if not immediately upon acquiring theory of mind. Moreover, this assumption will allow me to by-pass a number of unimportant complexities.

Still, it will be worth digressing briefly in the rest of this section, to note that *general* notions of truth and falsity may not themselves be required for the sort of deliberate attempt to improve epistemic rationality that I am interested in. In this essay I have been talking about 'reliability-for-truth' as such, because I have been considering the epistemic goodness of belief-forming methods from a general point of view, abstracting from any particular features to do with particular subject matters. However, particular epistemic agents concerned to improve themselves do not have to aim for truth in the abstract. Instead they might simply want the answers to specific questions.

Thus they may want to know *whether* the tiger is in the tree, or more generally *where* it is, or perhaps *how many* tigers are in that copse. 'Whether', 'where', 'how many' . . . here point to disjunctive aims which are indisputably available to any being with a theory of mind, even if the more abstract aim of truth requires some extra sophistication. Thus, to want to know *whether* the tiger is in the tree is to want that: you believe the tiger is in the tree, and it is, *or* that you believe it is not in the tree, and it is not. (Similarly, to want to know the *where*abouts of the tiger comes to wanting: you believe it is in the tree, and it is in the tree, *or* you believe that it is in the cave, and it is in the cave, *or* . . .; and, again, to want to know *how many* is to want that: you believe there is one, and there is one, *or* you believe there is two, and there are two, *or* . . .)

Philosophers familiar with redundancy-style accounts of truth may note here how wanting to know 'whether' the tiger is in the tree ('where', 'how many' . . .) is rather like aiming for a restricted kind of redundancy truth (truth-in-L, where L is restricted to terms for talking about the tiger and the tree). But, whether or not we take this notion of restricted truth seriously, it is clear enough that any being who can pass the false belief test can set itself the aim of finding out whether such-and-such (or set itself 'where' aims, or 'how many' aims . . .). Moreover, if it can devise a strategy for achieving these aims, then it will *de facto* have devised a strategy to bring it about that it gains true beliefs and avoids false ones. This would be quite enough for the deliberate improvement of epistemic rationality I am interested in. Whether these epistemic agents also think of themselves as aiming to gain *truth* and avoid *falsity* is an optional extra. The important point is that the strategies they devise to achieve their aims will in fact improve their reliability-for-truth on certain matters, whether or not they explictly think of it in these terms.[11]

8 Means–End Reasoning

Let me now turn to what I regard as the more difficult issue, the availability of means–ends reasoning to human beings. The notion of means–end thinking is so familiar that it may seem as if there can be no problem here. Isn't it obvious that humans often figure out which possible actions are the best means to their ends? Indeed, isn't it obvious that this is true of many animals too? Given this, surely there is no special biological puzzle about humans applying means–end thinking to the specific task of improving their reliability-for-truth. Aren't they just deploying an ability which emerged fairly early in evolutionary history, and which can therefore be taken for granted when

[11] It is interesting to contrast truth with probability here. While we have no doubt had the intellectual resources to pursue truth for at least 100,000 years, and quite possibly a lot longer, the concept of probability has only been around since 1654. (Cf. Hacking, 1975.) I think that this is why our culture encompasses many everyday techniques designed to help us track the truth, but is very bad at teaching ordinary people to reason with probabilities. It is no accident that most of the 'irrationality' experiments trade in probabilities.

we are trying to identify features which differentiate humans from other animals?

But I don't think we should take means–end thinking for granted in this way. I take it to be a genuinely open question whether non-human animals really perform means–end reasoning. Indeed I take there to be serious questions about the extent to which even humans do this. Of course, much hinges here on exactly what is required for 'really performing means–end reasoning'. But the issue is by no means solely a definitional one. However we resolve the definitional question, there will still remain relevant issues about which cognitive mechanisms are responsible for which behaviours in which animals, and about the emergence of these mechanisms in the course of evolution.

In the following essay in this collection I address the issue of means–end reasoning at length. In the course of that discussion, I consider a number of different ways of defining means–end reasoning; I argue that means–end reasoning in one interesting sense may well be peculiar to human beings; and I explore various possible ways in which this kind of means–end reasoning might have evolved.

The central notion I develop is of a cognitive mechanism which takes in representations of general causal information and processes them in such a way as to select *novel* actions—that is, roughly speaking, actions which have not previously benefited the individual organism in question nor its ancestors. I contrast 'means–end reasoning' in this sense with older cognitive systems of stimulus-response links laid down by genetic hard-wiring and associationist conditioning.

As it turns out, this contrast needs to be developed with some delicacy. The idea of a 'novel action' is less than clear-cut, and on some readings the performance of 'novel actions' is found throughout the animal world, and clearly does not demand any sophisticated mechanism which selects behaviour on the basis of representations of general causal information. Still, in the course of the following essay I refine my initial definition of 'means–end reasoning' in various ways, focusing in particular on the *kinds* of general causal information that different organisms are capable of processing. More specifically, I suggest that most animals, perhaps all except humans, can only deal with causal information which features their own potential actions as causes, and previous individual or ancestral rewards as effects.

However, rather than go into details here, let me content myself with one specific observation which will become important in the next section. It is no part of the position defended in the next essay that, once humans *are* able to do means–end thinking in the sense I specify, then this will somehow permeate all their cognition and transform it with higher intelligence. On the contrary, I argue that nearly all our activities will continue to be driven as before, by stimulus-response links which are automatically triggered by opportunity and drive. The means–end system is simply added on to the side of the existing stimulus-response architecture, as it were, leaving the rest as before. The only change I postulate is that sometimes, when the stakes are high and time does not press, the means–end system will be prompted to identify the best course of action in the light of the general causal information available to it. This identification will then feed back into the pre-existing stimulus-response architecture, by setting new input–output links so as to trigger some particular behavioural output when certain cues are next encountered.

So I don't think of means–end reasoning as some kind of 'central control' unit which *replaces* the evolutionary older stimulus-response links as the mediator between perceptual inputs and behavioural outputs, allowing intelligent reasoning to choose actions where previously they had been driven by blind reflexes (cf. Fodor, 1983). Rather means–end reasoning stands alongside the older structures which drive behaviour by standing stimulus-response links. The only difference that comes with means–end reasoning is that we have some new and powerful ways of *re-*

setting these links, in addition to the old methods of genetic hard-wiring and associationist learning. From this perspective, means–end reasoning is an evolutionary add-on, an extra way of adjusting stimulus-response links. For the most part, we can assume, the old ways of setting these links will be adequate. But sometimes it is helpful, for those organisms that can manage it, to allow these links to be set differently, in ways which do not depend so directly on the past successes or failures of the individual organism or its ancestors, but rather takes into account deductions from an indefinite range of relevant information, derived from third-person observation, testimony, and theorizing.

9 Means–End Reasoning and Theoretical Rationality

Let me now return to theoretical rationality. Recall that I argued, in response to the 'explanatory problem', that humans can avoid doxastic error by deliberately aiming to improve their reliability-for-truth. However, I have yet to address the question, which I flagged at the end of Section 6, about how this deliberate pursuit of truth is supposed to *supplant* the older 'quick and dirty' methods of belief-formation.

On the face of it, there certainly seems to be a problem here. If humans are innately predisposed to use certain 'quick and dirty' mechanisms to deliver answers when faced with certain problems, then how is it possible for them deliberately to *stop* these mechanisms operating? After all, it is a familiar philosophical point that our doxastic behaviour is not under the control of our will. So we might expect the automatic, older mechanisms to continue operating willy-nilly, even after we form the intention to improve our doxastic performance. But then, if this is right, it remains unclear how humans *can* improve their doxastic performance, given that the automatic mechanisms will continue to churn out the bad old answers as before.

However, consider now the point made at the end of the last section, namely, that means–end reasoning does not eliminate the older structures that drive behaviour, but is rather added on to the side of them. This gives us room to manoeuvre on the issue of whether it is in our *power* to improve our doxastic performance, given that the hard-wired and automatic belief-forming 'modules' threaten to force beliefs on us willy-nilly. As a first step, note that a decision to improve doxastic performance in such-and-such circumstances ('do the sums, don't just guess') is itself a special case of an *output* of means–end reasoning. Our general causal information implies that, if we want to avoid error, we had better do the sums, or whatever, and our desire to avoid error then leads us to set certain dispositions to action accordingly. We set ourselves to perform a certain sequence of actions (mental arithmetic, paper and pencil calculations . . .) whenever we are triggered by the relevant problem situations (problems involving probabilities, logic, arithmetic . . .).

If we look at it in this way, there is no suggestion that the new belief-forming methods need somehow *replace* or *abolish* the old fast and frugal modules. There are some interesting issues here, but the simplest assumption will be that the old modules will continue to run, quickly and frugally, alongside the improved belief-forming methods which we are now disposed to follow when triggered by the relevant problems.

This means that in certain cases, the ones where the fast and frugal methods go astray, we will in a sense 'end up' with two conflicting answers. The fast modules will continue to 'tell us' that it is likely that Linda is a feminist bank teller, and that we have cancer, and that we needn't turn over the odd number, even while the deliberate methods deliver the contrary answers.

Described like that, it may sound weird, but I think that it is quite faithful to the facts. Consider the familiar case of knowingly experienced visual illusions. The Muller–Lyer lines are the classic example. The two lines look different lengths to you, and moreover continue to do so *even when you know they are the same length*. There is an obvious modular explanation for this phenomenon. We have a fast and frugal object identification module, which delivers the conclusion that the lines are different lengths. We also have more deliberate and accurate ways of deciding the question, using measurements, which delivers the conclusion they are the same length. Deciding the question the deliberate way does not block the operation of the fast module, which is why the illusion persists even when you know it is an illusion.

As with the visual example, so in the more general case. Don't we continue to 'feel the pull' of the judgements that Linda is a feminist bank teller, that we have cancer, and that we needn't turn over the odd number, even when our more deliberate reasoning gives us the contrary answers? I would say that this is because our hard-wired modules are still generating their erroneous answers, alongside the more deliberate belief-forming processes that deliver the right ones. We know the quick answers are 'cognitive illusions', but our hard-wired modules continue to press them upon us.

There may still seem to be a problem. If I am now saying we *don't* in fact block the bad old modules when we decide to use better belief-forming methods, since the old modules are still running, then in what sense can I claim that we *succeed* in giving ourselves the new improved beliefs? After all, I have just insisted that the old modules continue to press their bad answers on us, while the new methods give us the contrary claims. So won't we end up with self-cancelling contradictions, rather than unequivocally improved new beliefs?

Here we need to distinguish between the different *uses* of module-driven and deliberate judgements, in addition to distinguishing their sources. The language of 'belief' starts to break down at this point. Consider the vision case again. Do I 'believe' that the lines are different lengths or not, when I 'knowingly experience' the Muller–Lyer illusion? Yes and no. Certain parts of my behaviour will be driven by the judgement that they are different lengths, as when I am asked to point quickly and without warning to the longer. But other behaviour, such as betting a large sum on their lengths, will be driven by the deliberative judgement that they are the same length. Similarly, I would suggest, with the other cognitive illusions. When we have to act in a hurry, our behaviour will standardly be driven by the fast illusory judgements. When we have time to think about what to do, we act on the basis of the deliberative judgements.

So the different sources of the two kinds of judgements are mirrored by the different uses to which they are put. At a first pass, we can expect that the 'beliefs' which emerge from quick-and-dirty modules will drive behavioural routines to which they are tied by hard-wired or conditioned links, even when deliberation indicates that those judgements are illusory. By contrast, 'beliefs' issuing from deliberate means–end reasoning will be distinguished, not just by being *outputs* of the means–end system, but also by providing distinctive *inputs* to that system. The main roles of deliberative judgements will be to feed further information back into the means–end system, and thus to improve future means–end decision-making.[12]

My idea here is thus that we should understand the possibility of our simultaneously holding contradictory 'beliefs' by distinguishing two species of 'belief'. When we simultaneously 'believe' both that the Muller–Lyer lines are different in length and that they are the same, or simultaneously 'believe' that Linda is more likely to be a feminist and that she is not, we harbour two different states in each case, which play different roles in our cognitive architecture: the former 'belief' in each example will be primarily tied to

---

[12] Of course, the means–end system will also acquire many judgements via the old fast modules, in cases where we have no reason to distrust those modules. But judgements issuing from the deliberate pursuit of truth will play a dominant means–end role, in that they will override doubtful modular judgements, within the means–end system at least, when there is any conflict.

immediate stimulus-response links, while the latter 'beliefs' will play a role in further means–end reasoning.

10 *Knowledge-Seeking and Biological Design*

So far I have simply presented our ability to achieve high levels of theoretical rationality as a spandrel. Once you can identify the end of truth (from your understanding of mind), and can figure out which strategies are the best means to this end (from means–end reasoning), then you will therewith have the ability to adopt reliable belief-forming methods in pursuit of true beliefs, without any further biological evolution needed.

In this section, however, I want to consider whether there has been any biological selection for truth-seeking itself. Have certain genes been favoured specifically because they make us better at seeking out reliable belief-forming processes?

One reason for pursuing this thought is that there has been a gap in my story so far. I have spoken of *identifying* the end of truth, and have argued that this falls out of theory of mind. But note that what falls out of theory of mind is the concept of truth, if anything, not a desire for truth. To be able to think about truth isn't yet to *want* truth, but it is only wanting truth that will make you seek reliable belief-forming processes.

Why might people seek truth? One reason has been implict in much of the argument so far, but has not yet been explicitly mentioned. If you act on true beliefs, you will generally get the results you want, but this does not hold if you act on false beliefs. So people who reflect on what's generally needed to satisfy their desires, and figure out that they need to act on true beliefs to be confident of this, will want truth as a means to satisfying their desires.

But this is rather a lot of reasoning to ask of our rather dull ancestors. They would need to start thinking about their aims, and about the general connection between possessing true beliefs and success in achieving what they want. Perhaps this connection will fall out of the theory of mind (it would be interesting to test small children on this), but it is not obvious that it should do so.

So, if it was not manifest to our ancestors that they needed true beliefs to succeed in action, then they may have had means–end thinking in general, yet mightn't have sought truth via reliable methods, for lack of thinking through the reasons for wanting truth as a means.

Still, it seems clear that they would have been much more successful the more true beliefs they were able to feed into their means–end system. So any gene that made them desire truth in itself would have been strongly favoured by natural selection.

Note that this would just be a special case of the logic by which natural selection makes us desire anything. There is a perspective from which it can seem puzzling that natural selection has designed us to desire anything except reproductive success. After all, natural selection favours traits just to the extent that they contribute to reproductive success. So why should it be a biologically good idea to design us to pursue proximate goals like food and warmth and sex, rather than reproductive success itself? Why not just set us the single aim of reproductive success, and leave it to us to figure out how best to achieve it?

The answer, of course, is that the relevant connections are often obscure, if not to us, then certainly to our ancestors. Natural selection couldn't trust our ancestors, so to speak, always to identify the best means to reproductive success. So instead it set them some more immediate goals, like food, warmth, and sex, and which had correlated reasonably well with eventual reproductive success in the evolutionary past, and which were immediate enough for our ancestors to figure out effectively how to pursue them.

Similarly, I would like to suggest, with truth. True beliefs will correlate well with reproductive success (since they will correlate with desire satisfaction which correlates with reproductive success). But, if our ancestors were unable to discern this connection (or more to the point, to discern the connection with desire satisfaction, given that evolution had already set them to pursue various proximate goals, rather than reproductive success *per se*), then it would have been greatly to their biological advantage to be instilled with a desire for truth *per se*. Then they would have pursued truth in any case, whether or not they saw the connection with further success in action, and so reaped the rewards of such further success as a side-effect (intended by evolution, so to speak, but not by themselves).

One obvious piece of evidence in support of this conjecture is the natural tendency of many human beings to seek out the truth on matters of no obvious practical concern. Consider investigations into the origin of the universe, or the evolution of species, or abstract metaphysics. It is not obvious, to say the least, how these investigations might be motivated by the thought that true beliefs will enable us to succeed in our practical projects. Of course, the tendency towards such research might be due to culture rather than any genetic selection. But we should not rule out the possibility that such pure research owes its existence to the fact that natural selection couldn't trust us to tell when the truth was going to be useful to reproductive success, and so made us seek it willy-nilly.

How seriously should we take talk of evolution selecting certain *desires*? This depends in part on how we understand desire talk. For most of the past few sections I have avoided 'belief' and 'desire' talk, because of philosophical controversies surrounding its interpretation. But in this section I have not been able to resist the expository convenience. Let me now make this talk of 'desires' good by explaining that I mean nothing but the *preferences revealed by means–end thinking*. This notion was implicit in my conception of a means–end system, which after all is a system which takes in representations of general causal facts, figures out what they imply for the consequences of the various actions available, and then selects one such option. Such a system, by its nature, favours certain consequences over others, and so to this extent can be said to embody a 'desire' for those consequences. This is all I mean when I say that natural selection may have instilled a 'desire' for truth in us. All I mean is that natural selection did something which increased the likelihood that the means–end system would select actions that it assumed would lead to true beliefs.

At this stage it will be useful to make a rather different point about genetic selection for a trait like desiring the truth. So far I have presented this as an alternative to the view that the pursuit of truth was *invented* by some stone-age decision theorist, some prehistoric genius who saw for the first time that people who had true beliefs would generally be better at achieving their ends. But in fact the two possibilities are not in conflict, and indeed the invention scenario adds hugely to the plausibility of the genetic story.

Suppose, for the sake of the argument, that some prehistoric ancestor did first see that it would be useful to get at the truth. Perhaps the idea spread some way, to the family of the immediate inventor, or to his or her hunter-gatherer band. This would be a wonderfully useful practice, and those who cottoned on to it would fare well. Indeed those who cottoned on to it quickly would be at a huge reproductive advantage. So there would be immense selective pressure in favour of any genetically based quirks of cognitive development which aided the acquisition of this trick.

One way to achieve this would be to jiggle the development of the means–end system slightly, in such a way as to make it more likely to acquire a preference for truth *when* the surrounding culture sets an example. It seems independently plausible that our adult prefences should depend upon our developmental experience, yielding derived preferences for things which in our experience have led to reinforcing results. And it is also independently plausible that surrounding cultural practices will influence which such derived preferences get set up. Now, when some such culturally influenced derived preference is also biologically advantageous, then natural selection is likely to come to the aid of the party too, by favouring genes that make it easier for this particular preference to be acquired. This genetic alteration needn't be advantageous in the absence of the surrounding culture. It may not be selectively positive when, in the absence of a supporting culture, there is no real chance of developing a preference for truth. Yet, if such a genetic alteration were selected within the context of a surrounding culture, then this would still constitute selection of a desire for truth, in the sense I intend. For certain genes would have been favoured because they increased the likelihood that the means–end system would select actions which promised to yield true beliefs.

It is important not to think of all biological selection as requiring complexes of genes which on their own specify elaborate end-products, in the way an architect's drawings specify a building. All an advantageous allele need do is increase the likelihood that some advantageous trait will develop *in the normal range of environments*. Indeed all genes will depend on some features of the environment to help bring about the effects for which they are selected. In the special case of organisms with cultures, the features of the environment which might combine with the gene to help produce the advantageous effects might be very complex and specific. The gene 'in itself', so to speak, might have no obvious connection with a desire for truth, to return to our example, except that it causes some non-specific change in the brain that happens to make you better at learning to pursue the truth *when others in your society are already setting an example and encouraging you to follow it*. But once there is a culture with this last-mentioned feature, then this gene will be strongly selected for. (What is more, once it is selected for, then there will be scope for more elaborate developments of the cultural practice, since everybody has now become better at cottoning on to it, which will create extra pressure for genes which make you good at learning the more elaborate practice . . .)

Let me now conclude by briefly considering a rather different way in which natural selection may have favoured the pursuit of belief-forming strategies which are reliable for truth. Apart from fostering a desire for truth, it may also have given us an input module dedicated to the identification of reliable sources of belief. I do not intend this as an alternative to the hypothesis of a biologically enhanced desire for truth, but as something which may have occurred in addition. (Moreover, the points about culture–gene interaction just made in connection with the desire for truth will also apply to the biological selection of an ability to identify reliable sources of belief. Let me now take this as read, without repeating the story.)

This further suggestion should strike an immediate chord with philosophers. Anybody who has tangled with the baroque philosophical literature on the *concept of knowledge* will know that humans make unbelievably detailed and widely consistent judgements about which people count as *knowers*. They can judge, in a way that seems to escape any straightforward philosophical analysis in terms of necessary and sufficient conditions, whether true beliefs derived in all kinds of recherché ways are tightly enough linked to the facts to qualify as knowledge. I would like to suggest that these judgements issue from a biologically favoured input module whose task is to identify those routes to belief which can be trusted to deliver true beliefs. When we ask, 'Does X really *know* about p?', or 'Wouldn't we *know* whether p if we went and examined those tracks carefully . . .?', we are arguably deploying a notion which has been designed to help us decide whether some route to the belief that p is a reliable source of truth. From this perspective, then, judgements about knowledge are the products of an input module which has been encouraged by natural selection because it yields a fast and frugal way of identifying strategies which are reliable for truth.

Recall a point I made in Section 4.1, that the everyday notion of 'knowledge' focuses exclusively on reliability-for-truth, and abstracts from the cost or significance of the belief in question. The man *knew* how many blades of grass he had, even if he was wasting his time on a trivial matter. This bears on one common objection to my suggestion that biological evolution may have favoured truth-seeking as such. A number of colleagues have contended (standardly citing Peter Godfrey-Smith's 'Signal, Detection, Action', 1991) that it is implausible that evolution should have encouraged the aim of truth as such. Since there are serious costs to a high degree of reliability, wouldn't we expect evolution to have balanced the worth of truth against the cost and significance of acquiring it?

This is a reasonable point, but we should not forget that evolution isn't a perfect engineer, and often has to settle for less than the best. I have already explained why evolution may have given us a desire for truth, just as it has instilled desires for other proximate goals other than reproductive success, in cases where these goals correlate reasonably well with reproductive success but the connection would have been obscure to our ancestors. Well, maybe the need for true beliefs was *so* important that evolution didn't want to obscure its pursuit, so to speak, by introducing complications to do with cost and significance. Perhaps a more sophisticated cognitive design would have avoided ever making truth *per se* one of our doxastic aims, but only truth weighed by some mix of cost and significance. But my suspicion is that evolution couldn't take the risk, so to speak, that the pursuit of truth might be diluted in this way. (Compare: maybe it would be even better if sex as such were never one of our aims, but only sex that is likely to lead to healthy offspring; here too evolution has clearly found it better not to be too fancy.)

I take the striking salience of the everyday concept of knowledge to lend support to the idea that truth-seeking *per se* has been selectively advantageous in our biological history. The complex concept of knowledge comes so easily to humans that it seems likely that there is some genetic component in its acquisition. Yet this concept focuses exclusively on reliability-for-truth, in abstraction from any other desiderata on belief-formation. If I am right to suggest that judgements about knowledge are the products of an input module which has been encouraged by natural selection, then this at least is one case where evolution has decided that the important thing is to get at the truth, whatever the cost or significance.

A prediction follows from the hypothesis that judgements about knowledge are the products of an input module. On this hypothesis, we ought to suffer 'cognitive illusions' with respect to judgements about knowledge. There should be situations where the quick but dirty module takes a view on whether some belief is or isn't 'knowledge', but our more deliberate reasoning disagrees on whether this belief stems from a reliable source.

I think there are cases just like this, and they will be familiar to philosophers. Consider the 'intuitions' that are standardly thought to count against reliabilist theories of knowledge. These are precisely cases in which some true belief has been arrived at by a reliable process, and yet, in the immediate judgement of ordinary people, does not really qualify as 'knowledge', or vice versa. I have no view (nor do I really care) whether this disqualifies reliabilism as a philosophical theory of knowledge. But it does fit the hypothesis of a dedicated module whose function is to identify reliable sources of belief. For, like all fast and frugal modules, it will cut some corners, and end up making some judgements it ought not to make. Philosophical epistemologists may wish to continue charting such mistakes in the pursuit of the everyday notion of knowledge. But naturalist philosophers of psychology will be happy to note how their existence perfectly confirms the hypothesis of a biological module dedicated to identifying reliable sources of truth.[13]

[13] I would like to thank Peter Carruthers, Peter Goldie, David Over, Kim Sterelny and Stephen Stich for comments on this essay.

REFERENCES

Barkow, J., Cosmides, L., and Tooby, J. (1992), *The Adapted Mind* (Oxford: Oxford University Press).

Carruthers, P., and Smith, P. (eds.) (1996), *Theories of Theories of Mind* (Cambridge: Cambridge University Press).

Cherniak, C. (1986), *Minimal Rationality* (Cambridge, Mass.: MIT Press).

Cohen, L. J. (1981), 'Can Human Irrationality be Experimentally Demonstrated?' *Behavioral and Brain Sciences*, 4.

Cosmides, L., and Tooby, J. (1992), 'Cognitive Adaptations for Social Exchange', in Barkow *et al.* (1992).

Davies, M. and Stone, T. (eds.) (1995a), *Mental Simulation* (Oxford: Blackwell).

—— —— (eds.) (1995b), *Folk Psychology* (Oxford: Blackwell).

Evans, J., and Over, D. (1996), *Rationality and Reasoning* (Hove: Psychology Press).

Fodor, J. (1983), *The Modularity of Mind* (Cambridge, Mass.: MIT Press).

Godfrey-Smith, P. (1991), 'Signal, Detection, Action', *Journal of Philosophy*, 88.

Gould, S., and Lewontin, R. (1979), 'The Spandrels of San Marco and the Panglossian Paradigm: A Critique of the Adaptationist Program', *Proceedings of the Royal Society*, B205.

Hacking, I. (1975), *The Emergence of Probability* (Cambridge: Cambridge University Press).

Kahneman, D., Slovic, P., and Tversky, A. (1982), *Judgement under Uncertainty: Heuristics and Biases* (Cambridge: Cambridge University Press).

Nisbett, R., and Stich, S. (1980), 'Justification and the Psychology of Human Reasoning', *Philosophy of Science*, 47.

Papineau, D. (1987), *Reality and Representation* (Oxford: Blackwell).

—— (1993), *Philosophical Naturalism* (Oxford: Blackwell).

—— (1999), 'Normativity and Judgement', *Procedings of the Aristotelian Society, Supplementary Volume*, 73.

Samuels, R., Stich, S., and Bishop, M. (2001), 'Ending the Rationality Wars: How to Make Disputes about Human Rationality Disappear', in R. Elio (ed.), *Common Sense, Reasoning and Rationality*, Vancouver Studies in Cognitive Science, ix (New York: Oxford University Press).

Stein, E. (1996), *Without Good Reason* (Oxford: Clarendon Press).

Stich, S. (1990), 'Rationality', in D. Osherson and E. Smith (eds.), *Thinking: An Invitation to Cognitive Science*, iii. (Cambridge, Mass.: MIT Press).

3

The Evolution of Means–End Reasoning

1 Introduction

When I woke up a few days ago, the following thoughts ran through my mind. 'I need a haircut. If I don't get it first thing this morning, I won't have another chance for two weeks. But if I go to the barber down the road, he'll want to talk to me about philosophy. So I'd better go to the one in Camden Town. The tube will be very crowded, though. Still, it's a nice day. Why don't I just walk there? It will only take twenty minutes. So I'd better put on these shoes now, have breakfast straight away, and then set out for Camden.'

This is a paradigm case of what I shall call 'means–end reasoning'. In such reasoning, we consider the consequences of various courses of action, and choose the course best suited to our overall purposes. I take it to be uncontroversial that all human beings are capable of such means–end reasoning, and that this kind of reasoning guides many of our actions. Indeed I take it that this power of means–end reasoning is one of the most important differences—if not *the* most important difference—between humans and other animals.

Yet for some reason this topic has become unfashionable. Means–end reasoning seems to have disappeared from the theoretical agendas of many of those you would expect to be most interested, namely those who work on human cognition in a comparative or evolutionary context. There are now large industries devoted to theory of mind, to language, and to other 'modules' putatively characteristic of human cognition. But means–end reasoning itself gets brushed under the carpet, as somehow not quite the thing to talk about in modish theoretical society.

In this essay I want to make a plea for this somewhat old-fashioned topic. While language, and theory of mind, and no doubt other modules, have clearly played a crucial role in human evolution, I think that as good a case can be made for the significance of means–end reasoning. It is of course a tricky matter to chart the exact evolutionary dependencies between the different cognitive abilities peculiar to humans, and the remarks I make on this specific topic towards the end of this essay will be abstract and speculative at best. But by that stage I hope at least to have persuaded you that means–end reasoning is an evolutionarily important topic in its own right.

My first task will be to be more specific about what I mean by 'means–end reasoning'. Care on this point is obviously needed, if I am to persuade you that 'means–end reasoning' is important for human evolution. For, if we set the standards too low, 'means–end reasoning' will be widespread throughout the animal kingdom, and not a peculiarly human adaptation. After all, nearly all animals have *some* ways of selecting behaviours which are appropriate to current needs and circumstances. Nor, in the other direction, will it do to set the standards too high, as requiring literacy or calculation, say. For then there will no reason to suppose that 'means–end reasoning' has anything to do with human *biology*, however important it might be for the development of higher civilization.

Accordingly, in the next two sections I shall aim to specify an understanding of 'means–end reasoning' which is consonant with my claims about its importance for human evolution. After that I shall attempt to defend these claims.

Before proceeding, however, it will perhaps be worth commenting on one specific influence that has diverted current theoretical fashion away from means–end reasoning. In many contemporary minds, I suspect, 'means–end reasoning' is thought of as antithetical to 'modularity'. This is because means–end reasoning tends to be associated with the kind of general-purpose learner-and-problem-solver that traditional psychology took to be the seat of all animal intelligence. Enthusiastic advocates of modularity, however, reject this domain-general conception of animal intelligence, and argue that all real advances in cognitive power, and in particular the distinctive features of human psychology, consist of purpose-built 'modules' selected for specific intellectual tasks (cf. Cosmides and Tooby, 1992: 39 *et passim*). And so enthusiastic modularists tend to be impatient with talk of means–end reasoning, because they see it as a return to the bad old days of general-purpose learning and problem-solving.

However, I do not think of 'means–end reasoning' as opposed to modularity in this way. In so far as there is a well-formed antithesis between general-purpose traditional mechanisms and modules, I would be inclined to place means–end reasoning on the side of the modules. Means–end reasoning may be domain-general in its *content*, in the sense that there is no limit to the kinds of information that it can operate with. But the same could be said of our linguistic abilities, yet these are widely taken to be the paradigm of 'modular' powers.

Moreover, means–end reasoning, as I think of it, is not to be thought of as providing a general interface between perceptual inputs and behavioural outputs, along the lines of the non-modular 'central system' that Jerry Fodor interposed between perception and action in his original *The Modularity of Mind* (1983). Rather, I take means–end reasoning to be an add-on that arrived late in evolution, in service of specific needs, and which itself interfaces with whichever pre-existing mechanisms coordinate perception and action.

Sceptics often respond to the modularist metaphor of the mind as a 'Swiss Army knife' by asking what decides which blades to use in which circumstances. This is a reasonable enough question, and some of my remarks later will indicate possible answers. But means–end reasoning itself does not play this role. Rather, means–end reasoning is a specialized mechanism, which gets activated when appropriate by whichever processes do coordinate the different aspects of cognition. From this perspective, means–end reasoning is simply another fancy tool in the Swiss Army knife, not some meta-device that cordinates the whole show.

2 Before Means–End Rationality

These last remarks are intended only as a pointer to my overall story. Details of the plot will be filled in as we proceed. The first step is to explain in more detail what I mean by 'means–end reasoning'. In this section I shall attack this question from the bottom up, so to speak. I shall consider how behaviour might be adapted to circumstances in animals who clearly lack means–end reasoning in any sense. By this means I hope to identify a sense of means–end reasoning in which there are interesting questions about its evolutionary emergence. The strategy, in effect, will be to isolate an important sense of means–end reasoning by considering what is lacking in those animals who manage without it.

I shall proceed abstractly, and in stages. I shall only consider very general features of cognitive design. And I shall start with the simplest possible such designs, and then proceed to more sophisticated ones.

Level 0—'Monotomata'—**Do R**

At the very simplest level, Level zero, so to speak, would be the kind of animal that always does the same thing, **R**. For example, it might move around at random, blindly opening and closing its mouth parts, thereby ingesting anything that happens to get in its way.

Level 1—'Opportunists'—**If C, do R**

A step up from this would be animals who suit their behaviour to immediate conditions **C**, saving their energy for situations where their behaviour **R** will bear fruit. For example, they move their mouth parts only when they detect the presence of food. (In such cases we can expect also that the behaviour **R** will itself be 'shaped' by sensitivity to conditions. The frog's fabled fly-catching behaviour fits this bill. Not only do the frogs shoot their tongues out at specific *times*, namely when the environment offers some promise of food; they also shoot their tongues out in specific *directions*, towards the point where the food is promised.)

Level 2—'Needers'—**If C and D, do R**

At the next level will be animals whose behaviour is sensitive, not just to current opportunities, but also to current needs. For example, we can imagine insect-eaters who don't shoot their tongues out at passing targets *unless* they also register some nutritional lack. Apparently frogs are not like this, and so are prone to overfeed. Even after their nutritional needs are satisfied, they still shoot their tongues out at passing flies. Still, even if frogs manage without a need-sensitive cognitive design, it can manifestly be advantageous to evolve one, and many animals have clearly done so.

Before proceeding to the next level of complexity, it will be well to enter a word of caution. It is natural, and indeed often very helpful, to characterize simple cognitive designs in representational terms, and I shall do so throughout this essay. But there are dangers of putting more into the representational description than the specified design warrants, and mistaking overblown representational description for serious explanation. In principle we should always demonstrate carefully that attributions of representational content are fully warranted. It would make this essay far too long to do this properly at every stage, but I shall try as far as I can to ensure that my representational descriptions are grounded in explicit specifications of cognitive design.

By way of illustrating the danger, consider the distinction I have just introduced between **C**s, which signify sensitivity to environmental '*conditions*', and **D**s, which register current *needs* (and so might thus be thought of as akin to 'desires' or, more cautiously, as '*drives*'). It might seem entirely natural to distinguish informational **C**s from motivational **D**s in this way. However, nothing I have yet said justifies any such contrast. After all, **C** and **D** appear quite symmetrically in the schematic disposition which heads this subsection—**If C and D, do R**. So far we have been given no basis for treating these states as playing distinct roles in the regulation of behaviour.

Now I have raised this point, let me pursue it for a moment. To focus the issue, let me stipulate that both the **C**s and the **D**s are henceforth to be understood as *internal* states which trigger resulting behaviour **R**. (There must be some such internal states, if distal conditions and needs are to affect behaviour.) At first sight there may seem to be an obvious basis for distinguishing motivational **D**s from informational **C**s. If some **D** is triggered by low blood sugar level, say, then won't it play a distinctively motivational role, by contrast with an informational **C** that, say, registers passing insects? Isn't the **D** required to *activate* the animal, by contrast with the **C**, which just provides factual information, and so gives no motivational 'push'? But this is an illusory contrast. The **C** is equally required to activate the animal—however low its blood sugar, the animal won't stick its tongue out until there is something to catch. So far everything remains symmetrical, and both **C** and **D** should be counted as simultaneously motivational and informational—as 'pushmi-pullyu' states, in Ruth Millikan's terminology (Millikan, 1996). They can both be thought of imperatively, as saying 'Do **R** (if the other state is also on)', and also indicatively, as saying 'Here is an occasion for doing **R** (if the other state is also on)'.

A substantial division between motivational and informational states only arises when there is some extra structure behind the Cs and Ds. Without going into too much detail, let me give the rough idea. A state C will become informational rather than motivational when it ceases to be tied to any particular behaviour, and instead provides information that is used by many different behavioural dispositions. We can expect behaviourally complex animals to develop sensory states which respond reliably to external objects and properties and which are available to trigger an open-ended range of activities. This will be especially advantageous when animals are capable of learning (see Level 4 below). When an internal state C ceases in this way to be devoted to any specific behavioural routines, it will cease to have any imperative content, and can be viewed as purely informational. (Cf. Millikan, forthcoming.)

Motivational states can become specialized in a converse way. Here again the states will cease to be tied to particular behaviours. But in the motivational case this won't be because the states come to provide generally useful information, but rather because they acquire the distinctive role of signalling that certain *results* are needed. The reason this detaches motivational states from specific behaviours is that different behaviours will be effective for those results in different circumstances. Such motivational Ds can still perhaps be thought of as having some informational content— blood sugar is low, maybe—but they will be different from purely informational Cs, given that they will have the special responsibility of mobilizing whichever behaviours will produce some requisite result, whereas informational Cs will have no such result to call their own.

Level 3—'Choosers'—**If C_i and D_i, do R_i,** *when* **D_i is the dominant need**

Once animals have states whose role is to register needs, then there is potential for another level of complexity. It would be advantageous to have a mechanism to decide priorities when some C_i and

Di prompt behaviour **Ri**, and another **Cj** and **Dj** prompt incompatible behaviour **Rj**. The obvious system is somehow to compare **Di** with **Dj**, and select between **Rs** depending on which need is more important. It is not hard to imagine mechanisms which would so rank needs in either a qualitative or quantitative way.

> Level 4—'Learners'—*after* **experience shows that Ci, Di and R lead to reward, then (as before): If Ci and Di, do Ri, when Di is the dominant need**

So far I have implicitly been supposing that the prompting **Cs** and **Ds** are 'hard-wired' to the responsive behavioural **Rs**—that is, that the relevant **C, D→R** links have been established by intergenerational genetic evolution and will develop in any animal which matures normally. *Learning* adds a further level of animal sophistication. By 'learning' here I simply mean that the **C, D→R** links can be influenced by the animal's specific experience of which behaviours produce which results in which circumstances. The obvious way to allow this is via mechanisms which will reinforce **C, D→R** links just in case **R** in **D** and **C** leads to some specific result.

In the schema above I have characterized the relevant reinforcing result simply as 'reward'. This raises a number of issues. One is whether the removal, or reduction, of the need-registering **D** is always implicated in the 'reward' which reinforces the likelihood of **R** given **C** and **D** in future. A mechanism along these lines is suggested by the fact that many drives, like hunger, or thirst, have functions (ingestion of food, or water) whose fulfilments are standardly necessary and sufficient for the reduction of the drives themselves. So learning mechanisms in which these drive reductions led to reinforcement would thereby select behaviour which was suited to fulfilling the functions of the drives (that is, getting food, or water).

Still, it is not obvious that all drives are designed to produce results which will then, as a matter of course, assuage those drives. For example, when there are signs of danger, an animal will need to identify anything unusual in its environment. Suppose there is some drive **D**—alertness, vigilance—which registers the need to identify anything unusual, and whose function is to get the animal to make such identifications. It wouldn't seem a good idea for this drive to be assuaged whenever it succeeds in fulfilling its function. If you find something unusual, you should become more vigilant, not less (and, conversely, your vigilance should be quieted if you fail to find anything unusual). More generally, there seems no reason to rule out drives which will continue through their own fulfilments, or even be enhanced by them. However, if there are such drives, then any associated learning mechanisms will not be able to use the drive's disappearance as a source of reinforcement, since this disappearance won't provide a good proxy for the drive's fulfilling its function. Rather, the learning mechanism will have to work with some other sign of a behaviour's being an effective means to the drive's fulfilment (such as actually finding something unusual).

I am not sure whether nature has in fact bequeathed any such learning mechanisms to the animal kingdom, or whether all actual animal learning mechanisms work with drive reductions as reinforcers. A further issue, which arises whatever the answer to this question, is whether all animal learning derives from a single mechanism, which reduces all the drive-specific reinforcers (sating of hunger, quenching of thirst, perception of something unusual) to a common currency (the release of opiates, say), or whether there are a number of distinct learning mechanisms, one for each drive, each of which attaches behaviours to its own drive, depending on which behaviours have proved effective in past experience in fulfilling that drive's specific function. The latter option would allow the more sophisticated control of behaviour, but again it is an empirical question how far nature has availed itself of this opportunity.

At this stage I propose to stop my initial classification of cognitive structures. We have enough levels to be getting on with. They will provide a basis, in the next section, for an initial characterization of 'means–end reasoning'.

But before proceeding it will be worth pausing briefly to remark on the way that even these initial levels have shown the category of *drive* to be surprisingly many-sided. In a sense *drive* is a primitive version of *desire*, and I shall say a bit more in Section 4.5 below about the extra elements in desire. But even before we get to the more sophisticated level of desires, drives themselves turn out to have a confusing number of facets. At the primitive Level 1, when need-registering drives are not really distinguishable from states which register environmental conditions, 'drives' simply signal the current appropriateness of some specific behaviour. Once drives do become so distinguishable, at Level 2, as registers of need rather than conditions, they will function to prompt whichever behaviours will satisfy those needs in current circumstances. A further role, which characterizes Level 3, is to compete with other drives, when those other drives prompt incompatible behaviours. Note that the Level 2 role does not guarantee the Level 3 role: we can imagine an animal, like Buridan's ass, who functions well when only one need is active, but freezes in the face of more; more realistically, we can imagine animals who resolve competition between drives in some arbitrary non-functional way. And at Level 4 we find drives which play a yet further role, by reinforcing behaviours which lead to the reduction of drive (though this will only work, as I observed, for drives whose fulfilment leads naturally to their extinction). Again, this Level 4 role is not guaranteed by the roles at lower levels, since the lower roles can be present in animals who do no learning at all.

At first, the notion of 'drive' can seem simple enough. But it turns out to pack in a number of dissociable features, which won't always be found together in real animals.[1]

---

[1] This complexity generates a corresponding uncertainty about the precise representational content of drives. Even if we can distinguish drives as a kind from purely informational states, along the lines indicated when discussing Level 2, this does not yet decide which specific objects

3 General Knowledge

Let me now draw attention to one striking feature of animals at Levels 0 to 4 (I shall call these '*simple* animals' from now on). They nowhere explicitly represent any general information of the form 'All As or Bs', or generic causal information to the effect that 'As cause Bs', or even conditional information about present circumstances like 'If A were to occur, then so will B'. In line with this, let me now specify, as a first approximation, that by means–end reasoning we should understand the use of this kind of explicit general[2] information to guide action. This initial definition of means–end reasoning will soon need to be significantly refined and qualified, but it will do to get us started.

Note that I have defined means–end reasoning in terms of using *general* information to guide actions, rather than in terms of

drives aim at. Perhaps we should deem them to be directed at any specific behaviours they may prompt (feeding behaviour, say); or perhaps their content is the specific results they are designed to achieve (ingesting of food); or perhaps, again, they represent the possibly different effects which will reinforce associated behaviours (such as raising blood sugar). I myself would argue in favour of the second answer, the specific result the drive is designed to achieve, given that this is the most basic function of any state which properly qualifies as a drive. But the rationale for assigning specific contents is a messy business, not only for motivational states like drives, but also for informational ones, and in what follows I shall not aim explicitly to justify any such specific attributions. For those readers who feel queasy about loose representational talk, I can only say again that I shall always aim to ground my attributions of representation in explicit specifications of cognitive design. (In Papineau (1997) I offer an account of the determination of mental content which hinges on the way that informational and motivational states interact, once their roles become differentiated.)

[2] There are philosophical contexts in which it is important to distinguish between generalizations, generic causal claims, and particular conditional claims. For present purposes, however, nothing will be lost if we lump these together under the heading of 'general information'.

using *any* information. This is because even simple animals clearly use particular information about their circumstances to guide behaviour. From Level 1 upwards they have states whose function is to represent particular features of their environment. Even so, no simple organisms explicitly represent any *general* facts. It is one thing to be able to represent the whereabouts of a particular pond, or apple, or lion. It is another to represent that the ponds contain water, or that apples are a source of food, or that lions are bad for your health.

This last point means that we cannot equate my question of which animals have means–end reasoning with the perhaps more familiar question of which animals should be counted as having *beliefs*. For the issue is not whether the animals have *any* powers of explicitly representing information, but whether they have the power of explicitly representing *general* information. I have no objection to saying that simple animals, certainly from Level 2 upwards, have particular beliefs about particular circumstances. But this won't qualify them as means–end reasoners, on my defin-ition, given that they will still lack beliefs on general matters.

There is also a rather more abstract reason for not wanting to pose my issue of means–end reasoning in terms of the possession of beliefs. This is because many philosophers, most importantly Daniel Dennett (1978, 1987), take an 'interpretational' approach to the ascription of beliefs. Dennett holds that the attribution of beliefs answers to the 'intentional stance', as opposed to the 'design stance', and thus that such attributions are justified as soon as they help to make sense of behaviour, even if there is nothing corresponding to the attributed belief in the organisms' causal workings. On this view, even very simple animals might be held, not just to have beliefs about particular circumstances (here's a pond, apple, lion), but also to have general beliefs (ponds contain water, say). For it is arguable that even the behaviour of simple animals can usefully be rationalized by such general beliefs, even if nothing in those animals explicitly represents this information.

Fortunately, we can by-pass this largely terminological issue about the meaning of 'belief'. Suppose I concede to Dennett, for the sake of the argument, that even simple animals can have general 'beliefs' in his sense. It doesn't at all follow that they do means–end reasoning in my sense. For I did not define means–end reasoning in terms of general *'beliefs'*, but in design-level terms, as a matter of using general representations to guide behaviour. Whatever you think about the meaning of 'belief', there remains a substantial issue, namely, about which animals actually do use general representations in this way. In what follows I shall try to keep the waters clear by continuing to avoid the terminology of 'belief'.

Some readers may be wondering at this point why I am so sure, by my own lights, that simple animals *don't* use general representations to guide their behaviour. Isn't there a sense in which just such general representations are embodied in these animals' dispositions to behaviour? Take an animal who is disposed to drink from ponds when it is thirsty, precisely because in its individual or ancestral past this has proved an effective route to water. In this kind of case, there seems good reason (especially for those, like myself, who favour a selectionist perspective on semantic matters) to say that this disposition, which certainly guides the animal's behaviour, *represents* the fact that drinking from ponds will yield water. After all, it is precisely because this behaviour has produced this result in the past that the animal now has the disposition, and correspondingly it is precisely in so far as drinking will yield water in this case that the disposition will fulfil its biological function. Shouldn't we thus think of the disposition itself as the present embodiment of the general information that drinking from ponds will yield water?

I do not especially want to contest such attributions of content. I am happy to allow that this kind of disposition embodies information about the general response-to-outcome connection (**C&D,** **R→O**) which was responsible for instilling the disposition in the first place.

So, given this concession, I need to tighten up the definition of means–end reasoning, if this is to define a kind of thinking unavailable to simple animals. In my initial definition of means–end reasoning, I referred to '*explicit*' representations of general information. Maybe I can make something of this phrase, and argue that general information is only *implicitly* represented by dispositions to action, not explicitly. If means–end reasoning specifically requires explicit representations of general information, and mere dispositions to behaviour fail on this requirement, then it will no longer follow that simple animals automatically qualify as means–end reasoners.

One way of developing this thought would be to hold that genuine explicit representation requires some kind of sentence-like vehicle, some articulated physical state to which we can ascribe a content. Simple organisms' representations of particular facts, involving definite modifications of sensory processors, would be so explicit. But their putative representation by mere behavioural dispositions would fail on this score, so this thought would go, because such dispositions do not have the kind of physical tangibility required for fully explicit representation.

However, I don't think that there is much substance to this line of thought. After all, dispositions to behaviour must have some kind of physical embodiment. An animal who is disposed to drink from ponds must differ in some substantial causal way from an animal who hasn't yet learned to do this. So why not let this real difference, whatever it is, serve as the vehicle of the content 'pond drinking yields water'? Moreover this vehicle, whatever it is, will interact appropriately with representations of needs and conditions in generating behaviour. The animal will only drink from the pond when this vehicle (which we are taking to represent 'pond drinking yields water') engages appropriately with the state which represents the need for water and the state which represents the presence of the pond, along the lines of the classical practical syllogism. So, on all these counts, there seems no reason not to count the disposition as a perfectly explicit representer: it must have some physical embodiment; and moreover that embodiment will interact with other uncontroversial representers in a way appropriate to its putative content.

Still, perhaps there is another way in which such putative dispositional representers of general information fail to be sufficiently explicit. In more familiar cases, general representations can be combined, one with another, to deliver new general representations. We can take 'valleys contain ponds' and 'ponds contain water', to generate 'valleys contain water'. But there is nothing in simple animals to allow anything like this. Their behaviour dispositions may embody general information, but they have no system which processes these items of general information to yield new such general information. At most, as outlined in the last paragraph, these dispositional representers will interact with items of particular information ('here's a pond') and drives ('water needed') to generate particular behaviours, as in the standard practical syllogism.

To make the point graphic, imagine a simple animal who has information along the lines of *shaking those trees will yield apples* implicit in one behavioural disposition, and information like *throwing apple-sized objects will repel bears* implicit in another. If it is a simple animal, it will have no way of putting these together so as to figure out that it would be a good idea to shake a tree when a bear is prowling nearby and no suitably throwable objects are yet to hand. Of course, this information may itself come to be embodied implicitly in some disposition, if natural selection or learning instils a specific disposition to shake trees and throw the resulting fruit when bears are nearby. But the general point will still apply. While the organism will have various bits of general information implicit in its various behavioural dispositions, it will have no system for combining them and using them to infer the worth of behaviour that is not already directed by its cognitive architecture.

This represents an extremely significant limitation. It means that simple animals will never be led to perform behaviours except those which they, or their ancestors, have performed successfully in the past—that is, behaviours which have either been reinforced by psychological reward in individual ontogeny, or selected for enhancing reproductive success in ancestral phylogeny. The only items of general information that can enter into simple animals' practical syllogisms, so to speak, are of the form 'In **C**&**D**, **R** leads to **O**', where **R** is some behaviour previously performed when **C** and **D**, and **O** some outcome whose past achievement has led ontogenetically or phylogenetically to their present disposition to do **R** given **C** and **D**. There is no possibility of their inferring that some **R** will lead to some **O** in some **C** and **D** from other items of general information, and then acting accordingly. They are limited to acting on **C**&**D**, **R**→**O** connections that they or their ancestors have themselves enacted.

So let me now specify that means–end reasoning requires 'explicit' representation of general information in the specific sense that *such information can be processed to deliver new items of general information*. Whether or not behavioural dispositions in simple animals carry 'explicit' general content in other senses, they do not satisfy this requirement, since simple animals cannot combine their behavioural dispositions to generate new dispositions. Because of this, simple animals cannot perform novel actions. In effect, then, I have now defined means–end reasoning as the ability to perform novel actions. (The notion of 'novelty' required here merits further discussion. I shall return to this in Section 4.1 below.)

Given this definition, we are now finally in a position to consider the importance of means–end reasoning for the evolution of higher cognition. To focus this issue, let me propose the strong hypothesis that means–end reasoning in the sense now specified is a biological adaptation peculiar to human beings. This essay certainly won't provide a knockdown defence of this hypothesis, and indeed as we proceed various modifications will prove to be necessary. Still, it will provide a useful peg on which to hang the discussion.

In the rest of this essay, I shall consider two lines of objection to the claim that means–end reasoning is a biological adaptation peculiar to humans.

First, there are those who think that means–end reasoning is *too easy*, and therefore widespread throughout the animal kingdom. Against this I shall argue, in the next section, that non-human animals are sophisticated in many different ways, but that there is no compelling reason to think them capable of means–end reasoning in particular.

Secondly, there are those who think that means–end reasoning is *too hard* to have been selected directly in human evolution, and therefore no essential part of our biological heritage. On this view, no human traits have been biologically selected *because* they facilitated means–end reasoning. Rather, means–end reasoning is a side-effect of traits which have been selected for other more immediate purposes, a non-biological 'spandrel' which has spun off from other distinctive abilities that evolution has bequeathed to humans. Against this I shall argue, in the final section, that standard explanations of this form do not work, and that in any case there are general reasons why no spandrel could fill the role played by human means–end reasoning.

4 Non-human Sophistication

I suspect that many readers who have lived through the cognitive revolution in psychology will have started to feel increasingly impatient during the analysis of the last two sections. Don't we now know that most animals are far too sophisticated to be understood in terms of simple links between stimulating **C**s, driving **D**s, and responsive **R**s? That was the way the original behaviourists and their various neo-behaviourist successors tried to understand animals. But surely, so the thought would go, we now realize that animals are much more elaborate than that. Animals are blessed with any number of refined cognitive devices which enable them to deal with their environments by figuring out sophisticated responses to their circumstances in real time. As a result, animals have any number of behaviours in their repertoire which are manifestly inexplicable on behaviourist grounds, and clearly display levels of behavioural control unavailable to the simple creatures discussed in the last section.

The first point to make here is that there is nothing in my analysis so far to commit me to behaviourism about simple animals. I may have schematized matters in terms of **C**s, **D**s, and **R**s, but this in itself scarcely convicts me of thinking in behaviourist terms. Indeed a moment's thought will make it clear that there are a number of ways in which my simple animals transcend behaviourist limitations.

Behaviourism holds that all dispositions to actions (all **C**, **D**→**R** links) are instilled in animals by general learning mechanisms operating on spaces of sensory inputs and behavioural outputs. Nothing in my analysis of simple animals commits me to any such blanket view about the sources of input–output links. True, I have allowed, at Level 4, for the possibility of learning by instrumental conditioning. But this does not mean that simple animals cannot also have structured 'hard-wired' links between inputs and outputs which do not derive from learning. After all, input–output links must be so 'hard-wired' in animals below Level 4; and even at Level 4 there can be 'hard-wired' links alongside the learned ones. Moreover, nothing I have said about simple animals implies that, when there is instrumental learning, at Level 4, it must derive from 'content-free' mechanisms which are equally ready to link any perceptual inputs with any behavioural outputs. Instrumental learning may be highly constrained, with only a limited range of input–output paths being available for shaping by individual experience.

Similar points apply to the inputs and the outputs themselves. Behaviourism assumes minimally structured spaces of sensory qualities as inputs and behavioural atoms as outputs. But nothing commits me to this strongly empiricist picture. I have, it is true, assumed *some* distinction between perceptual inputs and behavioural outputs in Section 2 above (and I shall comment on this distinction further in Section 4.1 below). But beyond this I have said nothing to imply that inputs and outputs must be simple or unstructured. So I have left it open that simple animals may have highly structured hard-wired input devices (perceptual 'modules', if you like), and highly structured hard-wired output devices (behavioural 'modules').[3]

So, to repeat, nothing in my analysis commits me to behaviourism about simple animals. This clarification, however, is now likely to prompt a contrary reaction from committed cognitivists: 'All right, I see that when you say non-human animals are "simple", you are not saying that they are behaviourist dummies. You allow that their input and output modules, and the links between them, may be highly structured. But, if you allow this, why stop there? Why not credit animals with means–end reasoning as well? If you allow they have the mental wherewithal for sophisticated analysis of sensory stimuli, and for sophisticated control of behaviour, then why doubt that they can also figure out the best means to their ends? After all, it is clear that many specialized perceptual and

---

[3] When I talk of 'modules' in what follows, I intend no specific theoretical commitments. I shall use the term merely as a stylistic variant for 'mechanism' or 'system'. In my view, the technical notion of a 'module' is a theoretical mess. Fodor (1983) originally specified a number of necessary criteria for modularity, but omitted to tell us what to call the many interesting types of cognitive mechanism that satisfy some of these criteria but not others. Moreover, some of these criteria themselves turn out to involve a number of distinct and dissociable requirements: 'hardwired', 'domain-specific', and 'informationally encapsulated' have proved particularly troublesome in this respect.

behavioural systems in animals, like vision and navigation, involve complex computational processing of representations. Since this is clearly just the kind of processing required for means–end reasoning, wouldn't it be very surprising, to say the least, if evolution had never pressed such processing into the service of animal means–end reasoning? Means–end reasoning is manifestly a very powerful adaptive tool, once you have it. Given that the materials for such a means–end reasoner were readily to hand, so to speak, we should surely expect that evolution would have made use of them for just this purpose.'

This line of thought, however, is less than compelling. Evolution only precipitates traits that provide some selective advantage, and it is not immediately clear what selective advantage would accrue to most animals from a computational processor devoted specifically to means–end reasoning.

Note in this connection that simple animals will certainly be able to display a wide range of sophisticated behaviours, despite their lack of means–end reasoning. Nothing stops such creatures from being sensitive to the most intricate features of their environment and performing extremely complex routines under the guidance of this information. Their cognitive mechanisms can be highly structured, both within their input and output modules, and in the links between them. All they lack is a system whose purpose is to put together items of general information in order to draw out further general conclusions.

It is perhaps worth emphasizing that input and output systems, as I am thinking of them, can be very complex indeed. One point I have not yet made explicit is that learning can take place within peripheral systems, as well as between them. Thus there could be perceptual systems which have acquired the ability, during individual development, to recognize different kind of animals or plants, or cars or aeroplanes, or individual faces or gaits, or musical compositions, or lack of pawn cohesion in the centre. Again, there could be behavioural systems which have acquired the ability to execute a forehand, or multiply by ten, or make a sandwich, or drive to work, or be apologetic.

Other complexities are possible. Thus, on the input side, some perceptual systems could receive information from others; while others could lay down their findings in memory stores (allowing information about particular circumstances to guide actions over a temporal distance, as it were). And, on the output side, the execution of behavioural routines could be guided by real-time informational resources deriving from special informational channels; moreover, there could also be nesting of behavioural routines, with more complicated modules being built up from simpler ones.

The possibility of all these sophistications in simple animals undercuts the thought that there must have been strong selection pressure for means–end reasoning from an early stage in evolutionary history of simple animals. If simple animals could already deal intelligently with every circumstance their environments threw at them, then why should they have undergone the selectional disadvantage of building an expensive specialized means–end reasoner?

At this stage a new suspicion about my line of argument is likely to arise. If I am packing so much into 'simple animals', isn't there a danger that simple animals are already performing means–end reasoning in the sense I have defined it? They may not have a definite 'theorem-prover' in their heads, a specific device that takes in sentence-like premises and derives conclusions via some mechanical realization of the predicate calculus. But, given the amount of cognitive structure I am allowing them, won't they satisfy my requirements for means–end reasoning in any case, even without such a device?

In the rest of this section I shall consider five different ways in which this challenge might be developed, by examining different kinds of cognitive sophistication which are undoubtedly present in many non-human animals. I should admit at this stage that some of these will lead to significant modifications to my strong hypothesis of non-human simplicity. However, even if the position I am left with is not exactly my strong hypothesis as originally advertised, it will still amount to a substantial claim about the distinctive abilities that humans use to select actions.

4.1 Modular Combinations

The first thought I want to consider is that the combined operation of different elements in simple cognitive systems can itself amount to means–end reasoning as I have defined it. In particular, this arguably happens when input systems (or output systems) combine with input–output links to generate behaviour.

Recall how in Section 3 above I allowed that input–output dispositions to behaviour can properly be viewed as embodying general information. If an animal is disposed to drink from ponds when thirsty, because in its individual or ancestral past so drinking led to water, then I agreed that this disposition can properly be viewed as representing the general claim that drinking from ponds will yield water.

However, note now how a similar point could be made about dispositions *within* perceptual input modules. For example, suppose that an animal is disposed to judge that a pond is present, when it receives retinal stimulation X, as a result of ontogenetic or phylogenetic selection: some reinforcing result accrued, in its individual or ancestral past, precisely when it formed this judgement after being so stimulated. Given this, shouldn't I equally now allow that this perceptual disposition represents the general claim that stimulation X indicates ponds?

I am indeed happy to allow this. However, it now seems to follow that an animal will be performing means–end reasoning, in my sense, whenever the two dispositions just mentioned combine to constitute a third, derived, disposition—to drink when thirsty on receipt of stimulation X. For at the representational level this derivation amounts to combining the general claims that 'stimulation X indicates ponds' and 'drinking from ponds will yield water' to generate the further general claim that 'drinking after stimulation X will yield water'.

Note in particular that an animal could well have this derived disposition even if stimulation X plus drinking had never been followed by water in its individual or ancestral past. Provided stimulation X had previously been followed by pond-judgements, and (different) pond-judgements plus drinking had previously been followed by water, past experience would give the animal the premises, so to speak—which it could then put together to derive the experientially novel conclusion, that stimulation X plus drinking will be followed by water.

A similar point applies to dispositions which develop within behavioural output modules. Suppose an animal has a disposition to perform specific movements Y in circumstances Z because in its individual or ancestral past so acting constituted drinking from a pond. Then, as before, this disposition could be held to embody the information 'in circumstances Y specific movements Z will constitute drinking from a pond'. Suppose also that the animal also has an input–output disposition which embodies, as before, the general information that 'drinking from ponds will yield water'. Again these two items can combine to deliver the possibly experientially novel conclusion that 'in circumstances Y specific movements Z will yield water'.

My response to this line of thought is that while these derived dispositions are experientially 'novel' in one sense, there remains another important kind of 'novelty' which is possible for humans, but not simple animals. For note that the examples just given do not involve behaviour which is novel *from the perspective of the animal's perceptual and behavioural classifications*. After all, we are assuming an animal whose perceptual input system classifies different stimuli together as '*ponds*' when sending information to other cognitive systems. So at this level, the level of the animal's perceptual classifications, there is nothing new in the fact that another pond yields water, given previous experience of ponds yielding water. Similarly, on the output side, an action needn't count as 'novel' just because it involves some uniquely discriminable sequence of movements, if these are simply one instance of a behavioural type which has previously been triggered as such by behavioural control mechanisms.

So let me now specify that the kind of novelty required for genuine means–end reasoning is novelty relative to the structure of the animal's perceptual and behavioural systems. Genuine novelty requires some new pairing within the animal's own perceptual and behavioural typology.

Some readers may feel that this is resting a lot on the animal's typology. This raises large issues, but in the present context let me simply observe that we have been committed to the reality of such typologies from an early stage. As soon as we reached Level 2 animals, with specialized informational systems, we were supposing a repertoire of perceptual input judgements ('here's a pond', say) which maintain their identity across interactions with different drives and behaviours. And by Level 4 learners, if not before, we were supposing a repertoire of output responses ('approach', 'retreat', 'drink', 'eat', say) which maintain their identity across prompting by different drives and perceptions. Given that these classifications were introduced earlier, and moreover that I then sketched their motivations, there is nothing particularly ad hoc in now using them in characterizing behavioural 'novelty'.

4.2 Getting into Position

Ruth Millikan (forthcoming), following Randy Gallistel (1980), has pointed out how responses to conditions may be adaptive, not because they lead directly to advantageous outcomes, but because they are likely to put the animal in the way of some further condition which will then prompt a response which will lead to the advantageous outcome (or some further condition which will then prompt a response which is likely to put the animal in the way of some further condition . . . which will then prompt a response which will lead to the advantageous outcome). So a bird, once it feels hungry, will be prompted to fly, and then, if it sees a fruit tree, will be prompted to approach it, and then, if it sees a fruit, will be prompted to peck it.

At first sight this might look like means–end reasoning as I have characterized it. When the bird takes flight, the virtue of this action lies in the fact that it is a means to seeing and approaching a fruit tree, which is a means to finding and eating a fruit, which is a means to food.

However, this is not a real instance of means–end reasoning in my sense. This is because such general facts as that flight is a means to finding fruit trees need not be represented anywhere in this bird, even in the generous sense in which I have allowed that such information can be represented in behavioural dispositions.

To see this, note that, for all that has been said so far, the *outcome* which has instilled the disposition to fly when hungry may be nothing other than that so flying has led to *food* in the past.[4] If this is so, then the disposition shouldn't be counted as representing anything except that flying when hungry leads to food. In particular, it won't represent that flying leads to tree-finding which in turn leads to fruit-finding. True, it is only in virtue of these further facts about these means that flying does lead to food. But if the aim of flying, as fixed by phylogenetic or ontogenetic history, has been food, rather than these intermediary means, then there will be no rationale for taking the disposition to represent anything about these means. (That would be like taking my belief that aspirin

---

[4] It would be different if the bird were able to *acquire* desires for some of the relevant means, such as for finding fruit trees, since then a proximal behaviour like flying could be reinforced by achieving this desire, and not only by leading to food. I shall not be able to deal with the acquisition of desires fully in this essay, however, though I shall make some remarks on the subject in Section 4.5 below.

cures headaches to represent facts about brain chemistry about which I am quite ignorant.)

It might seem arbitrary to think of the flying as aiming directly at food, rather than at the intermediary means. But note that animals get hungry when food is needed, and that the specific function of this drive is correspondingly to prompt behaviour which will lead to food. Given this, the phylogenetic or ontogenetic selection of flying when hungry will hinge crucially on whether flying leads to food, and not on whether it leads to other outcomes. (After all, if flying led to fruit trees, but not food, it wouldn't be selected; but if it led to food, but not via fruit trees, it would be selected.)

There may seem to be a problem in supposing that a behaviour (like flying) can be selected by a pay-off (food) from which it is removed by a long series of intermediate means. But note how such behaviours can evolve by accretion. Once hungry birds are disposed to eat when they see fruit, this will create selection pressure for hungry birds to approach when they see fruit trees. And once they are disposed to do this, then this will create selection pressure to fly when they are hungry. Perhaps this kind of process will work better in intergenerational genetic selection than in ontogenetic learning. For an ontogenetic learning mechanism will need somehow to connect the behaviour with the distal pay-off, and if the time-lag is too great this may prove difficult. From the point of view of genetic selection, by contrast, this is not a problem: the behaviour will be selected as long as its connection with the pay-off reliably influences survival and reproduction, however long the time-lag.

4.3 Intra-Modular Means–End Reasoning

So far I have been assuming that means–end reasoning, if it is to be found anywhere, will somehow mediate *between* perceptual inputs and behavioural outputs (or perhaps, as in Section 4.1 above, arise from the *interaction* between peripheral modules and input–output links). But what about the possibility that means–end reasoning might be found *within* peripheral modules? In this section I shall consider this issue specifically with respect to behaviour-generating output systems, though similar considerations could be raised with respect to perceptual input systems.

Thus, for example, consider the special navigation abilities, common to many animals, which enable them to find their way back home, or back to previously perceived food, even when these targets are hidden and distant. It is possible that some animals do this by combining given items of general (causal, conditional) information to derive new general conclusions. For example, they might start with the information 'If I go west from here, I'll get to A' and 'If I go north from A, I'll get to the food', and use this to infer 'If I go west until I get to A, and then north, I'll reach the food'.

There are two possible responses I could make here. On the one hand, I could appeal to the line I took in Section 4.1 above in order to exclude such intra-modular inferences from the category of means–end reasoning. Recall that I there specified that means–end reasoning should yield input–output links which are novel *relative to the animal's typology of behaviour*. Similarly, I could here argue that navigational abilities do not constitute genuine means–end reasoning, because they take place *within* a behavioural output module, and so yield no new links *between* inputs and behavioural outputs. From this point of view, figuring out novel ways of 'going back home' will not count as means–end reasoning, on the grounds that 'going back home' will function as a primitive behavioural unit relative to the structure of the animal's motivational and learning systems. (Thus different drives might in different circumstances each prompt the 'going back home' routine; again, 'going back home' may be a response that can be encouraged or extinguished as such by instrumental learning.) In support of this exclusionary line, note that intra-modular inferential mechanisms are likely to be highly content-specific, by comparison with means–end reasoning in mature human beings, which can work with pretty much any kind of information. A navigation system, for example, will deal only with spatial information, and will only select spatial routes as means.

On the other hand, even if we now assume that routines like 'going back home' do indeed so function as primitive behavioural units in non-human animals (and it remains possible that the empirical data will show that this is not so), this seems a rather cheap basis for denying means–end reasoning to animals. After all, if animals do piece together different bits of general information *within* the systems which govern their behavioural routines, and thereby figure out what to do, this certainly seems a reasonable example of the kind of behavioural flexibility I have been concerned with in this essay. Such animals will be able to extrapolate beyond specific behaviours which have proved advantageous in the past, and will do so by combining separate items of general information into inferences. Why downgrade this, just because it can be regarded as taking place within 'modules', rather than between them? And, again, why does it matter that these inferences will only operate on a specific subject-matter? It isn't as if we could seriously have expected non-human animals to perform inferences across the same wide range of subjects as humans.

I do not propose to pursue this largely classificatory issue any further. In the remainder of this essay I shall continue to focus on means–end reasoning which mediates between input and output systems in general, and which correspondingly has no in-built limitations on the kinds of content it deals with. But in doing so I do not want to suggest that it is unimportant that similar inferential powers may be located within behavioural output modules. Even if my focus in this essay lies elsewhere, this is clearly a significant question about animal cognition in its own right.

Before leaving this issue, let me comment briefly on the substantial issue of whether animal spatial navigation does in fact involve content-specific intra-modular means–end reasoning. This is not entirely straightforward. It is uncontroversial that many animals, including birds and insects, form non-egocentric spatial maps of their environments and behavioural targets, and that they can place and orientate themselves with respect to such maps using landmarks. However, this doesn't necessarily add up to means–end reasoning as I have been conceiving it. It depends on how they use the maps to generate behaviour.

Perhaps their brains simply execute the analogue of drawing a straight line from their present positions to their targets (perhaps iterating this strategy as they approach their targets, and in particular after any detours to circumvent obstacles). This wouldn't amount to anything like means–end reasoning as I am conceiving it.

It would be different, however, with animals who cognitively performed some analogue of tracing out a continuous obstacle-avoiding path from their starting positions to their targets, prior to embarking on their journey, and then set themselves to follow these paths. This would seem clearly to qualify as intra-modular means–end reasoning in my sense. For it would be equivalent to combining separate items of causal information, in the way sketched above—'If I go west from here, I'll reach *A*, and then, if I go north from there, I'll reach the food'.

4.4 Classical Conditioning

So far the only kind of learning I have considered has been instrumental learning, in which the disposition to perform some response **R** given some **C** and **D** gets reinforced because so responding has led to some reinforcing outcome in the past. However, there is also another kind of learning, classical or Pavlovian learning, where an animal learns to associate one stimulus **B** with another stimulus **C** after observing their past association, and shows this by now responding to **B** as it previously responded to **C**. (Note that classical conditioning involves no feedback from previous 'rewards'; all it requires is that perceptual 'nodes' which were previously co-activated now come to activate each other.)

This now gives us another candidate for means–end reasoning. Take an animal who initially responds to **C** (and **D**) with **R**, and then after classical conditioning of **B** with **C** comes to respond similarly to **B**. I have previously agreed that the initial disposition here can properly be understood as representing the information '**R** in **C** (and **D**) will yield **O**' (where **O** is the relevant advantageous result). Given this, it is natural to regard the classical conditioning as yielding the extra information that 'All **B**s are **C**s', which is then combined with the prior information to generate '**R** in **B** (and **D**) will yield **O**'.

Indeed there is nothing to stop such inferences being iterated. An animal could learn that 'All **B**s are **C**s' and then—separately— that 'All **A**s are **B**s', and consequently become disposed to behave on perceiving **A** in ways it originally behaved only on perceiving **C**. It is an empirical question how far such inferential chains might stretch in any actual animals. But one would expect any mechanism underpinning classical conditioning to allow some such iteration.

These kinds of cases cannot be dismissed on the grounds that the extra general information lies *within* perceptual systems, as in Section 4.1. For the new items of general information which get combined with the prior behavioural dispositions are now embodied in links *between* outputs of perceptual systems, not in structures within such systems. (Note how this point will not be sensitive to any particular rationale for identifying 'perceptual modules'. However we decide to discriminate 'modules', a general mechanism for associative learning will build links between them.)

I can see no reason not to allow that associative learning will in this way give rise to means–end reasoning as so far defined. Note, however, that animals who can perform means–end reasoning only in this specific sense will still be cognitively extremely limited, by comparison with mature human reasoners. This is because they can only draw inferences about the *conditions* which render actions appropriate, and not about the *consequences* actions may have. They can use their general information to figure out that **B** provides just as good an opportunity for **R**-ing in pursuit of **O** as **C** does. But when it comes to figuring out what **R**-ing might be good for in the first place, they still lack any inferential powers. They are stuck with information of the form '**R** will yield **O**', where **R** is some item from their behavioural repertoire, and **O** the outcome which in the past has instilled the disposition to **R**. In particular, they have no power to reason along such lines as: '**R** will yield **M**' and '**M** will yield **O**'—therefore, '**R** will yield **O**'.

The point is that associative learning can allow animals to figure out that new conditions are suitable for old behavioural dispositions, but it can't generate any new behavioural dispositions. When it comes to information 'causally downstream' from behaviour, so to speak, the only means of representation available so far is embodiment in behavioural dispositions. And the only mechanism for forming such dispositions is still phylogenetic or ontogenetic selection of some **R** which led to some **O** in the past. As yet we have seen no way to acquire the information of the form '**R** will lead to **O**', except via such direct selection.

Both Gopnik, Glymour, and Sobel (forthcoming) and Millikan (forthcoming) have compared this limitation to egocentricity in spatial mapping. An egocentric spatial map locates objects solely in terms of their relation to the subject's own position and orientation. Now, as I mentioned in the last section, many animals transcend this spatial egocentricity, and represent the spatial world in objective terms, in terms of maps in which they themselves are simply one item among many. However, animals who are spatially objective in this way may still be *causally egocentric*. In particular this will still be true of the Pavlovian animals we are currently considering. Despite their classical associative powers, they will lack any conception of objective 'causal space', as containing many objectively interacting items, of which their actions are just one special case. Instead the only information they can bring to bear on happenings causally downstream from their behaviour will be egocentric in form, with some piece of their own behaviour **R** at one end of the relation, and some reinforcing result **O** at the other.

So, at this stage, let me raise the stakes for full-fledged means–end reasoning once more, to include some degree of causal non-egocentricity. Let me now require that it involve, not just any use of general information to infer new general conclusions, but specifically that it allow animals to infer new behaviourally downstream causal facts of the form '**R** will lead to **O**' from other general facts. From now on, then, full-fledged means–end reasoning will in this sense use non-egocentric causal facts to figure out which behaviours will produce which novel results.

4.5 Dickinson's Rats

Now that this issue is in focus, the obvious question is whether there is any direct evidence for non-egocentric awareness of causal relations in non-human animals.

As it happens, the few studies which have attacked this question head-on suggest that even apes and other primates are very limited in their ability to appreciate objective causal connections. While apes can certainly learn to use tools in novel ways, they don't seem to represent causal connections in a way that can inform means–end reasoning. There is no direct evidence that non-human primates ever take the knowledge that some intermediary cause **M** produces end result **O**, combine this with knowledge that behaviour **R** leads to **M**, and use the two items of information together 'to devise novel ways of producing the intermediary and thus the end result'. (Tomasello and Call, 1997: 390. See also the rest of their chs. 3 and 12.)

At the same time, however, there is also some very detailed work in the animal learning tradition, especially from Anthony Dickinson and his associates, which at first sight suggests that rats can perform exactly the kind of inference I am now asking for (Heyes and Dickinson, 1990; Dickinson and Balleine, 1999).

Consider this experiment. (This is just one of a range of related rat experiments, but it contains the essential points.) Rats are trained while hungry but not thirsty, in an environment where they gain dry food pellets from pressing a lever, and a sucrose solution from pulling a chain. Both the pellets and the sucrose solution satisfy hunger, but, as it happens, only the sucrose solution would satisfy thirst. Now make some of these rats thirsty, and give them the choice of pressing the lever or pulling the chain. With one important qualification to be entered shortly, the thirsty rats will straightaway display a preference for chain-pulling.

Since nothing during their training reinforced chain-pulling over lever-pressing, this experiment provides prima-facie reason to suppose that the rats are explicitly storing the causal information that chain-pulling yields the sucrose solution, which they then combine with the fact that the solution quenches thirst, to derive the conclusion that chain-pulling will satisfy thirst.

It may seem as if there is a loophole in the argument. Even if the rats weren't thirsty during training, wouldn't their thirst-drive, low as it was, have been yet further reduced by the liquid-from-chain-pulling, but not by the pellets-from-lever-pressing? If the rats had a drive-specific learning mechanism (cf. the discussion of Level 4 above), then they may on this basis have acquired a preferential disposition to chain-pull when thirsty. (The idea here would be that certain behaviours—here chain-pulling—get attached to specific drives—thirst—not because they were generally rewarding in the past, but specifically because they *quenched thirst* in the past.)

However, this story is inconsistent with a further fact about the experiment. This is the rider I mentioned a moment ago. The trained rats won't chain-pull, even when thirsty, unless they are first given an opportunity to drink the sucrose solution *when they are thirsty*, and thereby discover that it quenches thirst. On the story just suggested, this further experience ought not to be necessary, for on that story the result of the initial training should already be to chain-pull *when thirsty*.

So it seems undeniable that the rats are somehow deriving from their training the information that chain-pulling leads specifically to sucrose solution, even though the difference between sucrose solution and food pellets is as yet of no motivational significance to them. Then, later on, the rats acquire the further information that sucrose solution quenches thirst. And at that point the rats combine the two pieces of information, to infer that chain-pulling as opposed to lever-pressing is a means to satisfying thirst. They thereby acquire a novel disposition to behaviour, a disposition that has never itself been reinforced for satisfying thirst.

So described, the rats would seem clearly to be capable of non-egocentric causal thinking, of the kind I am now requiring for full-fledged means–end reasoning.[5] But perhaps there is another way of viewing their cognitive achievements, a way that will distance them less from simple animals. Suppose we regard their exposure to the sucrose solution when thirsty, not as giving them the factual information that sucrose solution quenches thirst, but rather as instilling in them a new 'acquired drive' for sucrose solution.

On this way of looking at things, the rats are not so different from simple animals after all. We can view the preferential chain-pulling behaviour as the upshot of (*a*) a drive to get sucrose solu-

---

[5] Dickinson himself distinguishes sharply between creatures that process symbolic representations and mere conditioned learners, and takes his experiments to show that rats are in the former category. As the arguments of this essay will have indicated, however, I regard this distinction between representing and conditioned learning as a false dichotomy: there is plenty of representation in conditioned learners. The real issue is: exactly what kinds of representation do the rats embody, and exactly how do these representations guide behaviour?

tion and (*b*) a behavioural disposition to chain-pull in pursuit of sucrose solution when this drive is active. The rats will thus be prompted to act by just the same kind of practical syllogism as operates in other animals. Provided the 'acquired sucrose solution drive' is activated whenever the rats are thirsty, this model predicts just the same behaviour as a means–end reasoning model.

Of course, we will still need to acknowledge that the rats differ in very important ways from any simple animals discussed so far. Most obviously, we are now crediting them with an ability to *acquire* drives, where previously all drives were assumed to be innate. This is in fact a huge extension of cognitive power. Since there seems no reason why rats should not have the potential to acquire drives for any circumstance that they are capable of *recognizing*, we have here graduated from animals whose ends are limited to a few basic outcomes to animals that can embrace pretty much anything as an end. If we want to draw a sharp line between 'drives' and 'desires', this seems as good a place as any.

In addition, and even more interestingly, we must also acknowledge that the rats are capable of acquiring a disposition to do **R** (chain-pull) in pursuit of **O** (sucrose solution), *even though **R**'s so leading to **O** has never previously satisfied any drives.* The line I am now pushing is that the information '**R** leads to **O**' needn't be embodied anywhere except in a disposition to do **R** when a drive for **O** is activated. But it is striking, to say the least, that such a disposition can be acquired even before any internal representation of **O** has yet acquired the status of a drive.[6]

[6] [Footnote added for this collection: It now seems to me that I missed an important beat when I first wrote this essay. If animals acquire desires for those circumstances that they experience as preceding the satisfaction of pre-existing desires, then the rats would already have acquired a desire for sucrose solution in the initial training phase of the experiment, since they there experienced sucrose solution as preceding hunger satisfaction. And this would then explain why they already embodied the information that **R** (chain-pull) leads to **O** (sucrose solution): once they acquired a

It may seem, especially given this last point, that I am trying to build a distinction out of thin air. If I am admitting that somehow the **O**-productivity of **R** must be representable even when **R** isn't yet wired up to be triggered by a drive for **O**, then doesn't this already grant the rats the essential cognitive power at issue? However, a crucial limitation may still lie in the fact that this causal knowledge needs to be embodied in a disposition-ready way, so to speak. Before the rat has any drive directed at **O**, it is already able somehow to link behaviour **R** with an internal representation of **O**. But this link may consist in nothing more than that the rat would do **R** were its representation of **O** to acquire 'drive-active' status. If this is right, then the rats will still suffer from a form of causal egocentricity. The only causal information available to them will still have an item of their own behaviour **R** at the front end.

If we do see the rats in this way, it will have the advantage of explaining why their powers of means–end reasoning are limited as they are.[7] In my terms, Dickinson's rats are certainly capable of

desire for sucrose solution, they would then have learned, in the initial training phase, that chain-pulling is a good means to satisfying it, via standard instrumental conditioning. From this point of view, the rats' exposure to sucrose solution when thirsty serves only to dispose them to have their acquired sucrose-solution desire activated by thirst as well as by hunger, and not to instil this desire for the first time. More generally, this perspective reinforces this section's overall thesis about the rats' cognitive limitations: while the acquisition of desires certainly multiplies the possibilities of novel action, the rats are still limited to performing **R**s which *they* have experienced as preceding **O**s which *they* have experienced as preceding the satisfaction of . . . non-acquired desires. As I would now put it, the rats are limited to learning from *personal experience*, and have no way of using general information acquired from *observation* (or testimony) to draw inferences about potential causal consequences of their behaviour. I would like to thank Gianmatteo Mameli for putting me on the right track here.]

[7] Moreover, it will also allow us to explain the above-mentioned limitations of apes and other primates. Since primates will presumably share

novel actions. By combining their stored knowledge that **R** will lead to **O** with some newly acquired drive for **O**, they can be led to actions they have not previously performed. However, if their **R**→**O** information must always be stored in a 'dormant disposition', in the way just suggested, then the generative power of their overall cognitive system will be limited by their ability to acquire new drives. This is not the place to start considering details of the mechanisms by which animals acquire new drives (an issue which seems to me crucial, not just for understanding rats, but also for understanding humans). But if, as seems plausible, these mechanisms must work by some kind of direct association with pre-existing drives, then the causally egocentric rats will be capable of far less behavioural novelty than reasoners who are also able to derive **R**→**O** information from an unlimited range of non-egocentric causal links.

5 Reasoning by Accident

Overall, the previous section was a response to the thought that means–end reasoning is too easy to be a peculiarly human adaptation, and so must be widespread through the animal kingdom. I now want to address the converse thought, that means–end reasoning is too hard to be a biological adaptation, and so has only become available to humans as a side-effect of other biological developments.

On this view, means–end reasoning would be like arithmetic or music. Proficiency at these practices may well have yielded a reproductive advantage in the period since they emerged, in the sense that adepts may have had more children on average. But this doesn't make them evolutionary adaptations. Other abilities, with

any cognitive sophistications present in rats, we will be hard pressed to explain the poor primate performance, if we allow full-fledged means–end reasoning to rats.

independent evolutionary explanations, fully enable us to explain the emergence and preservation of arithmetic and music, once they get into our culture.[8] And in any case there probably hasn't been enough time since these practices started for any genes favouring them to be significantly selected.

On this model, then, means–end reasoning rests on other abilities with a biological purpose, but has no such purpose itself. In the terminology made famous by Stephen Gay Gould and Richard Lewontin (1979), it would be a 'spandrel'. The idea that means–end reasoning is a spandrel is perhaps found more often in conversation than in print. But it is popular among a surprisingly wide range of theorists, from official 'evolutionary psychologists', through Dennettians, to neo-associationist experimentalists.

5.1 Understanding of Mind

This general 'spandrel' suggestion can be combined with different hypotheses about the crucial prior ability. One fashionable candidate is 'understanding of mind'. Once our 'understanding of mind module' emerged, so this story goes, we would then have had the intellectual wherewithal for means–end reasoning, along with other cultural spin-offs like promising.

However, this particular suggestion seems to me to owe far more to intellectual fashion than serious analysis.[9] There is an obvious reason why means–end reasoning cannot have piggy-backed evolutionarily on understanding of mind. This is that the standard accounts of understanding of mind only make sense if

[8] Which is not to deny that these explanations themselves can be informed by biological facts. *Which* practices are preserved by 'culture' depends crucially on which dispositions have been bequeathed to us by natural selection. Cf. Sperber (1996).

[9] However, see Sperber (1997) for some interesting specific suggestions about the connection between understanding of mind and logic in general.

we suppose that 'mind-readers' are *already* capable of means–end thinking. This applies to both the 'simulation-theory', which holds that understanding of mind rests largely on the ability to simulate the decision-making of others, and the 'theory-theory', which holds that understanding of mind derives from an articulated theory of mind.

The point is perhaps most obvious in connection with the 'simulation-theory'. The central assumption of this theory is that 'mind-readers' proceed by simulating others' beliefs and desires and then mimicking their decision-making 'off-line'. But such 'decision-making' is nothing but the means–end reasoning we are trying to understand. Presumably an ability to perform such reasoning 'off-line' presupposes a prior ability to do it on-line. So this version of the story simply assumes what we want to explain.

The 'theory-theory' version of understanding of mind fares little better. On this version, 'mind-readers' anticipate others' reactions by drawing predictions from an articulated theory of mind. That is, they attribute beliefs and desires to others, feed these in as initial conditions to a set of general assumptions about the mind, and on this basis figure out their best strategies for dealing with others' behaviour. But this is then nothing but a special case of means–end reasoning as we have been considering it. Once more, the story simply begs the question.[10]

[10] [Footnote added for this collection: It remains possible that the evolution of means–end reasoning was facilitated by some *part* of understanding of mind, in particular, some part which does not itself presuppose means–end reasoning. For example, my final suggestion below is that means–end reasoning may derive from a combination of visual imagination with an ability to copy others' successful actions. But perhaps an ability to copy others' successful actions depends in turn on your being able to *empathize* with their successes (for otherwise why should *their* successes reinforce *your* dispositions to action?). Note that postulating such empathetic abilities on their own is not yet to postulate a system which predicts others' behaviour by using some pre-existing power of means–end reasoning.]

5.2 Language

A rather more plausible version of the 'spandrel' approach would be that means–end reasoning piggy-backs, not on understanding of mind, but on language. But here too there are difficulties. To start with, this story too seems to be in danger of assuming what needs to be explained. The worry here would be that the primary biological purpose of language is to increase each individual's stock of information. But such extra information wouldn't be any use to creatures who can't yet do means–end reasoning, since they wouldn't be able to use it to draw any extra conclusions about appropriate behaviour.

Perhaps this is a bit quick. Maybe language first evolved as a device for passing around pieces of *particular* information ('a tiger is coming', 'there are fruit in that tree' . . .). Since even simple creatures are guided by particular information about their circumstances, the utility of this information doesn't yet call for any means–end reasoning. So maybe means–end reasoning only emerged after our ancestors had first developed a relatively sophisticated language for reporting particular facts. Building on this basis, perhaps language *then* biologically evolved to report and process general claims.

The problem now, however, is to explain this last bit—what exactly was the extra biological pressure which led to language reporting and processing general information? If the answer is that language evolved this feature to facilitate means–end reasoning, then this will mean that means–end reasoning is not a spandrel after all. It may have been largely dependent on language, in the sense that its emergence had to wait on the biological selection of prior linguistic abilities. But in so far as certain genes were then selected specifically because they helped us to do means–end reasoning, means–end reasoning will qualify as an adaptation in its own right, not a spandrel.

On the other hand, if the answer is that language evolved the ability to represent and process general information for some independent reason, then there are more problems. Most immediately, we will need an explanation of *why* language should have been selected to report and process general claims, if this was not to facilitate means–end reasoning. But there is also a more fundamental problem. If we suppose that the linguistic processing of general claims first served some purpose independent of means–end reasoning, then we will need some some story about how this independent ability was then parlayed, spandrel-like, into means–end reasoning. Suppose that our ancestors first became able to formulate general claims, and draw novel causal conclusions from them, for reasons quite independent of means–end reasoning. How exactly would these novel theoretical conclusions then have come to make a difference to their practical activities?

The point here is that means–end reasoning must exert some control over *behaviour*. However, pre-existing cognitive architectures, of the kind present in simple animals, have no place for anything to issue in behaviour except dispositions to behave in certain ways when triggered by perceptions and competing drives. Somehow the ability to process general representations has to be able to *add* to this set of dispositions (either temporarily—'next time I see a post box I'll insert this letter', or permanently—'from now I'll eat fish instead of meat'). However, an ability to draw conclusions from general claims, even conclusions about means to ends, will not by itself ensure this. In addition, the outputs of such reasoning will have to intrude on the control of behaviour. Without being able to alter our behaviour-guiding programme in this way, means–end reasoning won't make any difference to what we *do*.

5.3 Why Means–End Reasoning Can't be a Spandrel

As it happens, this line of argument seems to me to present a difficulty, not just to the specific idea that means–end reasoning piggy-backs on language, but to any version of the view that it is a non-adaptational spandrel. The problem is to understand how a new power to alter behaviour could arise without some basic biological alteration. It scarcely makes sense to suppose that a pure spandrel could intervene in some unprecedented way in the biological systems that direct action. Prior to means–end reasoning, behaviour is controlled by a set of dispositions that are laid down either by genes or by conditioning. Somehow means–end reasoning, however it is realized, must involve the power to create new such dispositions. It is hard to see how this could happen without some biological selection, some alteration of our biological design, which allowed the output of deliberative decisions to reset our dispositions to action.

Note that this is not yet an argument for supposing that there is some quite separate mechanism in the human brain specifically devoted to means–end reasoning. There may well be such a mechanism, and I shall return to this possibility in my final remarks. But the argument I have just given supports only the far weaker conclusion that there must have been *some* biological selection for means–end reasoning. This could have been quite minimal, a matter of a few genetic alterations allowing some pre-existing cognitive activity to start exerting an influence on behaviour. The most obvious possibility would be the one suggested above: a linguistic ability to report and process general information evolved for some independent reason; once that was in place, then a further evolutionary step allowed its outputs to influence behaviour.

5.4 Means–End Reasoning as a Module

In the Introduction to this essay, I said that, if I had to choose, I would place means–end reasoning on the side of the 'modules', rather than with general-purpose cognitive mechanisms. I am now rather better placed to explain the thrust of this remark. My intention, in classifying means–end reasoning as modular, was not to claim that there is some dedicated processor in the brain which was built solely to perform means–end reasoning. As I have just said, this may be so, but it is not something I am insisting on. Rather, my concern was only to emphasize that means–end reasoning is a cognitive mechanism which is activated in specific circumstances to serve specific needs. It is not some meta-system which controls all human activity, constantly selecting whichever behavioural outputs are best suited to current perceptual inputs.

An implicit assumption of much philosophical thinking is that all human behaviour, apart perhaps from crude reflexes, is selected by just this kind of meta-systemic means–end thinking. However, this is not the picture that emerges from this paper. I see no reason to doubt that behaviour in humans is determined in the first instance in just the same way as it is in simple animals. We have a set of standing dispositions, which get triggered by current percep-tual information and competing drives. The only difference is that we humans have an extra way, beyond genetic inheritance and conditioning, of adjusting those dispositions. Sometimes we take time out, to consider the pros and cons of various options, and we figure out that the best way to get **O**, under conditions **C** and **D**, is by **R**-ing. And then we *reset* our standing dispositions, so that we become disposed to do **R** next time **C** and **D** arise.

Looking at things this way, we can see that it would probably not be a good idea for means–end reasoning to act as a constant mediator between perceptual inputs and behavioural outputs. Means-end reasoning takes time, and action cannot always wait on deliberation. If we always stopped to check whether we were doing the best thing, the time for action would normally be gone. So for the most part we simply allow our standing dispositions to guide us. But sometimes, when the issues are weighty, and time does not press, we delay acting, and instead activate our powers of means–end reasoning. (Think of this itself as a standing disposi-tion, triggered by the issues being weighty and by time not being pressing.) Then, after means–end reasoning has done its job, we alter our current dispositions, and once more allow them to guide us.[11]

5.5 Concluding Speculations

Let me finish this essay with some brief further reflections on the evolutionary emergence of means–end reasoning. So far I have maintained only that means–end reasoning must have played at least some role in biological evolution.[12] As I argued a moment ago, even if means–end reasoning was biologically posterior to language, there must still have been some selection for means–end reasoning as such, to account for its power to influence behaviour. Still, as I observed, this is consistent with means–end reasoning being a small biological add-on, as it were, to a language faculty that had evolved for quite independent reasons.

However, it is also possible that means–end reasoning may have played a more significant role in evolution. Even if we stick with the idea that language is the sole medium of means–end reasoning,[13] there is the possibility that means–end reasoning is the primary function of language, and that communication is the spandrel, which spun off after language had initially evolved to

---

[11] Note how this model, in which means–end reasoning 'resets' our dispositions to action, can easily accommodate *plans*, that is complicated sequences of actions needed to achieve some end. This would only require that the means–end system be able to produce multiple action settings, settings which will trigger a sequence of behaviours as a sequence of cues are encountered (some of which might simply be the completion of previous behaviours).

[12] At the same time, I take it to be uncontentious that, once means–end reasoning had emerged biologically, it then came to play a major role in the non-biological development of human civilization.

[13] I should perhaps make it clear that by 'language' I mean to include mental processing of internalized sentences of public languages, as well the overt expression of those sentences.

facilitate means–end reasoning. More plausibly, means–end reasoning and communication might both be biological functions of language. This idea is most naturally filled out in a co-evolutionary model: once the first small biological step along the linguistic path had been taken, to facilitate communication, say, then this would have made possible a further step, which facilitated means–end reasoning, which would have made possible a further step, which facilitated communication, and so on.

To complicate the picture still further, note that different aspects of language might call for different evolutionary models. Earlier I distinguished the language of particular facts from the language of general facts. Perhaps the language of particular facts evolved entirely for communicative purposes, as suggested earlier, while the language of general facts evolved primarily to serve means–end reasoning. Or perhaps the language of general facts evolved under the co-evolutionary pressure of means–end reasoning and communication. Or so on. It is not hard to think of further possibilities.

All these last suggestions assume, in one way or another, that means–end reasoning arrived only with language. And this is indeed an attractive assumption. For one thing, the combinatorial structure of language lends itself naturally to the kinds of inferences which are central to means–end reasoning. Moreover, this assumption explains immediately why means–end reasoning should be restricted to humans.

Still, it is also interesting to speculate on whether some forms of means–end reasoning might not initially have evolved independently of language. One obvious hypothesis would be that an initial stage of means–end reasoning made use of visual imagination. Our ancestors played out various scenarios in their 'mind's eye', and used this to choose between alternative courses of action.

This use of visual imagination is so familiar that it is often taken for granted in theoretical contexts. But this familiarity is deceptive.

There are any number of theoretical puzzles here. Is means–end thinking the primary function of visual imagination? How does this kind of 'visual anticipation' relate to visual memory? Is the use of visual imagination for means–end reasoning a generalization of domain-specific uses like spatial manipulation of objects, or, indeed, of spatial navigation as discussed earlier? And, to return to a central theme of this section, how did the upshot of visual imaginings acquire the power to influence pre-existing structures of action control?

In response to this last point, here is another hypothesis. Perhaps a crucial evolutionary step came when our ancestors acquired the ability to copy successful actions from others. This would require them visually to represent what their teachers were doing, and to appreciate the successful upshot, and then to translate this information into action. Once this was possible, it may then have been a small evolutionary step to translating an imaginative visual representation of your own prospectively successful behaviour into action.

These are enough speculations to be getting on with. They already provide the agenda for a number of other papers. I hope that this essay has at least shown that means–end reasoning is a topic worth pursuing further.

REFERENCES

Cosmides, L., and Tooby, J. (1992), 'The Psychological Foundations of Culture', in J. Barkow, L. Cosmides, and J. Tooby (eds.), *The Adapted Mind* (Oxford: Oxford University Press).

Dennett, D. (1978), *Brainstorms* (Cambridge, Mass.: MIT Press).

—— (1987), *The Intentional Stance* (Cambridge, Mass.: MIT Press).

Dickinson, A., and Balleine, B. (1999), 'Causal Cognition and Goal-Directed Action', in C. Heyes and L. Huber (eds.), *The Evolution of Cognition* (Cambridge, Mass.: MIT Press).

Fodor, J. (1983), *The Modularity of Mind* (Cambridge, Mass.: MIT Press).

Gallistel, R. (1980), *The Organization of Behavior* (Hillside, NJ: Earlbaum).

Gould, S., and Lewontin, R. (1979), 'The Spandrels of San Marco and the Panglossian Paradigm: A Critique of the Adaptationist Program', *Proceedings of the Royal Society*, B205.

Gopnik, A., Glymour, C., and Sobel, D. (forthcoming), 'Causal Maps and Bayes Nets: A Cognitive and Computational Account of Theory-Formation'.

Heyes, C., and Dickinson, A. (1990), 'The Intentionality of Animal Action', *Mind and Language*, 5.

Millikan, R. (1996), 'Pushmi-pullyu Representations', in J. Tomberlin (ed.), *Philosophical Perspectives IX* (Atascadero, Calif.: Ridgeview Press).

—— (forthcoming), 'Some Different Ways to Think'.

Papineau, D. (1997) 'Teleosemantics and Indeterminacy', *Australasian Journal of Philosophy*, 75.

Sperber, D. (1996), *Explaining Culture* (Oxford: Basil Blackwell).

—— (1997), 'Intuitive and Reflective Beliefs', *Mind and Language*, 12.

Tomasello, M., and Call, J. (1977), *Primate Cognition* (Cambridge, Mass.: MIT Press).

4

Probability as a Guide to Life

Co-authored with Helen Beebee

1 *Subjective Rationality*

Let us assume that people's degrees of belief conform to the probability calculus. This is an idealization, but it will not matter for the purposes of this essay. In line with normal usage, we will refer to these degrees of belief as subjective probabilities. Then we can say that agents are *subjectively rational* if they choose those actions which their subjective probabilities imply are most likely to achieve what they want. More precisely, given that agents normally attach different utilities to a number of different ends (another useful idealization), subjectively rational agents will choose those actions which will maximize their subjective expected utility.

An example will be useful for what follows. Suppose Alma offers you her £2 to your £1, with you to win all the money if a coin lands heads. Should you accept or decline the bet? If you have no aversion to betting, and your utility function varies linearly with money for these small amounts, then subjective rationality dictates that you should accept her bet if your subjective probability for heads is greater than $1/3$ (for example, if you think the coin fair), and you should decline if it is less than $1/3$.

Note that in this example the possible outcomes (heads/tails) are causally and probabilistically independent of the choice of actions (accept/decline). We shall concentrate on examples like this throughout, in order to by-pass the debate between causal and evidential decision theory. A fully general account of subjective rationality needs to specify whether decisions should depend on the degrees to which an agent believes that certain actions will *cause* certain outcomes, rather than on the agent's conditional degrees of belief in those outcomes given those actions. This is an important issue, but it cuts across our present concerns: the points we make will apply equally to the degrees of belief invoked by causal and by evidential decision theories. (In the examples we shall focus on, where outcomes are independent of actions, both theories agree that choices should depend on agents' simple degrees of belief in outcomes.)

2 Objective Correctness in Degrees of Belief

Whatever view is taken on the causal-evidential issue, there is clearly little point in being subjectively rational if your degrees of belief are objectively inaccurate. (Cf. Mellor, 1982.) Consider Betty, who has ordinary non-probabilistic beliefs about ordinary coins, yet believes to degree 0.9 that such coins will land heads when tossed. Betty will put up large sums of money against small ones on any ordinary coin coming down heads. There is a clear sense in which this is a bad thing. Yet Betty is still subjectively rational, since she chooses those actions which maximize her subjective expected utility.

Betty is subjectively rational. Moreover, she need not have any false beliefs, since believing to degree 0.9 that the coin will land heads isn't the same as (fully) believing that in some sense its probability of heads is 0.9, and we can suppose Betty does not believe this. Nevertheless, there is something objectively unsatisfactory about Betty's degrees of belief. They will lead her to act in a way that is subjectively rational yet objectively inadvisable. In this essay we shall investigate objective desiderata on subjective probabilities. We shall consider what can be said about which degrees of belief are objectively *correct* as a basis for decision. After exploring various possible principles governing objective desiderata on degrees of belief, we shall eventually conclude that the correct degree of belief in an outcome is not necessarily equal to its single-case probability, but rather to its *relative probability*, by which we mean the *objective probability* of that outcome *relative* to features of the situation which the agent knows about.

Let us stress immediately that we are concerned here with the correctness of degrees of belief from a *prudential* point of view. Our question is: which are the right degrees of belief to act on, given that you want such-and-such results? Other philosophers start with a more epistemological question: which degrees of belief ought you to adopt, given that you have such-and-such information which bears on the occurrence of the outcome? (Cf. Pollock: 1990, 22–3, for this distinction.) We are interested here in the first, prudential question. Moreover, we take this question to be different from the evidential question. Degrees of belief are made prudentially correct by objective features of the world, and are correct in this sense even for agents who are in no epistemological position to adopt those degrees of belief. Of course, only those agents who are fully informed about the relevant objective features of the world can *ensure* they have the correct degrees of belief. But, even so, you don't need to have such knowledge in order for the relevant notion of correctness to apply to you. It would be correct, in our sense, for you to give up smoking, if you want to avoid cancer, even if you have never heard about the smoking–cancer link.

This last point marks an important difference between our approach and that of the tradition of writers on 'direct inference', such as Reichenbach (1949), Kyburg (1974), Levi (1977), and Pollock (1990). These writers, like us, address the question of which degrees of belief agents ought to adopt towards outcomes. And they are in agreement with our eventual conclusion, at least to the extent that they hold that agents ought to set their degrees of belief equal to the relevant relative probabilities when they are in an epistemological position to do so. However, it is not clear that writers in this tradition share our central concern with prudential rationality. Writers on direct inference tend simply to take it for granted that you ought to set your degrees of belief equal to the relative probabilities if you can. Their real focus is rather on the evidential issues which arise when you cannot do this, because you do not know the requisite objective probabilities, but only have incomplete evidence about them. By contrast, according to our sense of 'correctness', the degrees of belief of an agent who has no knowledge of the relevant objective probabilities are still constrained by those objective probabilities, in the sense that the matching degrees of belief are still the correct ones for the agent to act on, whether the agent knows it or not. Evidential issues which arise for agents who lack full knowledge of the relevant objective probabilities are important, but they lie beyond the scope of this essay. Our concern is to show that certain objective features of the world, namely relative probabilities, make it prudentially correct to adopt corresponding degrees of belief. How far agents can achieve this, and what they should do if their lack of information hampers them, are further questions which we shall comment on only in passing.

3 The Perfect Principle

Our aim, then, is to specify what makes certain degrees of belief correct from a prudential point of view. The first idea we want briefly to consider is the principle that the correct degrees of belief are those that match the truth. According to this principle, if outcome o_k is going to occur, then the right degree of belief in o_k is 1, and if o_k is not going to occur, the right degree of belief in o_k is 0. Thus we would have:

(1) *The Perfect Principle.* If the kth outcome of mutually exclusive outcomes $\{o_i\}$ is going to occur, then the correct subjective probability for o_i is 1 for $i = k$, and 0 otherwise.

However, we take it that this is not a satisfactory account of which degrees of belief are objectively correct from a prudential point of view. If determinism is false, it is not in general fixed at the time of decision what the outcome will be. So even an agent who is omniscient about the laws of nature and current state of the universe would not be able to implement the Perfect Principle. In many decision situations, then, the prudentially correct degrees of belief must be fixed by the objective probabilities of outcomes, rather than what is actually going to happen.

4 The Objective Principle

The obvious alternative to the Perfect Principle is to say that the correct degrees of belief are those that match the objective probabilities:

(2) *The Objective Principle.* The correct subjective probabilities for outcomes $\{o_i\}$ are those that match the objective probabilities of those outcomes.

Note that agents who have the right degrees of belief in the sense of Principle (2), and are also subjectively rational[1] will act in

---

[1] We shall take this qualification about subjective rationality as read

such a way as to maximize not just subjective expected utility, but also objective expected utility.

The obvious question about the Objective Principle is how to understand its reference to 'objective probabilities'. This will be our focus in the rest of this essay. We shall argue that the best interpretation of the Objective Principle requires us to read 'objective probability', not in the most obvious sense of *single-case probability*, but rather as *probability relative to a description* of the decision situation.

5 Single-Case Probabilities

The nature of single-case probabilities will be discussed further in what follows. For the moment let us simply think of them as the rock-bottom metaphysical probabilities fixed by all probabilistic laws and all particular facts about specific situations. Quantum events provide the paradigm. The 0.5 probability of a radium atom decaying by AD 3615 is a single-case probability, in that there are no further contemporary facts about the radium atom or its surroundings which ensure that the probability of its decaying by AD 3615 is different from 0.5.

Note that if determinism were true, then single-case probabilities would never be different from 0 or 1. Non-degenerate single-case probabilities require outcomes whose occurrence or non-occurrence is not fixed by present circumstances and laws.

Note also that such non-degenerate single-case probabilities change over time. This happens when circumstances relevant to the outcome, but not themselves previously determined, either occur or fail to occur. Thus the single-case probability of a given radium atom decaying by a particular time will decrease as time

henceforth. Note that this warrants our using phrases like 'setting your degrees of belief equal to such-and-such objective probabilities' interchangeably with 'acting on such-and-such objective probabilities'.

passes and the atom does not decay, but will suddenly jump to one if the atom does decay. To take a more everyday example, due to David Lewis (1980), imagine people who move through a multi-path, multi-exit maze, deciding at each branch point whether to turn left or right by some quantum-mechanically random procedure. When they start, their reaching a given exit on the other side of the maze will have a given single-case probability different from o or 1. But this single-case probability will increase or decrease, depending on which choices they actually make as they pass through the maze, until it is determined where they will come out, by which time the single-case probability will have become 1 or 0.

6 *The Single-Case Principle*

One obvious way to read 'objective probabilities' in Principle (2) is as the single-case probabilities at the time of the agent's decision. If you are betting on where someone will come out of the maze, don't you ideally want to know the *current* single-case probability of their emerging from each of the various exits? This suggests the following principle:

(3) *The Single-Case Principle.* The correct subjective probabilities for an agent to attach to outcomes $\{o_i\}$ are equal to the single-case probabilities of the $\{o_i\}$ at the time of the agent's decision.

Note that this Single-Case Principle is equivalent to the Perfect Principle in all those cases where there is any practical possibility of humans using the Perfect Principle. For we can only now know whether some future outcome is going to occur if that outcome is already determined; and in such cases the single-case probability of that outcome will already be 0 or 1.

It may seem obvious that, if there is a right and a wrong about which degrees of belief you ought to act on, then it must be as specified by the Single-Case Principle, for the only way to attach a unique number to the objective probability of an outcome at the time of some decision is to equate it with the single-case probability at that time. So it seems to follow that acting on the single-case probability is the only way to guarantee that you will always choose the action that will maximize your objective expected utility.[2]

Nevertheless, despite this plausible line of reasoning, we think that the Single-Case Principle is not the right way to link degrees of belief with objective probabilities. We think there are many situations where the objectively correct degrees of belief do not match single-case probabilities. We shall formulate a different principle, which we shall call the Relative Principle, which will cover these cases as well. This more general principle will assert that in general the correct degrees of belief do not match single-case probabilities, but rather a kind of probability we shall call *relative probability* (because it is relative to a description of the set-up facing the agent).

The relation between our preferred principle, the Relative Principle, and the Single-Case Principle, is analogous to that between the Single-Case Principle and the Perfect Principle. We earlier rejected the Perfect Principle in favour of the Single-Case Principle on the grounds that the Perfect Principle does not cover all cases of prudentially correct choices. We reject the Single-Case Principle for the same reason. There are prudentially correct choices beyond those recommended by the Single-Case Principle.

In what follows we shall first illustrate the Relative Principle

[2] Of course degrees of belief other than those that match single-case probabilities can lead to the right choice in *particular* decision situations. The point of the Single-Case Principle is rather that it ensures maximization of single-case expected utility in *every* decision situation. (Analogously, in non-probabilistic contexts, while a choice of means recommended as effective by false beliefs will *sometimes* lead to desired results, those so recommended by true beliefs will *always* do so. Cf. Papineau, 1993: ch. 3.)

with examples, and explain how it works. We hope these examples will help make the Relative Principle plausible. But our ultimate rationale for favouring this principle over the Single-Case Principle will be that it turns out to yield a simpler overall theory of prudential rationality. By the time we reach the end of the essay, we will be able to show that the Relative Principle yields a uniform and integrated account of prudential rationality, while the Single-Case Principle does not.

Although we oppose the Single-Case Principle, we suspect that it captures many people's intuitive understanding of prudentially correct degrees of belief. However, even if this suspicion is right, it is difficult to find any straightforward expression of the Single-Case Principle in the philosophical literature. Those authors who come closest to arguing that the right degrees of belief must match the single-case probabilities do not generally adopt the simple version of the Single-Case Principle given above. Instead they defend more complicated formulations, designed in part to block some of the difficulties we are about to raise. Thus D. H. Mellor (1971, 1982), David Lewis (1980), and Wesley Salmon (1988) all forge a central connection between degrees of belief and single-case probabilities, but in each case via something more complicated than the simple Single-Case Principle given above. We shall comment on these writers in due course. But for the moment we shall retain the Single-Case Principle as our target. This is because our disagreement is not on matters of detail, but rather over the whole idea that the objectively correct degrees of belief are those that match the single-case probabilities. It will be easier to make our objections clear if we start with a simple version of this idea.

7 Relative Probabilities

It is high time we explained what we mean by the Relative Principle.

(4)   *The Relative Principle.* The correct subjective probabilities for an agent to attach to outcomes $\{o_i\}$ are the probabilities of the $\{o_i\}$ relative to the agent's knowledge of the set-up.

To illustrate this Principle, and the associated notion of relative probability, consider this example. Alma tosses a fair coin and places her hand over it as it lands. We shall say that the relative probability of finding heads when Alma's hand is removed, *in relation to the description just given of this situation,* is 0.5. Note that this probability of 0.5 is not a single-case probability, since the single-case probability of heads is already either 0 or 1. Yet it is clearly the right probability to act on if you haven't seen under Alma's hand, in line with the Relative Principle. For example, it is the right probability for working out that you should accept the bet we earlier described Alma as offering, since this 0.5 probability implies that the bet offers an expected gain of 50p.

It is not essential to the point we are making that the relevant result has occurred already. Suppose Alma tosses the coin and then offers her bet when it is in the air. Let us assume, as seems plausible, that the result, though still in the future, is by now determined. So the single-case probability of heads is already 1 or 0. Yet the relative probability of 0.5 is still clearly the probability you ought to act on.

Nor is it essential to the point that the single-case probability of the relevant outcome already be 1 or 0. Suppose that Alma has a machine that makes one of two kinds of devices at random. On each run of the machine, a radioactive source decides with probability 0.5 whether the machine will make device *A* or device *B*. Each device will then print out 'heads' or 'tails', again on a quantum-mechanical basis. Device *A* gives 'heads' a single-case probability of 0.8. Device *B* gives 'heads' a single-case probability of 0.2. You know that the device in front of you is made by the machine, but you don't know whether it is an *A* or a *B*. Again, it seems obvious that you ought to decide whether to accept Alma's bet on the basis of the relative probability of 0.5 for 'heads', even though the single-case probability is already 0.8 or 0.2.

8 Probabilistic Laws

It will be helpful to be more explicit about relative probabilities. For this we need the notion of a *probabilistic* law. We shall take as the basic form of such a law: 'The probability of an *A* being a *B* is *p*' ('The probability of a tossed coin concealed under a hand turning out to be heads is 0.5'). We take it that there are many objective truths of this form. Moreover we take it that many of these are known to be true, on the basis of inferences from statistical data about the proportions of *B*s observed in classes of *A*s.

Given a particular situation which satisfies description *D* and a particular exemplification *o* of type *O*, the probability of *o* relative to *D* is *p* if and only if there is a probabilistic law 'The probability of a *D* being an *O* is *p*'. Note that these relative probabilities are like single-case probabilities in that they attach to a particular outcome (a particular exemplification of a type), rather than to the type itself. But they don't attach to it *simpliciter*, but rather to the pair of the outcome and some description of the decision situation.

Single-case probabilities can be thought of as a special case of relative probabilities, namely as the relative probabilities fixed by *all* the relevant features of the situation. If we think of single-case probabilities in this way, then the single-case probability at *t* of *o* is *p* if and only if, for some *D* applying to the relevant situation at *t*, it is a law that the probability of a *D* being an *O* is *p*, and *D* is maximal in the sense that, for any further *E* applying at *t*, the probability of a *D&E* being *O* is *p* as well. (Note how the maximality of such a *D* explains why *D* will exhaust all the *relevant* features of a particular situation; for if *D* is maximal then any further *E*s will not alter the relative probability of *o*.)

Note that the Relative Principle concurs with the Single-Case

Principle in those cases where agents have information that fixes the single-case probabilities. This follows from the fact that single-case probabilities are special cases of relative probabilities. Consider agents who know all the relevant features of the particular decision situation. The relative probabilities of outcomes fixed by these agents' knowledge of the set-up will coincide with their single-case probabilities, and so these agents will conform to the Single-Case Principle by conforming to the Relative Principle. However, the above examples make it clear that this is not the only kind of case where the Relative Principle specifies the correct degrees of belief to act on. Often agents' relative probabilities will not be single-case probabilities, yet agents should act on these probabilities in just the same way.

Note that the Relative Principle accommodates any number of sensible choices that the Single-Case Principle excludes. When informed people make real-life choices (whether to stop smoking, say, or to take some medication, or not to draw to an inside straight), they characteristically act in line with the Relative Principle, but not the Single-Case Principle. However detailed their knowledge of their specific situations, there are always further unknown features (about their metabolism, say, or the next card in the pack) which mean their relative probabilities are not single-case probabilities. But this is no reason to condemn their actions as prudentially incorrect.

There is more to be said about the choice between the Relative and Single-Case Principles, and we shall return to this in Sections 11 to 14 below. But first we would like to clarify some other points.

9 The Range of the Relative Principle

Some readers might be tempted to raise the following objection. It seems implausible to suppose that there is a probabilistic law of the form 'the probability of a D being an O is p' for *every* property

D that the agent might know the set-up in question to have. But where there is no relevant probabilistic law to be had, the Relative Principle remains silent about how the agent's degree of belief in the outcome is objectively constrained.

Suppose, for instance, that you are presented with a black box which you are told makes coins and asked for your degree of belief that the next coin it produces will land heads when tossed. You know nothing further about the box. You just knows it is a black box which manufactures coins. We take it that there is no true probabilistic law stating that the probability of heads on a coin from any coin-manufacturing black box is *p*. The category of coin-manufacturing black boxes is too open-ended and heterogeneous to sustain any serious general patterns. So, given our explanation of relative probabilities in the last section, there is no objective probability of heads relative to your knowledge of the set-up, which means that the Relative Principle specifies no prudentially correct degree of belief in this case.

Doesn't this show that the Relative Principle does not cover all decision situations, and hence that it does not say everything there is to be said about how degrees of belief in outcomes are objectively constrained? We say no. We are happy simply to concede that not all degrees of belief are so constrained. If the features of the set-up the agent knows about do not constitute the antecedent of any probabilistic law about the outcome in question, then there is no objective constraint on the agent's degree of belief in that outcome. In the above example, there is no prudentially correct degree of belief in heads on the next coin from the black box.

10 *Philosophical Interpretations of Probability*

Most relative probabilities are not single-case probabilities. Does this mean that the notion of relative probability presupposes the frequency theory of probability? If so, the notion of relative probability is in trouble, for the frequency interpretation of probability is no good.[3] We do not think this is a good reason for rejecting relative probabilities. The topics discussed in this essay, and in particular the notions of relative probability and non-maximal probabilistic law, are independent of disputes between alternative philosophical interpretations of probability. It is true that, if you are interested in philosophical interpretations of probability, then the frequency interpretation, which identifies the probability of an *A* being a *B* with the limiting frequency of *As* in the sequence of *Bs*, offers the most immediate explanation of relative probabilities and non-maximal probabilistic laws. And it is also true that the currently most popular alternatives to the frequency interpretation, namely, 'chance' or 'propensity' theories that take the notion of single-case probability as primitive (e.g. Lewis, 1980; Giere, 1973; Fetzer, 1977), have to do some work to account for relative probabilities and non-maximal probabilistic laws. But we certainly don't think that the notion of relative probability stands or falls (and so falls) with the frequency interpretation.

On the contrary, it seems to us a boundary condition on *any* satisfactory interpretation of probability that it make good sense of relative probabilities and non-maximal probabilistic laws. Note in this connection that standard statistical tests are indifferent to the maximality or otherwise of the probabilistic laws under investigation. There are well-established empirical methods for ascertaining the probability that a certain kind of machine part, say, will fail in circumstances of some kind. It does not matter to these methods whether or not there are further probabilistically relevant differences between parts and circumstances of those kinds.

Perhaps this is a good reason for preferring those versions of 'chance' or 'propensity' theories that in effect take our notion of relative probability as primitive, rather than single-case probability

[3] See Papineau (1995) for a quick account of the central flaw in the frequency interpretation of probability.

(cf. Hacking, 1965; Levi, 1967; Gillies, 1996). But we shall not pursue this topic further here. We shall simply take the notion of relative probability and probabilistic law as given, and leave the philosophical interpretations of probability to look after themselves.

11 *In Defence of the Relative Principle*

We claim that the Relative Principle is the fundamental prudential truth about the correct degrees of belief for agents to act on. It may strike some readers as odd to accord the Relative Principle this authority. After all, many agents will have relative probabilities that differ from the single-case probabilities, and as a result the Relative Principle may specify that they should choose actions other than those that maximize the single-case expected utility.[4]

For example, imagine that you accept Alma's £2 to your £1 that 'heads' will be printed out by a device from the machine that makes devices *A* and *B*. You do so on the grounds that your probability for 'heads' relative to your knowledge of the situation is 0.5. But in fact this is a device *B*, for which the single-case probability of 'heads' is already 0.2. So declining Alma's bet would have a higher *single-case* expected utility than accepting it (0p instead of −40p).

Here the Relative Principle seems to advise the choice that is objectively inferior. Why then do we say it is superior to the Single-Case Principle? On the face of things, it looks as if the Relative Principle will only give the right advice in those special cases where it coincides with the Single-Case Principle.

Despite this, we maintain that the Relative Principle says all we need to say about correct degrees of belief. Even in cases where

[4] When we speak of 'an agent's relative probability' for some outcome, this should be understood as shorthand for the relative probability of that outcome in relation to *D*, where *D* is the agent's knowledge of the set-up in question.

your relative probabilities do not coincide with single-case probabilities, it is objectively correct for you to set your degrees of belief equal to the relevant relative probabilities, and act accordingly.

Our attention can be distracted here by a point we shall later discuss at some length. There is a sense in which it would be prudentially better if you could *find out* about the single-case probabilities before you choose between the alternative actions on offer. But this does not show that there is anything incorrect about setting your degrees of belief equal to merely relative probabilities when you *haven't* found out those single-case probabilities.

Indeed, as we shall see, the explanation of *why* it is prudentially better to find out about the single-case probabilities, if you can, is itself a consequence of the correctness of making choices on the basis of relative probabilities. We shall argue (in Sections 20 to 21, following Ramsey and Good) that the best understanding of why it is *better* to act on the single-case probabilities, if you can, is simply that it is correct, in the sense of the Relative Principle, to find out the single-case probabilities before acting, if you have the choice. It is certainly true that it is prudentially better to find out the single-case probabilities before deciding, if you can. But this truth, far from challenging the Relative Principle's notion of correctness, depends on it.

12 A Useful Comparison

We shall return to these complexities in due course. At this stage, however, some readers may still need persuading that there is *anything* worthwhile about the Relative Principle when it diverges from the Single-Case Principle. How can it be correct to act on relative probabilities when they advise actions different from those that would be advised by the single-case probabilities, as in the case where you accept Alma's bet not knowing the device in front of you is in fact a *B*?

The following comparison may be helpful. First suppose that, as above, you are offered Alma's bet on a device you know to be from the machine which makes As and Bs, but where you don't know which sort your device is. Now compare yourself with Dorinda, say, who is offered the same bet, but in connection with a device which she knows will print out 'heads' with a quantum-mechanical single-case probability of 0.5.

You and Dorinda will both accept Alma's bet, for you and Dorinda will both act on a probability of 0.5 for 'heads'. But where Dorinda is acting on a single-case probability, you are acting on a relative probability instead. Now, would you rather be offered Dorinda's bet than your bet? No. *People who make your bet will make money just as fast as people who make Dorinda's bet.* Even though Dorinda's bet is in line with the single-case probabilities, and yours is not, yours is objectively just as good a bet. Both of you are quite rightly wagering £1 because your expected repayment is £1.50. (How *can* we be sure yours is a good bet, given that you could well be betting on a device B, which would mean your *single-case* expected repayment is only 60p? But note that we could equally well ask—how *can* Dorinda's bet be a good bet, given that her device may well print out 'tails', which would mean her repayment is going to be 0p?)

We take this to show that it is objectively worthwhile to conform to the Relative Principle, even in cases where it could lead you to choose an action that will not in fact maximize the single-case expected utility. When you accept Alma's bet, knowing only the relative probabilities, but not whether you are betting on a B or an A, you are making just as good a choice as Dorinda, who knows the single-case probabilities, but not what the result will actually be. So if Dorinda is making a good choice, from a prudential point of view, then so are you.

13 'A Good Bet'

It may be helpful to expand briefly at this point on a notion that we assumed in the last section—the notion of an objectively 'good bet', a bet that is worth accepting rather than declining. This notion encapsulates the idea of the objectively correct choice that we are trying to explicate.

What makes a bet good? An initial temptation is to say that what makes a bet good is that it *will* make you money (a temptation to which we succumbed in the last paragraph, in the interests of dramatic emphasis, when we said that 'People who make your bet will make money just as fast as people who make Dorinda's bet'). But of course we cannot strictly say this, since even a good bet may turn out unluckily (your device may in fact print out 'tails'). Another temptation is to say that a good bet will make money *in the long run*. But this is little better, since any finitely long run of bets can still turn out unluckily.[5]

Once we resist these temptations, we realize that the only thing that can be said about an objectively good bet is that it is objectively *probable* that it will make you money; more generally, that the objectively right choice is that which offers the maximum *objective expected utility* among the alternatives open to you. It may be surprising that there is nothing more to be said, but it is a conclusion which a long tradition of philosophers addressing this question have been unable to avoid. (Cf. Peirce, 1924; Putnam, 1987.)

What is even more surprising, perhaps, is that it doesn't matter to the objective correctness of a choice whether the objective probabilities which make it correct are single-case or not. All that matters is that they are the objective probabilities relative to your knowledge of the decision situation. The comparison in the last section makes this point clear. It doesn't matter to the goodness of the bet offered by Alma whether the single-case probability of

---

[5] If you believe in the frequency theory of probability, you can argue that a good bet will definitely make money in the *infinite* long run. But, even for frequentists, it is not clear why this should *make* a bet good, given that none of us is going to bet for ever.

heads is currently different from 0.5. As long as you know the decision situation as one in which the relative probability of heads is 0.5, it will be right for you to accept the bet; and you will be just as likely to make money, in the objective sense of probability that matters to choice, as someone who accepts a similarly structured bet on the basis of knowledge that the single-case probability is 0.5.[6]

14 Decision Situations

One way of conveying our picture of prudential rationality would be to say that the practical predicament facing an agent cannot be separated from the agent's knowledge of his or her surroundings.

---

[6] Isn't there a danger, when betting on merely relative probabilities, that your opponent may know the single-case probabilities, and so have the advantage of you? (Alma may have a secret way of telling if the device is an *A*.) But note that in such betting situations you will have extra information apart from knowing about the structure of the betting device—you will also know, for example, that Alma is offering 2–1 against heads. So the recommendation of the Relative Principle in such a case depends crucially on the objective probability of heads *relative to the fact that someone is offering these odds*. If this is still 0.5, then your bet is fine. But if it is significantly less than 0.5 (as would be the case if people who offer attractive bets on 'heads' characteristically have a way of fleecing suckers) then you should avoid such bets.

We would all do well to remember the advice given by Sky Masterson's father in Damon Runyon's 'The Idyll of Miss Sarah Brown' (1946): 'Son, no matter how far you travel, or how smart you get, always remember this: Some day, somewhere, a guy is going to come to you and show you a nice brand-new deck of cards on which the seal is never broken, and this guy is going to offer to bet you that the jack of spades will jump out of this deck and squirt cider in your ear. But, son, do not bet him, for as sure as you do you are going to get an ear full of cider.' However, in what follows we shall simplify the exposition by continuing to assume, contra Mr Masterson Snr. and common sense, that the existence of attractive bets are in general probabilistically irrelevant to the relevant outcomes.

Let us use the admittedly inelegant term 'decision situation' for the context of a choice. It is tempting to think of such a decision situation as consisting solely of the particular objective set-up which will generate the outcomes of interest—such as, for example, some particular physical device which will print 'heads' or 'tails' with certain probabilities.

If we think of decision situations in this way, then it is natural to conclude that if there are correct degrees of belief, they must be those that correspond to the current single-case probabilities. For there is no way of identifying a unique probability for an outcome, given only the set-up in all its particularity, except as the probability fixed by all current features of the set-up—that is, the current single-case probabilities.

But suppose we think of the decision situation facing an agent as consisting of a set-up *plus* the properties the agent knows the set-up to have. Now there is another way of identifying a unique probability for an outcome—namely, the outcome's probability relative to all those properties that constitute the decision situation.

Note that on this view it is still an objective feature of the world that makes an agent's degree of belief correct, for it is a perfectly objective fact that the probability of outcome *o* relative to some property *D* of the set-up is *p*. Many such facts obtain quite independently of what agents know, or even of whether there are agents at all. Of course *which* such fact makes a particular agent's degree of belief correct will depend on that agent's decision situation. But it is scarcely surprising that which objective probabilities matter to decisions should be different for different decision situations.

15 The Principal Principle

It is an implication of David Lewis's 'Principal Principle' (Lewis, 1980) that, if you know the single-case probability of some outcome, and nothing else relevant (nothing 'inadmissible' in Lewis's terminology), then you ought to set your degree of belief equal to that single-case probability. It will be illuminating to compare the position we are defending here with Lewis's.

One immediate point is that Lewis seems as much concerned with issues of evidential rationality as with prudential rationality. His Principal Principle is part of a more general Bayesian account of the degrees of belief required of rational thinkers who have such-and-such evidence, and bears on questions of the prudential correctness of degrees of belief, if at all, only derivatively.

Even so, Lewis holds that connection forged by the 'Principal Principle' between degrees of belief and single-case probabilities exhausts the ways in which degrees of belief are rationally constrained by knowledge of objective probabilities. So it is natural to ask what would Lewis say about agents who know relative probabilities but not single-case probabilities. Take the case of the machine which makes devices A and B. As before, you know that the device in front of you comes from this machine, but not whether it is A or B. So you know that the probability of 'heads' relative to your information is 0.5, but you are ignorant of the single-case probability of this outcome. Lewis's Principal Principle would seem to have no grip here. Yet surely evidential rationality, just as much as prudential rationality, requires you to have a degree of belief of 0.5 in heads. (Cf. Levi, 1983; Kyburg, 1981.)

Lewis's (1986) response to this challenge hinges on the fact that the Principal Principle, unlike the Single-Case Principle, does not refer specifically to *current* single-case probabilities. Rather, it says that if you know the value of the single case probability for any time t, and nothing else relevant, then you ought to have a matching degree of belief, even at times other than t. In the case at hand, Lewis would argue that you know the single-case probability of heads was once 0.5 (before the machine opted between A and B), and you know nothing else relevant (since your later information tells you nothing about which device the machine made). So the

Principal Principle requires you to set your degree of belief equal to the relative probability of 0.5 after all.

16 A Modified Single-Case Principle?

The apparent success of Lewis's response might suggest that we were perhaps too quick to replace the Single-Case Principle by the Relative Principle. Perhaps we should have tried:

(5) *The Modified Single-Case Principle.* The correct subjective probabilities for an agent *currently* to attach to outcomes $\{o_i\}$ are equal to the single-case probabilities of the $\{o_i\}$ at those *earlier* times when only those conditions in D (the agent's current knowledge of the decision situation) were as yet determined, among conditions probabilistically relevant to the $\{o_i\}$.

This wouldn't require that the correct degrees of belief are the *current* single-case probabilities. Indeed this principle would agree with the Relative Principle, to the extent that it specifies that the correct degrees of belief are a function, *inter alia*, of which facts the agent now knows about. But it would at least retain the original idea of equating prudentially correct degrees of belief with single-case rather than relative probabilities.

However, this Modified Single-Case Principle won't do. Consider once more the case where you don't know whether the machine has given you device A or B. But now suppose that you have observed your device print out 'heads' as its first two results. What is the correct degree of belief in 'heads' next time? A simple calculation using Bayes's theorem will show that the probability of 'heads' next time on a device that has already produced two 'heads' is 13/17. This probabilistic law is a consequence of the other probabilistic laws already specified for this example. So the Relative Principle specifies, quite rightly, that the correct degree of belief for 'heads' on the next toss is around 13/17. Somebody who uses this figure to decide which bets to accept will make the correct choices.

But note that 13/17 is not, *nor ever has been*, the single-case probability of 'heads' next time. The single-case probability of heads on any toss was 0.5 before the device was made, and now is either 0.2 or 0.8. So even the Modified Single-Case Principle cannot cover this case. The only fully general principle governing prudentially correct degrees of belief is that they should equal the relative probabilities.

We should stress that this example does not *refute* Lewis's view. For Lewis is not committed to the Modified Single-Case Principle as the only principle governing reasonable degrees of belief. Rather Lewis's full theory of reasonable degrees of belief contains *two* principles which together accommodate cases that escape the Modified Single-Case Principle. These are (*a*) the Principal Principle by which he links reasonable degrees of belief to single-case probabilities, (*b*) a principle of Bayesian conditionalization for updating reasonable degrees of belief. So he can deal with the present example by saying that rational agents will first set their degrees of belief for *A* and *B* equal to 0.5, in line with the Principal Principle; and then they will update these degrees of belief by Bayesian conditionalization to get the right answer after they observe that their device has produced two 'heads' already.

Still, apart from demonstrating that prudentially correct degrees of belief can equal numbers which never were single-case probabilities (and thus that the Modified Single-Case Principle on its own is inadequate), our example also shows that there is a measure of theoretical economy to be gained by upholding the Relative Principle rather than Lewis's Principal-Principle-plus-Bayesian-conditionalization. The advantage is that we don't need to adopt conditionalization as a separate principle, at least in cases structured by objective probabilistic laws. For it can be shown that, in such cases, conditionalization falls out of the Relative Principle, in the way illustrated by our example: if you set your new degree of belief equal to the relative probability of getting the outcome in situations satisfying your initial-knowledge-plus-new-information, then you will automatically be conditionalizing. By contrast, note that conformity to conditionalization does not follow from the Principal Principle, but must be added as an independent requirement on rationality, since updated degrees of belief often won't match single-case probabilities, as in our example. It seems to us preferable to avoid postulating Bayesian conditionalization as an extra requirement, given the well-known difficulties of providing this principle with any satisfactory rationale.

17 Lewis and Determinism

In this section we would like to offer a different and more direct reason for preferring our Relative Principle to Lewis's package of Principal-Principle-plus-Bayesian-conditionalization.   Consider Elspeth, a convinced determinist, who is asked to bet on a certain coin coming down 'heads'. Elspeth has performed a large number of trials on coins of this manufacture and has overwhelming statistical evidence for a probabilistic law which says that the probability of 'heads' with coins just like this one is 0.9. Suppose also that determinism really is true. What ought Elspeth's degree of belief in the coin's landing 'heads' on the next throw to be? (Cf. Levi, 1983.)

Since Elspeth thinks that the single-case chance of 'heads' always was either 0 or 1, the full Lewisian story implies that her degree of belief in 'heads' should be the average of these two chances weighted by her degree of belief in each, which average will of course equal her degree of belief in the latter chance (since the former is 0). But what ought this degree of belief to be? To us it seems clear that it should equal 0.9. But there is nothing in Lewis's Principal Principle, nor in his principle of Bayesian conditionalization, to say why. The Relative Principle, on the other hand, can deal with the case: the objective probability of 'heads' relative to Elspeth's knowledge of the situation is 0.9, so 0.9 is the correct degree of belief for Elspeth to have.

There are two responses open to Lewis. The first possibility would simply be to deny that there would be any probabilistic laws if determinism were true. However, this seems to us a thesis that needs some independent argument in its favour. The other response would be to appeal to the notion of 'counterfeit chance'—a degree of credence that is resilient in the sense that it would not be undermined by further 'feasible' investigation—as a surrogate for the notion of a probabilistic law under determinism (cf. Skyrms, 1980; Lewis, 1986).

However, Lewis has severe doubts about this second response. Counterfeit chances have an indeterminacy that makes Lewis suspicious of their credentials as constraints on degrees of belief. He says: 'Counterfeit chances will be relative to partitions; and relative, therefore, to standards of feasibility and naturalness; and therefore indeterminate unless the standards are somehow settled, or at least settled well enough that all remaining candidates for the partition will yield the same answers. Counterfeit chances are therefore not the sort of thing we would want to find in our fundamental physical theories, or even in our theories of radioactive decay and the like. But they will do to serve the conversational needs of determinist gamblers.' (Lewis, 1986: 121.)

Put in our terms, Lewis is here appealing to the point that probabilistic laws will imply different probabilities for the same outcome, depending on what non-maximal descriptions of the set-up are used to specify the antecedent of the law. Lewis seems to be suggesting that such probabilities cannot therefore place objective constraints on agents' degrees of belief. But there is no good basis for this conclusion. It is only if you assume that such constraints must always be supplied by single-case probabilities that you will find their relativity to descriptions worrying. By contrast, from our point of view this relativity is just as it should be. We argue that the tie between degrees of belief and objective probabilities is forged by the Relative Principle, not the Principal Principle. And the Relative Principle invokes just that objective relative probability which is given by the probabilistic law which has the agent's knowledge of the set-up as antecedent.

Lewis gives no good reason to regard such non-maximal probabilistic laws as second-class citizens. We may not want to find such laws in our fundamental physical theories, but that doesn't mean that they are *only* capable of serving the 'conversational needs of determinist gamblers', and place no serious constraints on degrees of belief. On the contrary, the part which non-maximal probabilistic laws play in the Relative Principle makes them fundamentally important in understanding how degrees of belief in outcomes are objectively constrained. To deny this is to deny that there is any objective feature of the world that makes it correct for Elspeth to attach a 0.9 degree of belief to 'heads'.

18 Salmon's View

In 'Dynamic Rationality' (1988) Wesley Salmon argues forcefully that subjective degrees of belief ought to match objective probabilities. Although Salmon thinks of objective probabilities as long-run frequencies, he is sensitive to the distinction between single-case and relative objective probabilities: for him this is the distinction between frequencies in objectively homogeneous reference classes (genuine *chances*) and frequencies in merely epistemically homogeneous reference classes.

When he addresses this distinction (pp. 23–4) he argues that the fundamental external constraint on degrees of belief is that they should match the chances (the single-case probabilities); that is, his basic commitment is to the Single-Case Principle. He does recognize, however, that we need some account of the worth of choices informed by merely relative probabilities. His response is to view degrees of belief that match merely relative probabilities as the *best available estimates* of single-case probabilities. In effect, he views the Relative Principle as a matter of trying to conform to the Single-Case Principle under conditions of limited information.

This does not work. Consider the machine that makes As and Bs again. You have a device from this machine, but you don't know which kind it is. Your relative probability for 'heads' is 0.5. This does not seem a good estimate of the single-case probability—after all, the single-case probability is certainly either 0.2 or 0.8. At best Salmon could argue that the relative probability is a weighted average of the possible single-case probabilities. But then the weighting factors (0.5 for the 0.2 single-case probability, and 0.5 for the 0.8) are relative probabilities once more, and we are left once more with an unexplained appeal to the worth of matching degrees of belief to relative probabilities. Whichever way we turn it, Salmon does not give us a way of explaining the Relative Principle in terms of the Single-Case Principle.

19 Mellor's View

In *The Matter of Chance* (1971) D. H. Mellor argues that the correct degrees of belief are those that match the chances, and to that extent is in prima facie agreement with our Single-Case Principle. He then considers an example which is effectively equivalent to our machine that makes As and Bs. In connection with this example he appeals to another thesis defended in his book, namely, that chances are functions not just of specific outcomes ('heads' next time) but also of the *kind of trial* generating the outcome. So if the trial is (a) *the machine makes a device which displays a result*, then the chance of 'heads' is 0.5; but if it is (b) *this particular device (which came from the machine) displays a result*, then the chance of 'heads' is either 0.2 or 0.8.

So Mellor makes chances relative to kind of trial. What determines the kind of trial? If this depends on the agent's *knowledge* of the set-up, in such a way that the trial is of kind (a) whenever the agent doesn't know whether the device is an *A* or a *B*, and is of kind (*b*) whenever the agent does know this, then Mellor has effectively switched to the Relative Principle, for his 'chances' are equal to probabilities relative to the features of the set-up the agent knows about.

However, Mellor specifies that his 'chances' are not relative to knowledge, but rather to what 'counts as repeating the bet' at hand: if the bet is on the *device-generating machine*, so to speak, the 'chance' is 0.5, while if it is on *this device*, the 'chance' is 0.2 or 0.8. Mellor's resulting position is certainly different from the Relative Principle, since repetitions of a bet can presumably be on *this device*, rather than the machine, even though the agent doesn't know whether this device is an *A* or *B*. But for just this reason Mellor's position is unsatisfactory, since he is left without any explanation of why the prudentially correct degree of belief for this kind of agent is 0.5.

In his more recent 'Chances and Degrees of Belief' (1982) Mellor returns to this issue, and argues that such an agent should act on a 0.5 degree of belief after all, since of the two 'chances' that attach to the outcome 'heads' (0.5 relative to trial (*a*); 0.2 or 0.8 relative to trial (*b*)), this is the only one that the agent knows. We agree that this is the right answer, but would observe that Mellor is only able to give it because he has switched to the Relative Principle. In our terms he now holds that agents should act on the probabilities relative to the features of set-up that they know about, that is, that their degrees of belief should match their relative probabilities.

20 *More Information is Better*

We have argued that, if your degrees of belief match your relative probabilities, it is irrelevant to the goodness of your consequent choice whether or not these are also single-case probabilities.

Degrees of belief which correspond to the relative probabilities on one gambling device can be just as correct, from a prudential point of view, as numerically identical degrees of belief which match single-case probabilities on a different device.

However, as we admitted earlier, there is a different sense in which it *is* better to act on single-case probabilities, if you can find out about them. To pin down this sense, it will be helpful to consider, not two different gambling devices, but a single device, about which you might have more or less information. Imagine, for example, that you are facing a device from the machine that makes As and Bs. You are able *either* to act on your present relative probability for heads on a device from this machine, *or* to find out whether your device is an *A* or a *B*, and so act on the single-case probability of heads. In this kind of comparison, where the single-case probability involves *more* information about the *same* device, we agree that it is prudentially better to find out the single-case probability before deciding.

However, we deny that this point calls for any modification of, or addition to, the Relative Principle. That it is prudentially better to find out the single-case probabilities if you can, before committing yourself to action, is itself a consequence of the Relative Principle.

What is more, this corollary of the Relative Principle is simply a special case of a more general point—namely, that it is always prudentially better to act on probabilities relative to more rather than less information about a given set-up, if you can. Not only are single-case probabilities better than relative probabilities, but relative probabilities which are relative to greater amounts of information are better than relative probabilities which are relative to less. Indeed the same point applies within the category of single-case probabilities. As long as you can keep your options open, it is prudentially better to wait and see how the single-case probabilities evolve, instead of deciding straight off knowing only their initial values. Best of all, of course, is to wait until you know the outcome itself. If you can delay until Alma has removed her hand, then you can accept her bet whenever the coin shows heads, and decline whenever it is tails.

21 The Ramsey–Good Result

Let us first offer an example to illustrate why it is always prudentially better to act on probabilities relative to more rather than less information about a given set-up, if you can. We shall then sketch a general demonstration.

Imagine you are presented with three sealed boxes. You know that a ball has been placed in one, and that the other two are empty, and that some chance mechanism earlier gave each box the same 1/3 single-case probability of getting the ball. Felicity offers you her £3 to your £2, with you winning the total stake if the ball is in box 1. You can either accept or decline the bet now (option G, for 'Go'), or you can look in box 3 and then accept or decline the same bet (option W, for 'Wait-and-see').

If you take option G and choose now, you'll decline Felicity's bet (since you would be putting up £2 for an expected return of £1.67). So, since you will decline, the expected gain of option G is £0.

If you take option W, then 1/3 of the time you'll find the ball in box 3, and so decline the bet, since you would then be sure to lose it. But 2/3 of the time you won't find the ball in box 3, and in these cases you will accept the bet, since the expected return on your £2 will now be £2.50. Averaging over these two possibilities, weighted by their respective probabilities, you can expect to gain £0.33 if you take option W.

So option W is better than option G, since its expected value is £0.33 rather than £0. The reason is that option W gives you the opportunity of switching to accepting the bet in just the case where your extra information (no ball in box 3) indicates that this is worthwhile.

This example illustrates the general result. Suppose you are faced with alternative actions $\{A_i\}$, and have a meta-choice between deciding now (option G), or finding out whether C before acting (option W). If there is a non-zero probability that this extra information will affect which A_i you choose, and if the cost of acquiring this information is negligible, then the expected gain from option W is always greater than the expected gain from option G.

We shall sketch a proof (following F. P. Ramsey, 1990, and I J. Good, 1967) for the simple case of two alternative actions A_1 and A_2 (accept or reject some bet, say). If you take option G, then you will now choose one of these—A_1, say. Let $EU(A_1/C)$ be the expected utility of this action given the as-yet-unknown C. Then we can decompose the expected gain of taking option G and so choosing A_1 as

(4.1) $EU(G) = EU(A_1/C)Pr(C) + EU(A_1/\text{not-}C)Pr(\text{not-}C).$

Now suppose you take option W instead and find out whether C. The discovery that C might make you choose A_2 rather than A_1. Alternatively, the discovery that not-C might make you do this. (Both discoveries can't make you switch, otherwise you wouldn't have preferred A_1 to start with. But one of them must, since we specified there is a non-zero probability of switching.)

Suppose, without loss of generality, that discovering C makes you switch to A_2. Then

(4.2) $EU(W) = EU(A_2/C)Pr(C) + EU(A_1/\text{not-}C)Pr(\text{not-}C).$

But this must be larger than $EU(G)$, because if $EU(A_2/C)$ wasn't bigger than $EU(A_1/C)$, you wouldn't have chosen A_2 when you discovered C.

22 *More Information is Relatively Better*

We take this result to explain why it is better to find out the single-case probabilities before acting, when you can. More generally, we take it to explain why it is better to delay acting until you acquire more probabilistically relevant information, whenever you can.

It is noteworthy, though, even if not immediately obvious, that this explanation makes essential appeal to the Relative Principle, rather than to any Single-Case Principle. Waiting-and-seeing is better than Going because it has a higher objective expected utility from the point of view of your *relative probabilities prior to this choice*. In general, in equations (4.1) and (4.2), $Pr(C)$ and $Pr(\text{not-}C)$ will not be single-case probabilities, but probabilities relative to your initial information; and the same goes for the conditional probabilities $Pr(o_i/C)$ and $Pr(o_i/\text{not-}C)$ implicitly involved in the quantities $EU(A_i/C)$ and $EU(A_i/\text{not-}C)$.

We can illustrate the point with the example of the boxes. Here $Pr(C) = 1/3$ is the probability of finding the ball in box 3. This isn't the single-case probability of that outcome, for that is already either 0 or 1.[7] Rather it is the probability relative to your initial knowledge of the set-up. Similarly, the conditional probability $= 1/2$ of the ball being in box 1 (call this outcome o), given it is not in box 3, which is central to the expected utility calculations, is a relative conditional probability. It is calculated by dividing $Pr(o\ \&\ \text{not-}C) = 1/3$ by $Pr(\text{not-}C) = 2/3$, where these are again all probabilities relative to your initial information. (The *single-case* conditional probability of o given not-C—that is, $\text{Sing-}CPr(o\ \&\ \text{not-}C)/\text{Sing-}CPr(\text{not-}C)$—will already either be 0 or 1 or undefined—depending on whether the ball is in fact in box 2, box 1, or box 3 respectively.)

In effect, the Ramsey–Good result reduces the *superiority* of decisions based on single-case probabilities, and better informed probabilities generally, to the *correctness* of Waiting-and-seeing

---

[7] Wasn't $1/3$ *once* the single-case probability of C? Well, then consider an example where your relative probabilities of $1/3$ for each box is the result of conditionalizing on previous results, as in the kind of case discussed in Section 16 above.

rather than Going, whenever you have this choice. But, for this result to work, correctness must be understood in the sense of the Relative Principle, not the Single-Case Principle.[8]

23 Failing to Maximize Single-Case Expected Utility

We can highlight the dependence of the Ramsey–Good result on the Relative Principle by noting that the sense in which it is always better for you to acquire additional probabilistically relevant information, if you can, does not guarantee that you will end up choosing the action A_i which maximizes the *single-case* expected utility. Consider the above example again, and imagine the ball is in fact in box 2. You look in box 3, see nothing, and so accept Alma's bet, since it is now a good bet. But it was determined from the start that this bet would lose. So, despite the fact that it is better, from the point of view of the probabilities you will quite correctly act on, to Wait-and-see rather than Go, the single-case expected utility of Waiting-and-seeing in this particular case is –£1, by comparison with the single-case expected utility of £0 for Going.

This is simply a reflection at the meta-level of a point made in Section 11. The action that is specified as correct by the Relative Principle need not be the action which maximizes the single-case

---

[8] David Miller complains that the Ramsey–Good result fails to explain the Principle of Total Evidence (1994, ch. 7). Our view is that the Principle of Total Evidence should explain the Ramsey–Good result, not the other way round. We have no explanation of the Principle of Total Evidence, understood as the recommendation that you should act on the probabilities relative to *all* your information. That is the Relative Principle, and we take this to be a primitive truth about prudential rationality. However, if you want then to know why you should arrange to act on probabilities relative to *more* rather than less information ('Why should a Bayesian buy a bunsen burner?', as Miller memorably puts it), then there is an explanation in terms of the Principle of Total Evidence (alias the Relative Principle), via the Ramsey–Good result.

expected utility. Since the Ramsey–Good result explains the superiority of Waiting-and-seeing in terms of the Relative Principle, rather than any Single-Case Principle, it is unsurprising that there should be cases where Waiting-and-seeing does not maximize single-case expected utility.

24 Finding out the Single-Case Probabilities

Of course, in the special case where acquiring more information tells you about the current single-case probabilities, rather than just giving you better informed relative probabilities, then the A_i chosen after Waiting-and-seeing will indeed maximize the single-case expected utility, since you will then be acting on the single-case probabilities themselves. (Imagine that you can look in *two* boxes, or find out whether your device is A or B, before deciding on Alma's bet.) This may make some readers feel that in cases where you find out the single-case probabilities, at least, the rationale for Waiting-and-seeing is independent of the Relative Principle. Surely here the justification for Waiting-and-seeing is simply that this will enable you to act on the single-case probabilities.

However, this thought simply takes it for granted that it is better to act on the single-case probabilities if you can, without offering any explanation for this. We think it better to explain things, if you have the materials to do so, rather than taking them as primitive. The Ramsey–Good result explains why it is better to act on the single-case probabilities, rather than relative probabilities, when you have the choice. But it does so by assuming the correctness of acting on your initial relative probabilities, rather than your final single-case probabilities.

25 Conclusion

It is natural to think that the prudentially correct action is always the action which maximizes single-case expected utility. This in turn makes it natural to suppose that the Single-Case Principle specifies the basic notion of prudential correctness, and that the Relative Principle is at best some kind of derivative poor relation.

However, our analysis indicates that this has things the wrong way round. To see this, suppose you postulated the Single-Case Principle as a basic principle governing prudential correctness. You would then need to say something about agents who act on relative probabilities. Since relative probabilities need not be (nor ever have been) equal to single-case probabilities, you would need separately to introduce another notion of prudential correctness, as in the Relative Principle. This in itself is bad enough: your initial commitment to the Single-Case Principle forces you to introduce a second independent primitive principle, the Relative Principle, to cover the full range of cases; by contrast, you would need only one principle if you started with the Relative Principle, since the Single-Case Principle is a special case of the Relative Principle in all those cases where it is practically applicable.

However, it gets even worse. Suppose you have a choice between acting on the Single-Case Principle (by Waiting-and-seeing) instead of the Relative Principle (by Going). The question then arises of why it is *better* to be correct in the first Single-Case sense, than in the second Relative sense. You could take this to be a yet further primitive fact. But it would make more sense to explain it, via the Ramsey–Good result, as itself a consequence of the Relative notion of correctness. For note that you will in any case need to appeal to the Ramsey–Good result and the Relative notion of correctness to explain the more general point that it is always better to act on more probabilistically relevant information than less.

So, whichever way we turn it, the Single-Case Principle seems otiose. If we begin with the Single-Case Principle, then we will need to keep appealing to the independent Relative Principle to explain things the Single-Case Principle can't explain. By contrast, if we simply begin with the Relative Principle, we don't need to postulate a separate notion of Single-Case correctness, since agents who act on single-case probabilities are *per se* acting on relative probabilities. And the Relative Principle on its own will also explain why it is preferable to act on single-case rather than relative probabilities, and in general on probabilities relative to more information, when you can.

It may seem unnatural to regard the Relative Principle as more basic than the Single-Case Principle. But it has the support of theoretical simplicity.[9]

REFERENCES

Fetzer, J. (1977), 'Reichenbach, Reference Classes, and Single-Case Probabilities', *Synthese*, 2.

Giere, R. (1973), 'Objective Single-Case Probabilities and the Foundations of Statistics', in P. Suppes, P. Henkin, L. Joja, and A. Moisil (eds.), *Logic, Methodology and Philosophy of Science* (Amsterdam: North-Holland).

Gillies, D. (1996), 'Popper's Contribution to the Philosophy of Probability', in A. O'Hear (ed.), *Karl Popper* (Cambridge: Cambridge University Press).

Good, I. J. (1967), 'On the Principle of Total Evidence', *British Journal for the Philosophy of Science*, 17.

Hacking, I. (1965), *Logic of Statistical Inference* (Cambridge: Cambridge University Press).

Kyburg, H. E. (1974), *The Logical Foundations of Statistical Inference* (Dordrecht: Reidel).

—— (1981), 'Principle Investigation', *Journal of Philosophy*, 78.

Levi, I. (1967), *Gambling with Truth* (New York: Knopf).

—— (1977), 'Direct Inference', *Journal of Philosophy*, 74.

Levi, I. (1983), Review of R. C. Jeffrey (ed.), *Studies in Inductive Logic and Probability*, vol II, *Philosophical Review*, 92.

[9] We would like to thank Dorothy Edgington, Peter Milne, and especially Scott Sturgeon for comments on earlier versions of this essay.

Lewis, D. (1980), 'A Subjectivist's Guide to Objective Chance', in R. C. Jeffrey (ed.), *Studies in Inductive Logic and Probability, vol. II* (Berkeley: University of California Press).

—— (1986), 'Postscripts to "A Subjectivist's Guide to Objective Chance" ', in D. Lewis, *Philosophical Papers, vol. II* (New York: Oxford University Press).

—— (1971), *The Matter of Chance* (Cambridge: Cambridge University Press).

—— (1982), 'Chance and Degrees of Belief', in R. McLaughlin (ed.), *What? Where? When? Why?* (Dordrecht: Reidel).

Miller, D. W. (1994), *Critical Rationalism* (Chicago: Open Court).

Papineau, D. (1993), *Philosophical Naturalism* (Oxford: Blackwell).

—— (1995), 'Probabilities and the Many-Minds Interpretation of Quantum Mechanics', *Analysis*, 55.

Peirce, C. S. (1924), 'The Doctrine of Chances', in M. R. Cohen (ed.), *Chance, Love and Logic* (New York: Harcourt).

Pollock, J. . (1990), *Nomic Probability and the Foundations of Induction* (New York: Oxford University Press).

Putnam, H. (1987), *The Many Faces of Realism* (La Salle: Open Court).

Ramsey, F. P. (1990), 'Weight or the Value of Knowledge', *British Journal for the Philosophy of Science*, 41.

Reichenbach, H. (1949), *The Theory of Probability* (Berkeley: University of California Press).

Runyon, D. (1946), *Runyon à la Carte* (London: Constable).

Salmon, W. C. (1988), 'Dynamic Rationality: Propensity, Probability and Credence', in J. Fetzer (ed.), *Probability and Causality* (Dordrecht: Reidel).

Skyrms, B. (1980), *Causal Necessity* (New Haven: Yale University Press).

5

Causation as a Guide to Life

1 Introduction

In this essay, I want to re-examine the debate between evidential and causal decision theory. My immediate motivation for returning to this familiar issue derives from two recent papers, by Christopher Meek and Clark Glymour (1994), and by Christopher Hitchcock (1996). I shall argue that these papers are seduced by a plausible line of thought into a mistaken sympathy for evidentialism. A second motivation is to extend an account of non-causal probabilistic rationality developed earlier with Helen Beebee (Beebee and Papineau, 1997) to deal with causal contexts as well. By the end of the paper, I hope to have deepened our understanding of exactly why rational decision theory needs to attend to causes.

2 Maximizing Conditional Expected Utility

Once upon a time, before Newcomb's problem, it was easy to theorize about rational decision. Agents were simply advised to maximize conditional expected utility. In the simplest case, which will suffice for all the purposes of this essay, with only one end, R, and one choice, A or not A, they were told to do A just in case $P(R/A) > P(R/\text{-}A)$.[1] (Cf. Jeffery, 1983.)

3 Newcomb Problems

The deficiencies of this model were first exposed by the original Newcomb paradox, which made play with super-predictors and the like. (Cf. Nozick, 1969.) But the essential point is better displayed with more everyday examples.

Suppose there is a correlation between eating Mars Bars (A) and sleeping well (R), that is, $P(R/A) > P(R/\text{-}A)$. However, suppose also that you know that this correlation is due to the prior presence of some hidden hormone (H), which independently conduces both to eating Mars Bars and to sound sleep, and which therefore 'screens off' any direct association between these occurrences, that is, $P(R/A\&H) = P(R/H)$ and $P(R/A\&\text{-}H) = P(R/H)$. (Probabilities will be understood throughout this essay as the kind of objective probabilities introduced in the previous essay, 'Probability as a Guide to Life'.)[2]

---

[1] In the more general case, assume a range of available *actions* $A_1, \ldots, A_k$; a range of desired *results* $R_1, \ldots, R_m$, each with *utilities* $U(R_1), \ldots, U(R_m)$; and a set of conditional *probabilities* for R_i given action A_j, $P(R_1/A_1), \ldots, P(R_m/A_k)$. The choice which maximizes conditional expected utility is then the A_j for which $\Sigma_{i=1 \ldots m} U(R_i)P(R_i/A_j)$ is a maximum.

[2] This means that my basic notion of objective probability is manifested in statements of probabilistic law, such as 'The probability of a $\emptyset$ being an Ω is p', which I shall write as '$\text{Pr}_\emptyset(\Omega) = p$'. Note that these objective probabilities won't necessarily correspond to *chances*, or single-case probabilities. Given a probabilistic law, $\text{Pr}_\emptyset(\Omega) = p$, the single-case probabilities of particular $\emptyset$s being Ω might themselves always be p (when the reference class $\emptyset$ is 'homogeneous'). But it is equally consistent with such a law that there be different kinds of $\emptyset$ which fix varying single-case prob-

In this kind of case, the natural conclusion is that eating Mars Bars (A) does not itself cause you to sleep well (R). Rather, these two events are joint effects of the common cause, the hormone (H). Eating Mars Bars is a *symptom* that you are going to sleep well (since it is a symptom that you have H), but it is not a *cause* of sound sleep.

Even so, the simple theory of rational decision outlined in the last section advises you to eat Mars Bars if you want to sleep well. For the 'raw' conditional probability $P(R/A)$ is still uncontroversially greater than $P(R/\text{-}A)$. You are more likely to sleep well when you have eaten a Mars Bar than when you haven't (after all, you will then be more likely to have H).

abilities for Ω (then $\emptyset$ is 'inhomogeneous'). If you like, you can assume that all objective probabilities which aren't chances any longer were once chances. (For example, the 0.25 probability that the next card dealt will be a spade may derive from earlier chance mechanisms, in the brain perhaps, which influenced how the pack was shuffled.) However, I myself am equally happy to take the notion of probability displayed in probabilistic laws as basic. This is not the place to pursue these issues, but note that (i) a primitive notion of chance relies heavily on the ill-understood metaphysics of quantum-mechanical 'wave collapses', (ii) we can explain an effective notion of chance (that is, single-case probability) in terms of probabilistic laws with maximally relevant antecedents, as easily as explain probabilistic laws in terms of chances, and (iii) standard statistical inferences issue in conclusions about probabilistic laws, not single-case probabilities (thus, a typical such inference might inform us about the probability of a twenty-a-day male smoker of 60 developing cancer within a year, yet remain neutral on whether further divisions within this reference class will yield differing probabilities). I should make it clear, however, that taking the basic notion of probability to be that displayed in laws, rather than that of single-case chance, does nothing to commit me to the ill-conceived frequency interpretation of probability. My idea, to repeat, is that the law-displayed notion of probability is primitive, just as chance is primitive according to the chance interpretation of probability.

True, it is agreed on all sides that (a) this is a 'spurious correlation' which disappears when we consider cases with and without the hormone (H) separately, and that therefore (b) the Mars Bar doesn't *cause* the sound sleep. But the trouble is that the simple decision theory didn't say anything about spurious correlations or causes. It simply compares the raw conditional probabilities $P(R/A)$ and $P(R/\text{-}A)$, and recommends action A whenever the former is greater.

4 *Causal Decision Theory*

Obviously the simple theory is wrong. In the just-described case, you should not eat a Mars Bar in order to get a good night's sleep.

According to 'causal decision theory', the remedy is to introduce causal notions into the theory of rational decision. In its simplest version, causal decision theory requires that we first 'partition our reference class' by all combinations of presence and absence of other possible causes of the desired result R, and that we then act on the weighted average of the difference action A makes to R *within* each cell of this partition. If, as in our simple example, there is only one other cause H, this means taking the weighted average of the difference A makes given H and not H respectively, and then choosing A just in case this average is positive:

(5.1) $[P(R/A\&H) - P(R/\text{-}A\&H)] \times P(H) + [P(R/A\&\text{-}H)$
$- P(R/\text{-}A\&\text{-}H)] \times P(\text{-}H) > 0.$

The idea here is that rational agents need to consider all the different ways in which A might causally influence R, and then take a weighted average of these different differences A can make to R, with the weights corresponding to the probability of each kind of difference. Partitioning by 'other causes' will necessarily achieve this result, since anything which makes a difference to the way *A* influences *R* will thereby qualify as another cause of *R*.[3] (See Skyrms, 1980; Lewis, 1981.)

The problem with the simple 'raw' *A-R* correlation, from this causal point of view, is that it can be misleading about whether *A* makes any real *causal* difference to *R*. In particular, as in our example, we can find a positive 'raw' correlation between *A* and *R* even when *A* is itself causally irrelevant, simply because *A* is probabilistically symptomatic of the presence of some other cause of *R*.

5 Objectivity, Subjectivity, and Agents' Knowledge

As I said above, 'probability' in this essay will always refer to the kind of *objective* probabilities introduced in the previous essay (though not necessarily to single-case chances). This focus on objective probability contrasts with most other work in decision theory. Decision theorists standardly work with subjective notions. When they refer to probabilities, they mean subjective probabilities. They are interested in how you ought to act given that you attach certain *subjective degrees of belief* to given outcomes, whatever the objective probabilities of those outcomes. (Indeed a similar point applies to many of those who introduce causal notions into decision theory. When they demand a partition by other causes, they often mean a partition determined by the agent's *subjective beliefs about other causes*, whatever the accuracy of those causal beliefs.)

[3] Note however that we need to understand 'other causes' here as including only causes of *R* which are themselves causally independent of *A*. We don't want to partition by causes of *R* which are *effects* of action *A*, for this might suggest that *A* doesn't matter to *R*, when it does. If smoking actually causes lung cancer by altering certain DNA sequences, say, then you don't want to reason that, among people *with* those DNA alterations, smoking doesn't make any extra difference to cancer, and similarly among those *without*, and that therefore there is no point in giving up smoking.

I think that this subjective approach leaves out the most interesting issues. For we can also ask about which features of the objective world rational actions ought ideally to be sensitive to. From the point of view of getting what you want, which *objective quantities* ought to be tracked by your subjective degrees of belief and hence your actions? (Moreover, do you need to partition by *genuine causes* to arrive at the right decisions?)

While these objective questions introduce epistemological issues, the epistemology can be put to one side in the context of decision theory. The prior question is which objective facts we need to know about to make the right decisions. How we might find out these facts is a further issue.

In 'Probability as a Guide to Life' (1997, reprinted as the previous essay), Helen Beebee and I addressed this prior question in connection with decisions where Newcomb-like complications do not intrude, such as betting on games of chance. Since (unrigged) games of chance preclude any spurious correlations between actions (bets) and desired outcomes (pay-offs), we could ignore causal complexities, and concentrate instead on the question of which objective probabilities rational agents ought ideally to match their degrees of belief to.

A plausible first thought here might be that rational agents ought ideally to be guided by the *single-case probabilities* or *chances* which A and not-A would give R in the circumstances obtaining at the time of their decision. But Beebee and I argued against adopting this as a basic principle. It does not deal happily with gambles where the outcome is already determined but unknown to the agent, such as a bet on a symmetrical coin which has already been tossed but whose face is concealed (for here you should have a 0.5 degree of belief in heads, even though the chance is already either 0 or 1). Instead Beebee and I argued that the theoretically fundamental principle, somewhat surprisingly, is that rational agents should be guided by *relative probabilities*, by which we meant the probabilities of the desired results (R) given A and not-A *in the refer-*

ence classes defined by agents' possibly limited knowledge (K) of their situation. (For example, the probability of winning if you bet heads on-a-symmetrical-coin-which-has-been-tossed-but-not-yet-exposed.) Thus, in our view, agents should do *A* in pursuit of *R* just in case $P_K(R/A) > P_K(R/-A)$.[4] We called this the 'Relative Principle'.

This reference to agents' knowledge might seem to imply that the relevant probabilities are subjective after all. But this does not follow. Agents' limited subjective knowledge K may determine *which* relative probabilities matter to their choice, but there is nothing subjective about those probabilities themselves. It is not a matter of opinion that 0.5 is the probability of winning if you bet heads on-a-symmetrical-coin-which-has-been-tossed-but-not-yet-exposed. This an objective fact about the world, indeed a paradigm of an objective probabilistic law.

As advertised above, the probabilities I mention in this essay will all be of this kind—the probability of a given type of outcome in a given reference class, as specified by the relevant objective probabilistic law. If there is no explicit identification of a reference class,

---

[4] It is a nice question whether *A* and not-*A* should not also be written as subscripts, along with *K*. Having them as conditions in conditional probabilities, rather than as subscripts, implies that they themselves have well-defined probabilities, for example, the probability of an agent of kind *K* eating a Mars Bar. Such definite probabilities for actions are arguably in tension with the idea of agents choosing whether or not to perform those actions. At one time I thought that I could avoid probabilities for actions, since actions only appear as conditions in my probabilities, never as consequents (which means they could equally be written as subscripts). But Wolfgang Spohn pointed out in conversation that, since I am committed to $P_{K\&A}(H)$, $P_{K\&-A}(H)$ *and* $P_K(H)$, I can't reasonably avoid $P_K(A)$ and $P_K(-A)$. Still, while I accept my *theoretical* discussion does require $P_K(A)$s and $P_K(-A)$s, it is perhaps worth observing that these are not required by any of the *decision* processes I consider, since none of these uses *all* of $P_K(H)$, $P_{K\&A}(H)$ and $P_{K\&-A}(H)$. There is more to be said about this topic, but it is orthogonal to the issues discussed below, and so I shall simply continue with the familiar $P_K(R/A) > P_K(R/-A)$ notation.

then it should be taken to be the K given by the agent's possibly limited knowledge of his or her situation.

Beebee and I defended our Relative Principle for cases where there is no question of any spurious correlation between actions and desired results. This by no means decides how agents ought to choose when the question of spurious correlations does arise. The contention of causal decision theory, as I understand it, is that in such cases Beebee's and my Relative Principle does not suffice.[5] To do A in pursuit of R, according to causal decision theory, it is not enough that $P_K(R/A) > P_K(R/\text{-}A)$, where K includes everything you know about yourself. Action A should remain positively relevant to R when we take a weighted average of the difference A makes to R in each cell of the partition defined by the presence and absence of other causes.[6] Thus, in the simple case discussed above, you should do A only if inequality (5.1) holds.

[5] It is worth noting, however, that causal decision theory, as I am construing it, will characteristically share with the Relative Principle a commitment to probabilities which are objective but not necessarily single-case. This can be seen in connection with the $P(H)$ and $P(\text{-}H)$ which enter into inequality (5.1). In our simple example, let us specify that the hormone H is in fact either present or absent by the time agents decide whether to eat the Mars Bar. The single-case probability of H will thus either be 0 or 1. But these aren't the numbers that causal theorists recommend for calculating (5.1). When they say that agents should weigh the difference A makes in H (and not-H), by the probability of H (and not-H) respectively, they mean (or anyway should mean, if you ask me) the *probability of H and not-H among people of the kind the agents know themselves to be*, the kind of objective probability that would be evidenced by statistical surveys of such people. (The same point applies to the conditional probabilities, of R on combinations of presence and absence of A and H, which appear in (5.1). While objective, these needn't be single-case. But perhaps this isn't so obvious. I shall comment on this point in footnote 10 below.)

[6] Given that causal decision theory recognizes probabilities which are objective but not single-case, I can now be more specific about the causal

6 Evidential Decision Theory

Not all theorists are persuaded that causal notions are needed to deal with Newcomb-like cases. An alternative line is advocated by 'evidential decisions theorists'. Evidential theorists, as I shall understand them, argue that we don't need anything more than the Relative Principle outlined above to account for rational action.[7]

These theorists stick to the simple recommendation we started

requirement to partition by 'other causes'. Does this requirement refer only to factors which agents know with *certainty* to be potentially relevant to A's impact on R, or does it include any factors about whose relevance agents have some *non-zero credence*? (Cf. Skyrms, 1980; Lewis, 1981: sect. 8; Hitchcock, 1996: 517–18.) From my point of view, there is no significant difference between these two versions. This is because I take it to be worthwhile for agents to 'spread their credence' over different hypotheses about causal structure only if these credences correspond to objective relative probabilities (such as, the objective relative probability that you have inherited one kind of blood group, say, or perhaps the objective probability, again relative to all your knowledge, of a certain kind of theory being right about a causal structure). While agents may well 'spread credences' over different hypotheses even when their credences don't match anything objective, I don't see that they gain anything thereby. So I can read the casual requirement simply: use a weighted average of the probabilistic difference A makes to R in all causally distinguishable circumstances with a non-zero probability, weighted by that non-zero probability, where all probabilities are objective probabilities relative to the agent's knowledge.

[7] In one way this is unfaithful to standard evidentialism, since most actual evidential theorists work with subjective degrees of belief, rather than my objective relative probabilities, as I pointed out in the last section. But this is orthogonal to the issue which interests me in this essay: can we manage with the Relative Principle alone, without appealing to causal partitions? This question arises both for those who set things up subjectively, like standard evidentialists, and for those who assume that even evidential theory should work with degrees of belief that correspond to objective relative probabilities, as I shall throughout this essay.

with—namely, act on the 'raw' correlation given by the simple comparison $P(R/A)$ versus $P(R/-A)$—and aim to deal with the counter-examples by devoting appropriate attention to a *requirement of total knowledge*.

Such a requirement underlies the Relative Principle, in that this Principle specifies that you should always act on the probabilities you assign to various results *given your total knowledge of your situation*. And this feature then offers evidential decision theorists a possible way of blocking the causally ineffective choice in Newcomb-like situations such as the Mars Bar example. They can argue that agents will always know something *extra* (K) about themselves, such that within K the spurious correlation between A and R will disappear. Within K, A will make no probabilistic difference to R—$P_K(R/A) = P_K(R/-A)$—and so the original simple recommendation, plus attention to the requirement of total knowledge, will suffice to stop agents acting stupidly. Evidential decision theory thus maintains that, if we attend carefully enough to the kind of self-knowledge K possessed by rational agents, it turns out that Beebee's and my Relative Principle is all we need, without any supplementation by causal partitioning.

By way of illustration, consider the Mars Bar example again. Suppose, for the sake of the argument, that you *knew* you had the hormone H (or that you didn't). Then, by the principle of total evidence, you should act on the probabilistic difference A makes to R within H (or within not-H). And since it is agreed on all sides that this is zero—once you know H (or not-H), knowing A doesn't make R any more probable—evidential decision theory thus avoids recommending that you eat the Mars Bar.

Tyros are often bemused at this point. Both causal and evidential decision theory seem to solve the Newcomb problem by pointing out that the spurious A-R correlation disappears when we partition by H. So what's the difference?

The crucial point is that evidential decision theory, but not causal decision theory, requires agents to *know which* cell of the partition they are in.

Causal decision theory allows agents to reason thus: '*Either* I have *H, or* I don't, and either way *A* won't make a difference to *R*.' This either-or reasoning doesn't require the agents to know whether they are in fact *H* or not-*H*. However, this kind of reasoning isn't allowed by evidential theory. This is because evidential theory wants to avoid using causal notions in explaining rational decisions, yet the either-or reasoning needs to partition by precisely those factors that make a *causal difference* to *R* but are themselves *causally independent* of *A*.

Because of this, evidential theory aims to avoid any either-or reasoning. Instead it simply tells agents to consider whether *A* makes *R* more likely among people *such as they know themselves to be*. Provided agents know that they are *H*, or not-*H*, or indeed are in any category where the *A-R* correlation disappears, then nothing more is needed to make them do the right thing than the simple cause-free recommendation to do *A* only if it makes *R* more likely. So evidential agents aren't reasoning either-or, but simply acting on what they definitely know about themselves.

7 *Evidential Motivations*

This strategy means that evidential decision theorists face an extra commitment. They need to show that rational people are always sufficiently self-aware to be able to place themselves in a category where any spurious *A–R* correlations disappear.

It is natural to ask why evidential theorists should wish to enter into this commitment. It is not obvious, to say the least, that rational agents will always know themselves to be in some category within which any spurious correlation between *A* and *R* will disappear. Moreover, causal decision theory seems to offer a straightforward alternative account of how, even so, sensible people can avoid acting stupidly—even if they don't know whether or not they are H, they can see that in either case A won't make any difference to R. What have evidentialists got against this eminently sensible 'either-or' reasoning?

The official answer is that this reasoning is implicitly causal (since it only works if we partition by other causes of R), and that it is preferable not to build such a metaphysically doubtful notion as causation into the theory of rational decision.

I have always found this answer puzzling. After all, evidential decision theorists typically take causal notions for granted when they analyse Newcomb-type counter-examples, even if they don't attribute causal thinking to their agents. Evidential *agents* may be able to avoid 'either-or' reasoning, but evidential *theorists* are standardly found arguing that sufficiently self-aware agents will *either* know themselves to be in some category where the hidden *cause* is present, *or* in a category where it is absent, and that either way these agents will know that they are in a category where A ceases to be correlated with R.

The notion of causation may not be fully understood by metaphysicians. But if it is good enough for evidential theorists, it is hard to see why it should be denied to rational agents.

Still, perhaps there is a better way of motivating evidential decision theory, albeit not one that is prominent in the literature.[8] Evidentialists shouldn't say that causal thinking is bad. Rather they should say that evidential thinking is better, since it can justify causal thinking, while not standing in need of any justification itself.

Note first how the evidential recommendation seems self-evident. Evidential theory simply recommends that agents perform those actions that make desired results *most probable*. This recommendation doesn't seem to need any further justifi-

---

[8] But see the discussion of Hitchcock in Section 10 below, and of 'one-boxing' in Section 15.

cation. Doesn't everybody want it to be probable that they will get what they want? (True, the desired results will be probable specifically in reference classes defined by rational agents' knowledge of themselves. But then there is arguably an independent warrant for wanting actions which makes desired results probable in this specific sense: according to the Relative Principle, it is just these probabilities which pick out rational decisions in contexts where Newcomb-like problems do not arise.)

By contrast, it is not at all self-evident why rational agents should act on *causes*. Suppose it is indeed granted, in line with both causal decision theory and pre-theoretical intuition, that you ought to do A in pursuit of R only to the extent that A *causes* R. Even so, it still seems reasonable to ask *why* it is a good idea to act on causes in this way. It doesn't look as if this ought to be a basic truth about rational decision. What's so good about causes, that they should be acted on? It would be nice if we could give some explanation of the wisdom of acting on causes, some account of what makes causes good to act on.

Now, evidential decision theory promises an answer to just this question. For, if evidentialism can be made to work, it will in effect show that agents who act on causes are *more likely* to get desired results than those who don't. After all, evidential decision theory (at least in what I shall call its 'orthodox' version) aims to legitimate just the same class of actions as its causal opposition. Yet it hopes to do so by showing those actions are the ones which make desired results *most probable*. This then offers an immediate explanation of why it is wise to act on causes. Those who act on causes are more likely to get desired results.

In short, if evidential decision theory is viable, then it will *justify* acting on causes, by showing that such actions make you into the kind of person who is *most likely* to enjoy desired results. This would make evidentialism preferable to causal decision theory, which can offer no such justification.

8 Evidentialism and Probabilistic Accounts of Causation

If we were able to give this kind of evidential justification of causal decision-making, it would commit us to certain assumptions about the connection between causes and correlations. In particular, it would require us to assume that genuine causal connections will correspond to A–R correlations that *don't* disappear when we condition on rational agents' knowledge of themselves. For these are precisely the cases where evidential decision theory advises doing A in pursuit of R, and thereby aims to *justify* the causal thought that such As should be performed because they *cause* Rs. Conversely, the evidentialist justification would require us to deny causal status to any correlations which *do* disappear when we condition on rational agents' knowledge of themselves.

This evidentialist explanatory project thus has an affinity with views which seek to illuminate the nature of causation by pointing to the 'robustness' or 'invariance' of correlations between causes and effects. Such theories contrast 'robust' causal correlations with the kinds of non-causal correlations which can be dissolved or 'screened-off' by conditioning on further factors.

It is worth emphasizing, however, that, while some such connection between causes and robust correlations will be implicated in any evidentialist attempt to explain why it is good to act on causes, not all theorists who are interested in such connections between causes and robust correlations need endorse this evidentialist explanatory project. A story connecting causes with robust correlations is *necessary* for the viability of the evidentialist explanation, but is certainly not sufficient. I emphasize this point because some recent thinkers (Hitchcock, Meek, and Glymour: see Sections 10 and 11 below) seem to me to move too quickly from a connection between causes and correlations to an endorsement of evidentialism.

To see why a story connecting causes with robust correlations is not sufficient for evidentialism, we need only remember that the evidentialist explanation of the wisdom of acting on causes is premised, after all, on the assumption that evidentialism can be made to work in the first place. That is, it assumes that, when we condition on agents' knowledge of themselves, the only A–R correlations that we will be left with are those where A really causes R. And there is plenty of room to doubt this, even on the part of those who see some essential link between causes and robust correlations.

I myself, for example, am very enthusiastic about such a link, even to the extent of hoping that causation can be *reduced* to suitably robust correlations (Papineau, 1989, 1993a). Here I go beyond most other theorists in this area, who aim only to *connect* causes with correlations, not reduce them to correlations. My hope is that we can reductively identify causes with correlations that are robust with respect to certain kinds of conditioning. However, even given this, I don't uphold evidential decision theory, nor therefore the evidential explanation of why it is good to act on causes. For I don't think causes can be identified with those correlations which are robust with respect to conditioning *on agents' knowledge of themselves*. On the contrary, I think that, even after we condition on agents' knowledge of themselves, we will be left with some correlations which are spuriously non-causal, and so ought not to be acted on. Further conditioning, by hidden causes that agents don't know about, will display this spuriousness, but not conditioning on agents' knowledge alone.

So I don't think there is any non-causal explanation of why it is good to act on causes. It may seem surprising that we can't justify causal decisions by showing that, in a non-causal sense, those who make such decisions are more likely to get good results. But that's how it is. That you should act on causes, even if it makes you less likely to succeed, is a basic fact about rationality. Here, as in other places, bedrock turns out to be nearer the surface than we expect.

But I am getting ahead of the argument. I haven't yet discussed in any detail the strategies by which evidential theorists seek to show that spurious *A–R* correlations can be made to disappear, nor *a fortiori* have I shown that these strategies won't work.

What is more, I have also been ignoring in this section a more extreme form of evidentialism, which is so attached to the idea that the best action is the one which makes desired results likely that it is prepared to deny that causally recommended actions are always right. I shall call this 'radical' (as opposed to 'orthodox') evidentialism. Radical evidentialists admit that sometimes, albeit rarely, conditioning on total knowledge won't yield the same choice as causal decision theory, and say that in such cases we ought *not* to act on causes.[9]

I shall address the defensibility of these different versions of evidentialism in Sections 12 to 15 below. But first it will be illuminating to look more closely at the line of thought which has seduced some recent theorists, like Meek and Glymour, and Hitchcock, into evidentialist attitudes.

9 'Other-Cause Independent' Agents

This line of thought hinges on the idea that agents whose choices are *probabilistically independent of the other causes* of desired results will never be led astray by acting in line with evidential recommendations. This is indeed true, as the following calculations will show. (Intuitively, the point is obvious enough. There is only a danger of action *A* being *spuriously* correlated with *R* if it is itself correlated with the other causes of *R*; if it's not so correlated with any other causes of *R*, then any probabilistic association between A and R must be genuinely causal.)

---

[9] This extreme evidentialism won't of course aim to explain why it is *always* good to act on causes, since it doesn't believe that it is. But it can still try to explain why it is *normally* good to act on causes, given that it is only in special cases that it takes causal recommendations to diverge from those which make desired results most likely. Cf. Section 15 below.

Recall inequality (5.1), which specified this causal requirement for action A:

(5.1) $[P(R/A\&H) - + [P(R/A\&-H) -$
$P(R/-A\&H)] \times P(H) \quad P(R/-A\&-H)] \times P(-H) > 0$

Compare this with the simple evidential requirement that the raw correlation $P(R/A) - P(R/-A) > 0$. Since elementary probability theory tells us that

$$P(R/A) = P(R/A\&H)P(H/A) + P(R/A\&-H)P(-H/A)$$

and

$$P(R/-A) = P(R/-A\&H)P(H/-A) + P(R/-A\&-H)P(-H/-A),$$

we can rewrite the evidential requirement as

(5.2) $[P(R/A\&H)P(H/A) - + [P(R/A\&-H)P(-H/A) -$
$P(R/-A\&H)P(H/-A)] \quad P(R/-A\&-H)P(-H/-A)] > 0.$

Comparing (5.1) with (5.2), it is obvious that the two recommendations will coincide as long as A and H are probabilistically independent, that is, if $P(H/A) = P(H/-A) = P(H)$, and $P(-H/A) = P(-H/-A) = P(-H)$.

It may be helpful briefly to consider (5.2) from the point of view of causal decision theory. Causal theorists will say that the 'raw correlation' in (5.2) weighs the difference A makes to R, in H and not-H respectively, by the 'wrong' factors—instead of using the unconditional $P(H)$ and $P(-H)$, it is in danger of 'confounding' any real difference A makes to R with the tendency for A to occur when the other cause H of R is present.

Still, this danger will be absent if A is *not* so probabilistically associated with any other causes of R. In such cases the 'raw correlation' will give us a measure which can be agreed on all sides to be appropriate for rational action.[10]

---

[10] Note that there is therefore no need for causal theory to require agents to partition by the presence or absence of other causes I which are *not* themselves correlated with the action A. While A may well make different probabilistic differences to R in combination with different such

Given this, it may seem attractive to reason as follows. Surely the choices of *genuinely rational* agents *are* independent of the other causes of desired results. Presumably genuinely rational agents can choose *freely*, can arrive at decisions in ways that are unconstrained by extraneous causal pressures. Maybe the choices of unthinking, non-deliberative agents are indeed contaminated by inappropriate influences. But surely we can expect genuine deliberators to choose in ways that are probabilitistically independent of the other causes of their desired results.

If this is right, then we will be able to run an evidential justification of causal decision-making, of the kind outlined in the previous two sections. Agents who reason in causal terms, using the

other causes I, the independence of such Is from A will mean that the raw correlation $P(R/A)$ versus $P(R/-A)$ will already automatically equal the weighted average of such differences, as required by causal decision theory. Some corollaries: (1) This is why I said in footnote 5 that the conditional probabilities $P(R/A\&H)$ etc. which enter into the causal theory's calculations need not correspond to single-case probabilities. For a sensible causal decision theory need only require agents to partition by other causes *which are themselves probabilistically correlated with A*. There may be further Is which make further differences to the probabilistic impact of A on R. But, as long as these Is are uncorrelated with A, we will still get the right answer even if we do not enter them explictly into the calculations. (2) This point also illuminates the logic of randomized trials. In a randomized trial the experimenter aims forcibly to decorrelate the treatment T from any other unknown causes I of the result R. Assuming this doesn't affect the unconditional probabilities of these other causes, the T–R correlation in the so-contrived distribution is thus guaranteed to measure the appropriately weighted average of the different causal differences T makes to R in combination with presences and absences of these other Is. (Cf. Papineau, 1993b.) (3) Some theorists of probabilistic causation insist that probabilistic causes should increase the chance of their effect in *every* context, not just on weighted average across all contexts. 'Average effect is a sorry excuse for a causal concept' (Eells, 1991: 113). I reply that (a) average effect is precisely the notion we need for decision-making, and (b) the vast majority of intuitive causal claims implicitly average across unknown but independent causes.

quantities involved in inequality (5.1), won't of course be led astray. But this is simply because the causal (5.1) gives the same answers as the evidential (5.2) will give for genuinely rational and therefore other-cause-independent agents. Agents who reason in causal terms can thus be confident of doing the right thing, since they are thus guaranteed to reach the same decisions as rational agents who reason evidentially.

It is crucial, however, to realize that this is not the only possible reaction to the coincidence of (5.1) and (5.2) for 'other-cause-independent' agents. Let it indeed be agreed that other-cause-independent agents don't need anything beyond evidential decision theory to reach the right decisions. This needn't mean that all rational agents *are* 'other-cause-independent'. It might simply reflect the fact that, *when* agents are 'other-cause-independent', then the 'raw correlations' in (5.2) are guaranteed to measure the *causal* influence of A on R as in (5.1). And so, in such cases, but not when agents aren't 'other-cause-independent', evidential theory will succeed in shadowing the correct recommendations of causal theory.

I shall eventually defend this second, causalist response to the coincidence of (5.1) and (5.2) for 'other-cause-independent' agents. And I shall adopt the obvious strategy, of seeking out agents who are *not* other-cause-independent to serve as test cases. That is, I shall aim to show that such agents do indeed exist, and that for them the right recommendation is the causal (5.1) rather than the evidential (5.2). Before coming to this, however, let me comment on the papers by Christopher Hitchcock (1996), and Christopher Meek and Clark Glymour (1994), both of which go the other way, and offer versions of the first, evidential response.

10 *Hitchcock and Fictional Evidentialism*

In his 'Causal Decision Theory and Decision-Theoretic Causation' (1996), Christopher Hitchcock begins by noting that standard probabilistic accounts of causation take the causal influence of a putative cause C on some putative effect E to be measured by the probability that C gives E *within* the cells of the partition created by presence and absence of other factors which are causally relevant to E. Hitchcock then asks why is *this* such an interesting relationship between C and E? What is so special about conditional probabilities within this 'elaborately constructed partition' (p. 509)? '[W]hy should we be so interested in the conditional distributions that obtain *relative to the c-partition* . . ., which is so baroque in its construction?' (p. 512; emphasis in original).

In order to answer this question, Hitchcock makes the assumption that causes are recipes for achieving results. C is a cause of E just in case it is advisable to do C (if you can) if you want E. As Hitchcock explains, this is to adopt a version of the 'manipulability' theory of causation. We aim to analyse causation in terms of rational choice, in terms of the rationality of adopting a means C in pursuit of some end E.

However, as Hitchcock immediately observes, this strategy would be unattractively circular if we need to appeal to a prior notion of causation in explaining rational choice. If the definition of a rational choice of means were simply that the means be apt to *cause* the desired result, then the manipulability theory of causation would take us round a small circle.

Hitchcock thinks we can break out of this circle with the help of evidential decision theory. This theory will tell us which actions are rational *without* assuming anything illegitimately causal. Rational actions are those which bear such-and-such probabilistic relationships to desired results. We can then use this, plus the manipulability theory of causation, to infer that *this* kind of probabilistic relationship is characteristic of causal relationships. This thus yields a non-circular answer to Hitchcock's original question, of why probabilistic theories of causation should focus on just those probabilistic relationships. In short, they do so because those relationships are good to act on.

Hitchcock is thus committed to a version of the evidential

explanation of why causes are good to act on, as outlined in Sections 7 and 8 above. True, he doesn't aim to explain the wisdom of acting on causes as such, but rather why probabilistic theories of causation pick out certain specific probabilistic relationships as causal. But since the answer he offers, via his manipulability thesis, is that these peculiar probabilistic relationships are evidentially good to act on, his overall story also commits him to the evidential explanation of the wisdom of acting on causes.

So far, Hitchcock's project is entirely cogent. Things go wrong, however, when he explains how he understands evidential decision theory. In his version, evidential theory does not make the recommendation that agents should act on the 'raw correlation' $P(R/A)$ – $P(R/A)$. Hitchcock does not deny that this correlation may be spurious in many cases, even after we have conditioned on the total knowledge of self-aware rational agents. And he accepts that when raw correlations are spurious in this way, they will be a bad guide to rational decision.

So instead Hitchcock reads evidential decision theory as recommending that you should act on the A–R correlation that *would* obtain under the assumption that you *were* other-cause-independent. He accepts that this assumption will be false for many agents. But even so, he suggests, rational agents can reason *as if* they were other-cause-independent, and consider whether A would still be correlated with R in the fictional distribution fixed by this assumption.

In effect, then, Hitchcock is advising agents to act on the comparison given by inequality (5.1) above, rather than the actual raw correlation (5.2). He wants them to hold fixed the dependency of R on A within H and not-H, but imagine away any correlation between A and H.

We can all agree that this recommendation will give the intuitively right answers. What is not clear, however, is why Hitchcock thinks it a version of evidential decision theory. I would say that it is just causal decision theory in disguise.

Suppose we ask Hitchcock *why* people should act on this

assumption, given that for many of them it will be an inaccurate 'fiction'. Causal decision theorists of course have an immediate answer. For them correlation (5.1) simply identifies the overall causal difference that A makes to R. The 'fictional correlations' are thus guaranteed to equal the weighted causal difference A makes to R given the presence and absence of other causes.

However, there is no corresponding evidential answer. If it is indeed a fiction that some agents are other-cause-independent, then why, according to evidential theory, should they choose as if they were? For such agents, the fictional correlations won't correspond to the raw correlations evidential theory favours. The fictional correlation will be a bad guide to how often the good result R accrues to agents who do A. If Hitchcock were really appealing to evidential thinking, then surely he ought to urge such agents to act on the spurious correlation (5.2), not the casual difference (5.1).

This shows that Hitchcock cannot give any non-causal rationale for acting on his version of 'evidential theory'. Once we ask *why* anybody should act under the *fiction* that they are other-cause-independent, the only available answer is that this comes to the same thing as acting on causes.

This is why I said Hitchcock's decision theory is really causal decision theory in disguise. And, given this, his overall project collapses. Since his explanation of the significance of the relevant probabilistic relationships must in the end be that they are the relationships to which we are directed by the recommendation to act on *causes*, he can't give any non-circular explanation for why probabilistic theories of causation focus on just those probabilistic relationships. (All he can say is that 'those probabilistic relationships are important because they mean that C causes E'.) This is disappointing, for Hitchcock's original question is certainly worth asking. But disappointment will be inevitable, if there is no non-causal explanation of why we should act on causes.[11]

---

[11] One further comment about Hitchcock. While the above criticism

11 Meek, Glymour, and 'Intervention'

Christoper Meek's and Clark Glymour's paper, 'Conditioning and Intervening' (1994), is motivated by research about the possibility of deriving causal claims from correlations. In a number of recent works (Glymour *et al.*, 1987; Spirtes *et al.*, 1993), Glymour and

undermines his own argument, there seems to me to be a less ambitious version of his thesis which can survive. Suppose we simply take the recommendation to act on (5.1) as primitive, without trying to explain *why* we should so act, and in particular without saying that this will ensure we act on causes. Then we could non-circularly answer Hitchcock's original question ('Why do probabilistic theories of causation focus on precisely *those* baroque relationships?') by observing that these are just the relationships on which we ought to act, as specified by (5.1). (True, we would still be implicitly requiring that the *H*s mentioned in (5.1) are *other causally relevant* factors, but this element of circularity, according to Hitchcock, is only partial, and in any case is already present in probabilistic theories of causation, and so not damning in an explanation of why those theories pick out the relationships they do (p. 518).) The reason Hitchcock does not settle for this less ambitious story is that he demands some further *rationale* for the recommendation (5.1) (pp. 518–19). However, the only available options, if do want such a further rationale, are (i) that the actions so recommended will be *evidentially correlated* with R, or (ii) that they will be apt to *cause* R. Hitchcock is hoping to get away with (i), but his talk of 'fictional correlations' means that he can only really give a further rationale via (ii) and a prior notion of cause. (Which then once more collapses his answer to his original question into the empty 'those probabilistic relationships are important because they mean that C causes E'.) So it seems to me Hitchcock would do well simply to drop his demand for a further rationale for (5.1). Then he could settle for the useful point that probabilistic theories of causation focus on just those probabilistic relationships which the *right* decision theory recommends acting on (and which, moreover, given his manipulability thesis, thereby qualify as causal). There would be no need to bring in evidential decision theory or 'fictional correlations' to make this point. (As before, there would still be the partial circularity arising from the 'right' decision theory's commitment to partitioning by other relevant *causes*, but, as I said, Hitchcock is happy to live with this.)

others have shown that survey-derived unconditional and conditional correlations between sets of variables will often determine directed causal connections between those variables (given a few plausible assumptions about the relationship between causes and correlations).

Some commentators have queried the practical significance of such findings. Can these causal conclusions be used as a basis for action? Do they tell us what will happen if we 'wiggle' one variable in order to influence another? Let us accept, for example, that we can use correlational data derived from surveys to infer existing causal connections between parental income, type of school, pre-school test scores, and school-leaving abilities. Does this tell us what will happen if the government tries to improve leaving abilities by changing which types of schools children attend, say?

To answer this question, Glymour and his associates have introduced the notion of an 'intervention' (Spirtes *et al.*, 1993; Meek and Glymour, 1994). They define an intervention as something which directly controls some 'manipulated' variable, in such a way as to render that manipulated variable probabilistically independent of all its other causes, while leaving the rest of the causal structure the same. For example, a government 'intervention' could fix the types of school children attend, independently of usual causes like parental income and pre-school test scores, while leaving constant the connection between school type itself and leaving abilities. Glymour then shows how initial causal conclusions derived from surveys can allow us to infer the difference such an intervention will make to any further effect of interest.

For example, suppose we want to know how much government manipulation of types of school attended would affect school-leaving abilities, based on our prior knowledge of the causal connections between these and other relevant variables. Glymour's solution is to look at the probabilistic association between school type and leaving abilities that *would* be found if school type *were* controlled by an 'intervention' in the above sense. The point here is that we don't want to make policy decisions on the basis of the 'raw correlation' between school type and leaving abilities in the original probability distribution. Instead we need to work out what that correlation *would* be in a new distribution that preserves the original conditional probabilities of each variable given its direct causes (and the unconditional probabilities of independently caused exogeneous variables), but decorrelates the manipulated variable from all variables that it doesn't itself affect. This will enable us to eliminate any element of the 'raw correlation' which doesn't reflect a genuine causal influence of school type on leaving abilities, but is due rather to prior probabilistic associations between school type and other causes of leaving abilities, such as parental income, or pre-school test scores.[12]

There are obvious connections between Glymour's analysis and our earlier discussion. In terms of our simple *A–R–H* example, his analysis implies that the influence of *A*, eating the Mars Bar, on *R*, sleeping well, should be measured by the difference used in inequality (5.1), that is, the correlation we *would* find between *A* and *R* if *A* *were* independent of the other cause of *R* (the hidden hormone, *H*). Correlatively, his analysis implies that it would be a mistake to measure the influence by the 'raw correlation' displayed in (5.2), since that will compound any genuine influence *A* may have on *R* with the tendency of *A* to be more common among people with the hidden hormone *H*.

However, as I pointed out in section 9, there are two ways to respond to the generally agreed superiority of (5.1) over (5.2) as a guide to action. One response—the first, evidential response—is to

---

[12] Of course, this kind of calculation assumes that the 'intervention' doesn't change any causal connections in addition to those directed into the manipulated variable. A government decision to eliminate private schools, for example, might make rich parents devote yet more resources to home tuition, and thereby *enhance* the direct influence of parental income on school-leaving abilities. In this kind of case Glymour's calculation will give the wrong answer.

say that genuinely rational choices *are* independent of other causes of desired results, and so (5.1) is simply the special case of (5.2) that applies to rational agents. The other response—the causal response—is simply to say that (5.1), but not (5.2), measures the *causal* influence of A on R, and so is the appropriate guide to action, even for rational agents who are not 'other-cause-independent'.

Though it is not immediately obvious, a careful reading of Meek and Glymour reveals that they are simply assuming that the first, evidential reading is the correct one. Thus, in discussing the fact that causal and evidential decision theories can in principle issue in different recommendations, they say:

The difference in the two recommendations does not turn on any difference in normative principles, but on a substantive difference about the causal processes at work in the context of decision making—the causal decision theorist thinks that when someone decides when to smoke, an intervention occurs, and the 'evidential theorist' thinks otherwise. (1994: 1009).

Meek and Glymour are here suggesting that the rationale for the recommendations of causal decision theory is the causal theorist's commitment to the 'other-cause-independence' of agents. This follows from the definition of the notion of an 'intervention'. Remember, an 'intervention' is something that decorrelates a manipulated variable (smoking, in the above quotation) from any other causes it may have. So Meek and Glymour are here taking it that causal recommendations are justified only in so far as the deliberations of rational agents actually render their actions independent of the other causes of desired results.

12 Actions and 'Interventions'

Let us now focus on the two competing responses to the comparison of (5.1) and (5.2). The evidential line, recall, was that the causal

(5.1) yields good advice simply because it is the special case of the evidential (5.2) for other-cause-independent agents, and rational agents *are* indeed generally other-cause-independent. The causal line, by contrast, was that the evidential (5.2) will indeed agree with the causal (5.1) for other-cause-independent agents; but rational agents are *not* generally other-cause-independent, and when they are not the evidential (II) will lead them astray.

The obvious way to decide this issue, as I signalled earlier, is to consider whether there are any rational agents who are not other-cause-independent (that is, whose actions are not in fact 'interventions' in the sense specified by Meek and Glymour). If there are indeed no such rational agents, then evidentialists will be able to stick to their story that the worth of acting on causes derives from the fact that causal choices will always coincide with evidentially recommended choices. But if some agents are *not* other-cause-independent, if some rational actions are *not* interventions in Meek's and Glymour's sense, then the recommendations of causal and evidential theory will diverge, and the only option left to evidential theory will be the radical step of insisting that it is sometimes right to act contra-causally, that is, on spurious correlations.

Is there really an issue about whether actions are 'interventions'? Surely, one might feel, it is just obvious that humans 'intervene' in nature when they act. But this isn't obvious at all, in the sense which matters for present purposes. The terminology of 'intervention' is very misleading here. In an everyday sense, it is indeed uncontentious that governments can act, or intervene, to standardize schools, and individuals can act, or intervene, to get Mars Bars into their stomachs. But this by no means shows that they can 'intervene' in Meek's and Glymour's sense. For Meek and Glymour define 'interventions' as requiring *other-cause-independence*, and it remains to be shown that agents who act or intervene in an everyday sense are indeed 'interveners' in this technical sense.[13]

---

[13] This conflation can be discerned in ch. 5 of Dan Hausman's *Causal*

In fact, it is quite obvious that many rational choices are *not* other-cause-independent, and so not 'interventions' in the relevant sense, at least when the *population at large* is our reference class. This simply reflects the fact that many choices can be positively influenced, in a rational way, by the presence of a factor which also exerts an independent influence on the desired result.

This in itself is not a problem for evidentialists generally, nor perhaps for Meek and Glymour,[14] since evidentialists do not generally regard the population at large as the appropriate reference class. As explained earlier, evidentialists appeal to the general principle that agents should always act on probabilities in the reference class defined by their total knowledge of their situation. And their contention is that within this narrower class agents will always be other-cause-independent, and their actions will thus in this sense qualify as 'interventions' once more.

13 The Tickle Defence

Let me explain these points more slowly. This is relatively familiar ground, but it will be worth laying things out clearly.

I earlier aired the thought that the choices of free, deliberative agents must *per se* be other-cause-independent. But this thought does not stand up, if it is intended to establish other-cause-independence in the population at large. Maybe an extreme kind of

Asymmetries (1998). Hausman is not concerned with the evidential-causal debate, but in discussing agency theories of causation he assumes without argument that all human actions are 'interventions' in the technical sense.

[14] Meek and Glymour don't say much about reference classes. Their one relevant remark is: 'We agree with "evidential" decision theories that nothing but an ordinary calculation of maximum expected utility is required; we agree with causal decision theorists that sometimes the relevant probabilities in the calculation are *not the obvious conditional probabilities*' (1994: 1015, emphasis added).

libertarian freedom would decorrelate agents entirely from any other causes of their desired results. But there is no reason whatsoever to suppose that all deliberative, rational agents must be free in this extreme libertarian sense.

Consider again the connection between types of school and school-leaving abilities, not this time from the perspective of government policy, but from the perspective of individual parents deciding whether or not to send their children to fee-paying schools in order to enhance their leaving abilities. Assume, as seems highly plausible, that while school type makes some difference to leaving abilities, the wealth of parents is *another* distinct cause of this result, because of the extra educational resources found in wealthy homes. Now note that, on average rich parents are more likely to send their children to fee-paying schools than poorer parents, for the obvious reason that they can better afford it.

These facts alone mean that choices to send children to fee-paying schools will *not* be other-cause-independent in the population at large. Such choices will obviously be more likely among rich people who can afford the fees, that is, more likely when another cause (parental wealth) of the desired result (high leaving abilities) is present. But this certainly does not mean that the choices of the rich (or poor) parents are undeliberative, constrained, or in any other intuitive sense irrational. For all that has been said so far, the parents can be fully informed, highly sensible, and entirely able to work out how best to get what they want. The only reason parental choice of school type is not other-cause-independent is that wealth both (*a*) exerts a distinct influence on leaving abilities and (*b*) makes it easier to pay school fees.

We can expect just this structure in many other cases where there are non-causal correlations between deliberate choices and desired results. The presence of some other cause of the desired result will increase the probability of the choice, and so create a spurious action–result correlation, via some route which does nothing at all to discredit the deliberations of the agents involved.

Now, as I pointed out above, this kind of spurious population correlation isn't necessarily a problem for careful evidentialists, for they still have the option of arguing that such spurious population correlations will always disappear in the reference classes appropriate to rational agents, that is, in the reference classes defined by agents' total knowledge. Once parents take into account what they know of their own characteristics, then any spurious school–ability correlation should be eliminated, just as the spurious Mars Bar–sleep correlation was supposed to disappear when anxious insomniacs conditioned on their self-knowledge.

Thus, presumably rich people will know that they are rich. So, if they are interested in how much a private school will help *their* children's leaving abilities, they should look at the correlation between these two factors *among rich children*, and choose on that basis. This should remove any spurious association due to the fact that wealth affects both school selection and attainment level, and leave the raw correlation in this new reference class as a true measure of the educational value of private schools.[15]

[15] Should I be saying that the action–result correlation is *spurious* in the school-abilities example? After all, I specified that private schools do exert *some* genuine influence on leaving abilities. But note that this causal influence will be *less* than is indicated by the raw correlation, since the raw correlation will also be inflated by the association between private school and parental wealth, which separately influences leaving abilities by influencing home resources. The raw school–ability correlation is thus *partly* spurious, even if not entirely spurious. In this connection, it is worth observing that it is specifically cases of partial spuriousness, rather than total spuriousness, that generate other-cause-independence among fully informed rational agents (since in cases of total spuriousness fully informed agents who know about the total spuriousness will have *no* reason to do A in pursuit of R, where in cases of partial spuriousness they will know the A–R correlation is merely overinflated and so still indicative of *some* causal influence). The focus on total spuriousness in the philosophical literature may have created the fallacious impression that other-cause-dependence, even in the population at large, always indicates some

The obvious gap in this argument is the assumption that agents will generally know whether or not they instantiate any common causes of prospective choices and desired results. Do rich people always know how much they are worth, or insomniacs whether they have the hidden hormone *H*?

The standard evidential response at this point is to appeal to 'tickles'. The above examples all share a structure in which the common cause creates a spurious action-result correlation *by influencing the motives of agents*. Wealth affects choice of school because it means you don't *mind* spending the fees so much. The hidden hormone gets you to eat the Mars Bar by making you *want* to eat it. So, provided agents know their own minds, argues 'the tickle defence', they are guaranteed to know something that will render them other-cause-independent and so stop them acting on spurious correlations. Maybe they won't know directly whether they have the original common cause or not, but they will know whether or not they have the psychological 'tickle' by which that cause influences decisions, and so will be able to appreciate that, among people who are like them in this respect, the prospective decision will now be other-cause-independent, and so can't be spuriously correlated with the desired result.

At this point the argument gets more intricate. A natural objection is that there is no obvious reason why rational agents need to be so perfectly self-knowing. David Lewis (1981) complains that

kind of deficiency on the part of decison-makers. Huw Price (1991: 166), for example, in arguing for evidential theory, suggests that other-cause-dependence cannot survive among people who realize that their only reason for action derives from a spurious correlation. This may be true with totally spurious correlations, but it doesn't hold for partially spurious ones: rich parents will remain more likely to choose private schools than poor parents, even after they realize that the raw correlation between school type and leaving abilities is rendered partially spurious by this other-cause-dependence.

decision theory ought also to guide agents who are unsure of their own motives. To which evidentialists have responded that agents surely cannot help but be aware of their motives in the kind of case at issue, since we are explicitly concerned with agents who are *choosing* actions which they *believe* to be correlated with *desired* results (Horwich, 1987: 183). A further question which has been discussed is whether awareness of belief and desires is guaranteed to yield reference classes which render subsequent choices other-cause-independent, given that you could know your beliefs and desires, yet, remain unsure, in complex cases, how they will lead you to decide (cf. Eells, 1982; Horwich, 1987). Huw Price (1991) offers some plausible abstract arguments, beyond that mentioned in footnote 15, for the thesis that rational agents contemplating acting on a correlation can't help but view themselves as other-cause-independent.

14 Compatibilist Unfreedom

I am not going to pursue this line of argument. This is because there is a quite different kind of case which shows clearly, contra evidentialism, that agents are *not* always other-cause-independent, even within the reference classes defined by everything they know about their reasoning, and that when they aren't other-cause-independent they should act causally, not evidentially.

So far we have been considering agents who are at least free in a compatibilist sense, even if not a libertarian sense. That is, we are supposing that their actions are entirely controlled by their motives and subsequent deliberations, even if those motives are in turn affected by other factors (including factors that may exert a distinct influence on the desired results).

But what about agents who are not free even in this compatibilist sense? In particular, what about agents whose actions are partly influenced by their motives and deliberations, but also partly influenced by some entirely non-psychological route, some route that quite by-passes their self-conscious reasoning?[16]

It is not hard to construct plausible cases of this kind. Suppose you are considering whether to have a cigarette, and are concerned, *inter alia*, to avoid getting lung cancer. Whether or not you have a cigarette is a chance function of two factors, whether you consciously decide to smoke, D, and the probabilistically independent presence of a certain psychologically undetectable addictive chemical, H, in your bloodstream. (Thus, for example, you're 99.9 per cent certain to smoke if you decide to, and have H; 95 per cent if you decide to, and lack H; still 40 per cent likely to smoke if you decide *not* to, yet have H; and 1 per cent if you decide not to, and don't have H.) Now suppose further that H causes lung cancer, quite separately from inducing people to smoke. Smoking itself, however, doesn't cause lung cancer. Among people with H, cancer is equally likely whether or not they smoke, and similarly among people without H. And suppose, finally, that you know all this.

Should you aim to smoke or not (assuming that you'd quite like a cigarette, very much don't want cancer, and don't care about anything else)? I say obviously you should smoke. You know that smoking doesn't cause cancer. What matters is whether you've got H or not.

However, there seems no good way for evidentialists to recommend smoking. Given the above specifications, there will be a raw correlation between smoking and cancer (since smoking provides some positive probabilistic evidence that you have H, and H causes cancer). Moreover, this correlation will remain, however much

[16] There are brief hints at this kind of case in Lewis (1981: 312) ('a partly rational agent may well [have] choices influenced by something besides his beliefs and desires') and Horwich (1987: 181) ('we could simply have stipulated that cancer be correlated with smoking . . . *regardless of the agent's inclinations*' (emphasis in original)). But neither develop these quoted suggestions. And Horwich claims that there are no actual such cases.

you narrow the reference class by reference to aspects of your reasoning. For, whatever decision you reach, your actually ending up smoking would still provide some extra evidence that you have H, and thus that you are likely to get cancer.

Can't evidentialists say that agents in this kind of situation are not *fully rational*, since their actions are influenced by non-psychological factors, and that it is therefore unsurprising that 'rational decision theory' does not explain what they should do? But this will not serve. Even agents who lack full compatibilist freedom are in need of advice about how to reach decisions. Whether or not we call such agents 'rational' is a red herring. Whatever we call them, there is a right and wrong way for them to reason, and a normative theory of correct decision-making ought to account for this.

Imagine you are actually facing the issue of whether or not to aim to smoke, knowing you are the kind of agent specified in the above smoking-H-cancer example. (This shouldn't be too hard for anybody with addictive inclinations, or with a tendency to weakness of will.) Of course, you know that your resolving to smoke, say, will not be decisive on whether you actually smoke, since it is just one factor, along with H, which influences whether you smoke or not. But still, your decision will still have *some* influence in whether or not you smoke. And, given this, you would still like to get this decision right. So you face a live issue, on which normative decision theory ought to advise you, about *which* smoking-cancer dependency ought to provide an input to your practical reasoning. Should you aim not to smoke, because cancer is commoner given smoking among people who share your known characteristics? Or should you aim to carry on smoking regardless, because you know this correlation is spurious, and that smoking won't cause you any harm. I say the latter answer is clearly right, even if it runs counter to evidentialism.

It might seem as if evidentialists could argue that in this example we ought to think of agents deciding whether to *aim to smoke*, rather than whether to *smoke*. After all, this 'basic action' is within the agents' control, rather than smoking *per se*. Moreover, and precisely because *aiming to smoke* is within the agent's control, this shift of focus will restore the standard evidential ability to mimic causal decision theory and deliver the intuitively right answers. In the above example, there won't be any spurious correlation between aiming to smoke and getting cancer to start with, since H only affects whether you smoke, not whether you aim to smoke. And if we complicate the example so that H does affect whether you aim to smoke, by somehow also affecting your motives, then the spurious correlation which results will disappear when you narrow the reference class with the help of your knowledge of your own practical reasoning, as per the standard 'tickle' argument.

This is a reasonable response. But now let me change the example slightly, so that you become compatibilist-unfree 'all the way down', with no 'basic action' fully under the control of your motives. Thus make the undetectable addictive chemical H more insidious. It doesn't just affect what you do, but what you *aim* to do. It surreptitiously and undetectably biases you towards the decision to aim to smoke. So now aiming to smoke is itself the outcome of a probabilistic process, influenced partly by H, and partly by your desire to avoid cancer and your belief about the dependency of cancer on smoking. Readers can fill in some numbers themselves if they wish. The point is that even in this example there will be a question about *which* cancer-smoking dependency ought to influence your decision about whether to aim to smoke. True, even this decision will now be affected probabilistically by H as well. But, taking this as given, should the mere belief that smoking is *correlated* with cancer also weigh probabilistically against aiming to smoke? Or should you only be less likely to aim to smoke when you believe that smoking actually *causes* cancer?

Once more, this seems a clear normative question, on which

agents of this kind could use some good advice. Maybe their decisions (even about whether to aim to smoke) are less under the
control of their beliefs and desires than those of fully rational
agents. But, still, these agents would like to know, just as much as
fully rational agents, *which* beliefs would provide the better inputs
to their decision processes. And here it seems clear that the causal
beliefs would be better, and that beliefs about correlations among
people who share their known characteristics would direct them to
choose badly. These agents may be in a sad state. But they aren't so
sad as to want a smoking-cancer correlation to influence them to
stop smoking even when they know full well this correlation is
spurious.

15 Biting the One-Boxing Bullet

The only option which seems left to evidentialists is to bite the
bullet and deny the causal intuitions. They can admit that there are
examples where the tickle defence doesn't work, and non-causal
correlations cannot be made to disappear. And they can allow that
in such cases it may initially seem as if agents ought not to be
swayed by these evidential connections. But they can argue that
we should distrust these initial intuitions, and should instead stand
by the principle that agents do best by acting so as to render
desired results likely.

   This was of course the line adopted by the 'one-boxers' in the
original discussion of Newcomb's paradox.[17] An even clearer case
is Paul Horwich, in his *Asymmetries in Time* (1987), where he insists
that there are indeed possible cases where no amount of conditioning on self-knowledge will make non-causal correlations disappear, and who maintains that in such cases agents ought still to

---

[17] Of course 'one-boxing' is interesting only when it is specified that
the choice does not (backwardly) cause what was placed in the opaque
box. All can agree that one-boxing is rational given backwards causation.

choose those actions which will render desired results non-causally most probable.

It is also the line adopted by Meek and Glymour in 'Conditioning and Intervening'. I explained above how, in their view, causal recommendations are justified just in case actions are 'intereventions', that is, other-cause-independent. The obvious corollary is that agents who are not other-cause-independent ought to act on 'raw correlations', even when this would violate causal recommendations.

Meek and Glymour explicitly embrace this corollary. Speaking about Teddy Seidenfeld's view that an agent in the orginal Newcomb paradox ought to act evidentially, and take one box rather than two, they say that 'Seidenfeld's judgement is fully in accord with [Glymour's and Meek's mathematical analysis]; were it stipulated with Seidenfeld that there is no intervention, his judgement is also that which causal decision theory ought to give' (1994: 1014). And a bit later they say that, in cases where evidentialists like Seidenfeld differ from the causalists, this: '. . . is because they differ about whether an action is an intervention . . . If so, then a different event must be conditioned on than if not, and a different calculation results' (p. 1015).

The implication is clear. If an action is *not* an 'intervention', then we 'must condition on' an event which *is* associated with the other causes of the desired result, and so act on spurious correlations.

It is difficult to accept the contra-causal line here being advocated by Meek and Glymour, along with Horwich and one-boxers generally. Surely it is wrong for agents to act on correlations that they know to be causally spurious. In my original example, I took it to be simply obvious that you shouldn't eat a Mars Bars just because this is spuriously correlated with sound sleep. Standard evidentialists responded by bringing in total knowledge, tickles, and so on. But now we are told that, when this story runs out, as in cases of compatibilist unfreedom, then agents should be influenced by spurious correlations after all. This still seems absurd. Surely there is no virtue in an action that can make no causal difference to the result you want.

Radical one-boxing evidentialism does have one last arrow in its quiver. Recall the motivation for evidentialism discussed in Section 7. Evidentialism appealed to the simple thought that you ought to render yourself the kind of person who is most likely to get good results. By contrast, causal decision seemed to offer no independent justification for acting on causes.

Radical evidentialists can hold onto this thought even in the hard cases where evidential and causal recommendations diverge. They will point out that in these cases causal theory actually advocates actions that make it *less* likely you will prosper. (In Newcomb's paradox, those who take two boxes will find there is nothing in the opaque box, where one-boxers get the million pounds.) Given this, they will argue, surely we ought to question the causal intuitions. If causal theorists are so smart, they can ask, how come they are so likely to stay poor?

Of course, evidentialists can allow, causal theory *normally* makes you rich, even if not in the hard cases of compatibilist unfreedom. Causal answers shadow evidential answers in the vast majority of cases. Given this, it is unsurprising that everyday intuition should favour causal choices. It is a good rule of thumb to trust causal theory. But it would be foolish, and unfaithful to the rationale for those intuitions, to stand by them even in those cases where they recommend actions that make you less likely to prosper, such as in cases of compatibilist unfreedom. Or so bullet-biting evidentialists can argue (cf. Horwich, 1987).

16 An Evolutionary Digression

Despite this line of argument, I think that evidentialism is wrong. In trying to get clear about these matters, and in particular about decisions which are unconsciously biased by other causes of desired results, I have found it helpful to think about evolutionary examples where conscious decisions are not at issue.

My thinking here is that the human decision-making mechanism is an adaptation, bequeathed to us by natural selection, to enable us to figure out in real time whether particular actions have the virtue that selectively advantageous traits have for non-decision-making organisms. Given this, we should be able to cast light on the adaptive purposes of our decision-making mechanisms by reflecting on the virtues of selectively advantageous traits in general.

More particularly, we can consider whether natural selection will favour traits that do not themselves cause reproductive success, but which happen to be correlated with other causes of such success. If such traits are favoured by natural selection, then this would argue for the rationality of evidential choices which are themselves inefficacious but are correlated with other causes of desired results. On the other hand, if intrinsically inefficacious biological traits aren't favoured by selection, then this would argue against the rationality of evidential choices.

At first sight it might seem as if natural selection will indeed favour traits as soon as they are correlated with other causes of reproductive success. Thus consider a case of genetic pleiotropy in which a single allele G is responsible for two phenotypic effects, A and H: let H be some hormone which makes a big positive difference to reproductive success, say, and A some mildly disadvantageous symptom of H, such as some distinctive colouring. The distinctive colouring A will then be favoured by natural selection, despite its being no help to reproduction itself, for it will increase its frequency in the population, carried along for the ride when G is selected over competing alleles.

However, this is not the model we need. In such cases of genetic pleiotropy, the connection between A and H is taken as given, and not itself alterable by selection. But we are interested in inefficacious actions *A* which are correlated with some efficacious *H* in some wider population, but whose correlation with *H* can be *reset* as a result of a rational decision. The right model for our purposes is thus an inefficacious biological trait *A* which happens to be systematically correlated with some efficacious trait *H* in the existing population, but whose connection to *H* can itself be *undone* by selection.

So now suppose *H* is produced by *G* as before, but let the mildly disadvantageous colouring *A* be the result of an *interaction* between H and some other gene *G'* at some unrelated locus. If *G'* is present, then *H* makes *A* likely, but not otherwise. Now, will natural selection favour the distinctive colouring *A*? I say not. The colouring doesn't aid reproduction. So natural selection will select against the colouring, despite the existing correlation between this colouring and reproductive success.

Why so?[18] Won't the proportion of organisms with the colouring *A* increase over the generations, precisely because these organisms reproduce more often than those without? But this will only happen if the colouring is *unalterably* tied to the hormone *H*, and this does not apply in our revised example. Now natural selection will operate on the following variations: *H*s with the colouring *A*, *H*s without the colouring *A*, not-*H*s with the colouring *A*, not-*H*s without the colouring *A*. Of these, the organisms without *A* will be favoured over those with, since they will lack the disadvantageous extra visibility. Maybe a simple partition by the presence or absence of the colouring *A* alone would suggest that organisms with *A* will be evolutionarily more successful. But this is the *wrong* kind of partition to appreciate the workings of natural selection in this kind of case. We need to partition by the presence and absence of the *other cause H*, and then ask whether the colouring *A* makes success more likely within *H*, or without it. To understand natural

[18] I would like to thank Jessica Brown for helpfully pressing me on this point.

selection, it is essential to think in causal terms. Natural selection is a causal process, and favours things which make a causal difference, and not mere symptoms.

I take this evolutionary parable to carry a moral for decision theory. As I said, I take the human decision-making mechanism to be an adaptation, whose purpose is to select actions with the virtues possessed by selectively advantageous traits in general. If this is right, then it follows that the purpose of human decisions is to pick actions A which make a *causal* difference to desired results R, not those which are merely correlated with them, in the way that the organism's colouring is correlated with reproductive success.[19]

17 Conclusion

This evolutionary point is by no means conclusive. After all, there is no direct route from biological purposes to normative conclusions. Just because some human trait has been *selected* to do X, it does not follow that it *ought* to be so used (cf. Essay 1, n. 5.) So, even if you agree that the *biological purpose* of human decision-making is to pick causally efficacious actions, you may still remain unconvinced that this is how human decisions *ought* to be made.

Because of this, I accept that committed evidentialists need not be moved by my evolutionary digression. They can simply concede that decision-making abilties may have been selected for

---

[19] Ian Ravenscroft has pointed out to me that natural selection could well favour decision-making mechanisms that respond to *any* correlations, whether causal or not. Two points. (1) Even if that were true, it would still be the *purpose* of such mechanisms to track causal connections (since that's when they would aid survival). (2) I suspect that in humans at least the ability to discriminate between genuine and spurious correlations does have some genetic underpinning. It is very striking how easy it is for humans to grasp the causal significance of 'screening-off' statistics, even before any formal training.

causal ends, and yet continue to maintain that rational human agents can do *better*, by acting evidentially. Wouldn't it be better to get rich, they can ask, whatever our decision-making dispositions may have been selected for?

Perhaps there is not much more to say at this point. I have no further argument to offer in favour of causal decision theory, at least not one that does not assume what it needs to prove. Here we reach bedrock.

But it will be helpful to conclude by articulating an explicit causal response to the question 'If you're so smart, how come you aren't rich?'

At first sight it might look as if this challenge gives the argumentative advantage to evidentialism. After all, it offers a principled basis for evidentialism, against which the causal side can offer only intuitions. But on analysis this challenge can be seen to beg the question just as much as any causal intuitions.

The underlying issue here is the status of the thought that rational agents should do what will make desired results most likely in the reference class defined by their total knowledge of themselves. (Equivalent formulations of this thought employed in this paper have been the 'Relative Principle', and the recommendation to act on the inequality (5.2).) So far I have not explicitly questioned my earlier suggestion that this evidential thought is self-justifying. 'What could be more obvious than that agents should make it the case that good results will probably ensue?' I asked earlier, contrasting this with the apparently unwarranted idea that agents should pick actions apt to 'cause' good results.

I hope it is now clear that causal theorists should have resisted this suggestion of self-justification from the start. The basic truth about rational decision, causal theorists should insist, is that you should always perform the action best suited to *causing* good results. There is no independent virtue in the principle that you should make good results *probable*. When this is true, it is true only because it is a special case of the causal recommendation.

It might initially have seemed self-evident that you should make desired results most likely in the reference class defined by your total knowledge of yourself (conform to the 'Relative Principle', act on inequality (5.2)). But far from being self-evident, this is often false, and only true when it happens to shadow the causal choice of that action which makes the most causal difference to the desired result, on weighted average over the different causal possibilities. In some special cases, the action so causally chosen will happen also to be one which will render desired results most probable in the total knowledge reference class. But this will only be because, in these special cases, the action which is best correlated with the result will also be the one which is best suited to causing the result.

Earlier in this essay, I aired the possibility of justifying causal decision recommendations evidentially, by showing how causally recommended actions would in general render desired results probable. We can now see that, from the causal point of view, this project had things exactly back to front. Rather, it is evidential decisions that need to be justified causally. Evidential recommended actions are acceptable, when they are, only in virtue of their being apt to cause desired results.

There is one element of evidential thinking that does need to be retained, namely, that highlighted by Beebee's and my 'Relative Principle'. In originally defending this Principle, our aim was not to side with evidential thinking against causal partitions (indeed we deliberately side-stepped this issue). Rather we were concerned to show that 'relative probabilities' (probabilities in the reference class K fixed by the agent's total knowledge) are fundamental to decision, as opposed to single-case probabilities. This point still stands. Causal decision theory still makes essential use of relative probabilities, in particular when it weighs the different possibilities which might make a difference to A's causal impact on R. As I pointed out at the end of Section 5, these probabilities—$P_K(H)$ and $P_K(-H)$—will standardly not be single-case probabilities, but rather the probabilities of an inhomogeneous K being an H or not-H. Moreover, the arguments which Beebee and I used in our earlier essay to show that such agent-relative probabilities cannot be eliminated from the logic of decision will carry over to causal contexts.

Still, once we do turn to causal contexts, there is no question but that the Relative Principle *per se* is inadequate. Rational decision theory has ineliminable need of relative probabilities, but it also has ineliminable need of causal influences. Agents must evaluate their choices using probabilities relative to their knowledge. But they must also focus on the probabilities, in this sense, of their actions having different *causal* influences on desired results, and not just the probabilities of finding those results when those actions are performed.

Sometimes, to repeat, the action which makes the result most likely won't be the one which exerts most causal influence on average across the different causal possibilities. One-boxing renders you more likely to be rich, even though it won't *cause* you to have more money. Even so, we should stand by the basic principle that you should do what will have the greatest causal impact, on relative-probability-weighted average across the different causal possibilities. Maybe this action won't make you rich. But even so, it's still the thing to do, for the bedrock reason that it has the greatest causal impact, on weighted average across the different causal possibilities. This might seem a funny place to find bedrock. But that's how it is. There isn't anything more to say. There is no further reason for choosing this action, beyond the fact that it will serve you best on weighted average across the different causal possibilities.

REFERENCES

Beebee, H., and Papineau, D. (1997), 'Probability as a Guide to Life', *Journal of Philosophy*, 94.

Eells, E. (1982), *Rational Decision and Causality* (Cambridge: Cambridge University Press).

—— (1991), *Probabilistic Causality* (Cambridge: Cambridge University Press).

Glymour, C., Scheines, R., Spirtes, P., and Kelly, K. (1987), *Discovering Causal Structure* (New York: Academic Press).

Hausman, D. (1998), *Causal Asymmetries* (Cambridge: Cambridge University Press).

Hitchcock, C. (1996), 'Causal Decision Theory and Decision-Theoretic Causation', *Nous*, 30.

Horwich, P. (1987), *Asymmetries in Time* (Cambridge, Mass.: MIT Press).

Jeffrey, R. (1983), *The Logic of Decision,* 2nd edn. (Chicago: University of Chicago Press).

Lewis, D. (1981), 'Causal Decision Theory', *Australasian Journal of Philosophy*, 59, reprinted in his *Philosophical Papers* (Oxford: Oxford University Press, 1986) (page references to this reprinting).

Meek, C., and Glymour, C. (1994), 'Conditioning and Intervening', *British Journal for the Philosophy of Science*, 45.

Nozick, R. (1969), 'Newcomb's Problem and Two Principles of Choice', in N. Rescher (ed.), *Essays in Honor of Carl G. Hempel* (Dordrecht: Reidel).

Papineau, D. (1989), 'Mixed, Pure and Spurious Probabilities and their Significance for a Reductionist Theory of Causation', in P. Kitcher and W. Salmon (eds.), *Minnesota Studies in the Philosophy of Science*, xiii (Minneapolis: Minnesota University Press).

—— (1993*a*) 'Can We Reduce Causes to Probabilities?' in D. Hull, M. Forbes, and K. Okruklik (eds.), *PSA 1992,* ii (East Lansing: Philosophy of Science Association).

—— (1993*b*) 'The Virtues of Randomization', *British Journal for the Philosophy of Science*, 44.

Price, H. (1991), 'Agency and Probabilistic Causality', *British Journal for the Philosophy of Science*, 42.

Skyrms, B. (1980), *Causal Necessity* (New Haven: Yale University Press).

Spirtes, P., Glymour, C., and Scheines, R. (1993), *Causation, Prediction and Search* (New York: Springer-Verlag).

6

Uncertain Decisions and the Many-Minds Interpretation of Quantum Mechanics

1 Introduction

Imagine you are faced with a quantum-mechanical device which will display either *H* or *T* ('heads', 'tails') when it is operated ('spun'). You know that the single-case probability, or *chance*, of *H* is 0.8, and the chance of *T* is 0.2. (I could have taken a biased coin, but I wanted to make it clear that we are dealing with chances.)

You are required to bet at evens (your £1 to your opponent's £1, winner take all) but have a choice of whether to back *H* or *T*. What should you do?

Back *H*, of course. The expected gain of this option is £0.60 ((0.8 × £1) + (0.2 × –£1)), whereas backing *T* has an expected gain of –£0.60 (i.e. an expected loss).

But *why* is this the right choice? This looks like a silly question. Haven't I just shown that backing *H* will probably make you money, whereas backing *T* will probably lose you money? But we need to go slowly here. Note that any normal person wants to *gain money*, not *probably* to gain money. After all, what good is the bet that will probably make you money, in those cases where the device displays *T* and you lose a pound? So, once more, why should you choose the option that will *probably* make you money?

Even if this question looks silly at first, it cuts very deep. In this essay I shall proceed as follows. In Section 2 I shall show that there is no good answer to my question, and that this is puzzling. In the following section I shall show there is no good answer to a related question, and that this is even more puzzling. I shall then describe the 'many-minds' interpretation of quantum mechanics, and show that my puzzles simply disappear if we accept the many-minds view. Where this leaves us I am not sure. The many-minds theory is so counter-intuitive that it is difficult to take seriously. But it does have independent motivation in the philosophy of physics. Given this, it is at least noteworthy that it also dissolves one of the most deep-seated and difficult conundrums in the philosophy of probability and action.

2 *Probabilities and Pay-Offs*

My initial question was: why should we do what will probably get us what we want? To help clarify this request for an explanation, compare the following two standards by which we might assess which of a range of options is prudentially the best (that is, the best way for you to get what you want).

(*A*) The prudentially best option is the one which will in fact yield the greatest gain. (Call such options 'best$_A$'.)

(*B*) The prudential best option is the one which maximizes your probabilistically expected gain.[1] (Call these options 'best$_B$'.)

[1] The expected gain of an action is the weighted average of the gain that the action will yield in each alternative possibility (such as *H* or *T*),

Now, there seems an obvious sense in which (A) gives us the fundamental sense of prudentially 'best'. From the point of view of your getting what you want, the action which in fact yields the greatest gain is surely the best.

Given this, we can understand my initial question as a request for an explanation of (B) in terms of (A). On the assumption that the best$_A$ actions are primitively best, can we find some sense in which best$_B$ actions are derivatively best?

The initial difficulty facing any answer is that there is no guarantee that any particular best$_B$ option will also be best$_A$. You bet on H, as this is certainly best$_B$. But this choice will not be best$_A$ in those improbable (but all too possible) cases where the device displays T. So, once more, what is the worth of best$_B$ choices, given that they won't always be best$_A$?

Some readers might wish to object here that we often have no alternative to best$_B$ choices. In cases like our original example, we don't know what is actually going to happen, but only the chances of the alternative outcomes. Given that practical choices in these cases *can't* be guided by (A), isn't it obvious that we should use (B) instead? If we don't know which action will actually succeed, how can we do better than choose the action that will most probably succeed?

But this response doesn't serve. It doesn't connect (B) with (A). We haven't yet been told why the action that will *probably* get us what we want is a good way of aiming at what we *actually* want. Let us grant that we need *some* strategy for choosing actions when we can't use (A). Still, what is so good about (B)? Why not instead opt for the action which *minimizes* the positive expected gain, rather than maximizes it? This action might still give you what you

weighted by the *chances* of those possibilities. In this essay I shall stick to examples where the chances of the alternative possibilities do not depend on the agent's choice, so as to by-pass the debate between causal and evidential decision theory.

want. Of course, it is less *likely* to do so than the best$_B$ action. But this last thought does not explain (*B*), so much as simply restate it.

Can't we offer a *long-run* justification for (*B*) in terms of (*A*)? Won't repeatedly choosing according to (*B*) in situations of uncertainty yield greater actual gain in the long run than any other strategy? However, there are two objections to this argument.

(1) First, choosing according to (*B*) *won't* necessarily lead to the greatest gain in any finite long run of repeated choices. Suppose you repeatedly back *H* in our earlier example. This won't be the most lucrative strategy if you suffer an unlucky sequence of mostly *T*s. In that case repeatedly backing *T* would have done better. (What about the *infinite* long run? Won't (*B*) be guaranteed to maximize gains in an *infinite* sequence of repeated choices? Maybe so, if you buy the frequency theory of probability, but this resort to infinity only adds weight to the second objection.)

(2) The truth of (*B*) seems quite independent of any long-run considerations (and *a fortiori* independent of infinite long-run considerations). Let us agree that there is some sense (yet to be pinned down) in which the best option for an uncertain agent is indeed the best$_B$ option that maximizes expected gain. The advisability of this option surely doesn't hinge on what gains similar choices may or may not bring in the future. Suppose I expect the world to end tomorrow. Or, more realistically, suppose that I am a shiftless character with little thought for the future. I want some money *now*, and who cares what tomorrow will bring. Surely I have just as much reason as anybody else to bet with the odds rather than against. From the point of view of my desire for money now, the right thing is clearly to back the 80 per cent *H*, and not the 20 per cent *T*. My lack of interest in future bets surely doesn't lessen the advisability of my backing *H* in this case.

It seems that, whichever way we turn it, we cannot derive (*B*) from (A). In recognizing this, I am merely following a long line of philosophers. At first sight, it seems that we ought to be able to explain why it is good to act on probabilities. But there is no question-begging way of showing that the option which will most probably succeed is a good way of aiming for what you actually want. So philosophers from Peirce (1924) to Putnam (1987) have felt compelled to conclude that principle (B) is a brute fact about rational choice, which lacks further explanation. We should stop asking *why* it is is right to act on probabilities. This is just what it means to choose rationally in conditions of uncertainty.

Perhaps we should learn to live with this. Our spade must reach bedrock somewhere. But I find it very odd that we should have two independent principles for assessing choices. True, this independence engenders no practical conflict. For, as I observed earlier, in situations of probabilistic uncertainty there is no possibility of using (A), and so we simply use (B) instead. Even so, (A) still *applies* to uncertain decisions, and seems to give the fundamental sense of the prudentially best option. So it seems very odd that we should actually make uncertain choices via some quite independent standard for assessing actions, namely (B).

I want to explore a different path. So far we have started with (A) and tried to explain (B). What if we start with (B) instead, and take it to be fundamental that the best actions are those that maximize expected gain? Can we then explain (A) in terms of (B)?

The immediate problem facing this strategy is that the $best_B$ action sometimes isn't $best_A$, as when backing H turns out badly because of an unlucky T. But let us put this difficulty to one side for the moment, and note that there is one respect in which the (B)-first strategy works better than the earlier (A)-first strategy. If we take (B) as basic, then we don't have to invoke any other principle to explain all the prudential choices we actually make.

This is because (A) is only a practical guide to action under conditions of certainty. But under conditions of certainty (A) is a special case of (B). When agents know which outcomes will occur, then the chances of those outcomes are already fixed as o or 1, and the best$_B$ choice which maximizes probabilistically expected gain is identical with the best$_A$ choice which in fact yields the greatest gain.

This doesn't work the other way round. When we took (A) to be basic, we could of course immediately account for rational choices made under conditions of certainty. But (A) didn't help at all with choices made under uncertainty. The best$_B$ choices that maximize probabilistically expected gains certainly aren't always special cases of the best$_A$ choices that actually get you what you want, nor is it clear how they relate to them. This was the basic problem facing the (A)-first strategy. So, when we started with (A), we were forced to invoke (B) as *another* primitive principle, to account for uncertain choices.

I think this gives us some reason to suspect that (B), rather than (A), encapsulates the primitive truth about prudentially best choices. If we start with (B) we have *one* principle that explains all our choices. Whereas, if we start with (A), we can explain choices made under certainty, but then have to invoke another unexplained principle to account for uncertain choices.

Still, what about (A)'s assessments of decisions made under uncertainty, as in our basic betting example? As I said, (B) clearly doesn't explain these assessments, since the best$_B$ choice can diverge from the best$_A$ choice in such cases. Maybe (A) is of no practical use in such cases, which is why (B) alone is able to explain all our practical choices. But (A) still *applies* in these cases, and tells us that the best$_B$ action isn't always the best$_A$ action.

Given this, has anything really been gained by 'starting' with (B)? We can say (B) gives us the 'fundamental' sense of 'best', if we like, but don't we still face the problem of explaining what's so good about best$_B$ actions, if they don't always give us what we want?

I agree that the underlying problem hasn't really gone away if we still accept that (A) applies to decisions made under uncertainty.

However, there is a more radical option. Suppose we just ditch (*A*) altogether. We simply deny that it is a virtue in an action that it yields what you want. The only virtue in an action is that it will *probably* yield what you want. If we do this, then we will have no problem of squaring one standard of goodness with another, for we will only have one standard of goodness left.

At first sight this option scarcely makes sense. Surely there is *some* sense in which the action which gives you the greatest gain is 'best'. What could it *mean* to deny this? At this stage I can only ask readers to give me the benefit of the doubt. In due course I shall describe a metaphysical picture which will make my radical suggestion comprehensible, indeed mandatory. But for the moment I only want to make the abstract point that, *if* we could somehow ditch (*A*), then there would be no remaining problem of squaring (*B*)-assessments with (*A*)-assessments, and moreover (*B*) alone would explain all our practical choices.

3 Single-Case and Knowledge-Relative Probabilities

I have just promised that in due course I will make good the counter-intuitive suggestion that the only standard of goodness for choices is that they will probably yield what you want, not that they will actually do so. In fact it's even worse than that.

So far I have been assuming that uncertain agents at least know the *chances* of relevant outcomes. This assumption was built into principle (*B*), in that I defined 'maximum expected gain' as the average of gains weighted by the chances of the relevant outcomes. However, if we focus on chances in this way, then there will be yet another species of prudential optimality we can't account for, a species of optimality which often guides agents who don't even know the chances. So in this section I am going to argue that it is not even principle (*B*) that should provide the sole standard of optimal choice, but an even more surprising principle (*C*).

An example will help readers to see where I am heading. Imagine a machine that makes two kinds of quantum-mechanical devices. When operated ('spun') each device displays either H or T. The first kind of device is H-biased, giving H a 0.9 chance and T a 0.1 chance, say. The other kind is T-biased, giving H a 0.3 chance and T a 0.7 chance. In addition, let us suppose that the machine that makes the devices itself proceeds on a quantum-mechanical basis, and that on any occasion there is a 0.6 chance of an H-biased device, and a 0.4 chance of a T-biased one.

Now imagine that you are faced with a particular device; you know it is from the machine, but have no indication of which kind it is. You are offered the same bet as before: £1 at evens, you to choose which result to back. What should you do?

Back H, obviously. There's a 0.66 probability of H (0.6 × 0.9 + 0.4 × 0.3), and so a 0.34 probability of T, which means that backing H offers an expected gain of £0.32, while backing T offers an expected loss of £0.32.

However, note that this choice is *not* necessarily optimal according to principle (*B*). Principle (*B*) works with *chances*, yet the 0.66 and 0.34 probabilities which entered into the above expected gain calculation are not chances. The chance of H is now either 0.9 or 0.3, depending on which kind of device you now have, not 0.66. Moreover, if the chance of H is 0.3 (you have a T-biased device), then backing H is not the best$_B$ option, but backing T.

What kind of probability is the 0.66 probability of H, if it is not a chance? It is what I shall call a 'knowledge-relative probability'. This is a probability in the sense: how often does H tend to occur in situations-like-the-one-you-now-know-yourself-to-be-in: for example, how often does H occur when you spin a device from the machine? (Note that while it is subjective *which* knowledge-relative probability bears on some particular choice, since this depends on the agent's current information, such probabilities are themselves objective: for example, it is independent of anybody's opinion that

H tends to be displayed in 66 per cent of the spins of devices from the machine.)[2]

This notion of knowledge-relative probability allows us to distinguish the following two principles for identifying prudentially optimal choices:

(B) The prudentially best option is the one which maximizes the *single-case* expected gain. (Call such options 'best$_B$'.)

(C) The prudentially best option is the one which maximizes the *knowledge-relative* expected gain.[3] (Call these 'best$_C$'.)

If we compare these two principles for assessing choices, analogies of all the arguments from the last section present themselves.

In our current example you do not know the single-case probability of H, but only the knowledge-relative probability. So you have no choice but to assess your options by principle (C). But from a God's eye point of view, so to speak, principle (B) still *applies* to your choice, and moreover it seems to deliver a more basic sense of best option. After all, what you *want* is surely the option which is best$_B$. You want to back H if you've got an H-biased device, but not if you've got the other kind. In practice, of course, you'll go for the best$_C$ option, and back H, for you don't know which option is best$_B$. But you would clearly *prefer* to be able to decide by applying standard (B) rather than standard (C).

Given this, it seems natural to try to justify principle (C) in terms of principle (B): we feel that we ought to be able to show, on

---

[2] Although it is convenient to introduce knowledge-relative probabilities with talk of how 'often' given results tend to occur in given kind of situations, I do not endorse any kind of frequentist reduction of these probabilities. I think the frequency theory of probability is hopeless, for familiar reasons (cf. Papineau, 1995: 243).

[3] By 'single-case expected gain' I simply mean 'probabilistically expected gain' defined in terms of chances as in footnote 1; 'knowledge-relative expected gain' can then be defined similarly, but with the alternative possibilities weighted by their knowledge-relative probabilities, rather than their chances.

the assumption that best$_B$ actions are primitively best, that best$_C$ options are in some sense derivatively best.

However, this can't be done. The initial hurdle is that the best$_C$ option simply isn't always best$_B$. (In our example, backing H won't always maximize single-case expectation.) Nor does it help to appeal to the long run. The best$_C$ choices are only guaranteed to maximize single-case expectation in the *infinite* long run (and even then only if you assume the frequency theory). Moreover, it seems wrong to argue that the rationality of *now* choosing the best$_C$ option depends on how similar choices will fare in future.

So, if we take (B) as basic, we seem forced to postulate (C) as an additional and underived principle which informs our choices in cases where we know the knowledge-relative but not the single-case probabilities. This is cogent, but odd. Principle (B) still applies in these cases, and seems to involve a more basic sense of prudential worth. Yet we decide how to act via a quite unconnected standard for assessing actions, namely (C).

What if we start with (C) instead of (B)? Obviously principle (C) can't explain *all B* assessments, for as I have just observed, the best$_C$ option isn't always best$_B$. But it does at least account for all the *B*-evaluations we make in cases where we *use* (B) to guide our actions. For we only use (B) when we know the single-case probabilities. And when we know the single-case probabilities (B) is a special case of (C): for example, if you know the single-case probability is 0.8, then you know that H happens in 80 per cent of cases-like-the-situation-you-know-yourself-to-be-in. (Note that principle (A) is therefore also a special case of (C) in all those cases where *it* informs practical choices; for we have already noted that it is a special case of (B) in those cases.)

So perhaps we ought to take (C) as basic, rather than (B) (or (A)). However, there remains the fact that when we *don't* know the single-case probabilities, and so must act on (C), rather than (B), the best$_C$ option isn't always the best$_B$. So isn't the underlying problem still there? What's so good about the best$_C$ option, if it is all too possible that this option doesn't maximize single-case expectation?

However, consider the radical step of ditching (*B*) altogether (along with (*A*)). Then principle (*C*) would be the *only* standard for assessing actions; the only sense in which an action can be good would be that it maximizes knowledge-relative expectation. This may make little sense as yet. But for the moment simply note that (*C*) by itself would still be able to explain all the practical choices we ever make. And there would be no further problem of squaring (*C*)-assessments with other standards for assessing choices, if we jettison the other standards.

In the next section I shall begin to sketch a metaphysical picture which will make this radical option comprehensible. But first it will be worth noting that, even if (*C*) is our only principle, we can still do a kind of justice to the thought that it is good to act on knowledge of the single-case probabilities, if you can. Suppose that, as before, you are faced with a device from the machine, but don't know which kind, and that you have the choice of backing *H* or *T* at evens. But now suppose that you have a third, further option, *W* (for 'wait-and-see'): you are allowed to find out which kind of device it is, at no cost (you can turn it over and see if it is marked '*h*-series' or '*t*-series', say), and then you can decide whether to back *H* or *T* at evens. Given this three-way choice, *W* is clearly the best option. Where backing *H* immediately offers an expected gain of £0.32, and backing *T* immediately offers an expected loss of £0.32, *W* offers an expected gain of £0.64. (To see this, note that there is a 0.6 probability that the device is '*h*-series', in which case you will then back *H* and expect to win £0.80; and a 0.4 probability it is '*t*-series', in which case you will back *T* and expect to win £0.40; the weighted average over the two possibilities shows that *W* offers an expected gain of £0.64.)

This result is quite general. An argument due to I. J. Good (following F. P. Ramsey) shows that the option of getting-more-free-information-and-then-betting-on-your-new-knowledge-relative-probabilities always offers at least as great an expectation as any immediate bet. The general result applies to the discovery of probabilities relative to *any* extra information, and not just to the discovery of single-case probabilities. But since finding out single-case probabilities is a special case of finding out new knowledge-relative probabilities, the result applies in these special cases too (as in the above example).

This Ramsey–Good result thus shows that it is always better to find out the single-case probabilities and act on them, if you can (and the extra information is free), rather than to act on merely knowledge-relative probabilities. You might be tempted at this point to read this result as an argument for reinstating (B). Doesn't the Ramsey–Good result show that the best choice is the one informed by the single-case probabilities? But I think we should resist this reading. (After all, we don't *want* to reinstate (B) alongside (C), since this would also reinstate the awkward divergence between many (C) assessments and (B) assessments.)

If we consider the matter carefully, we can see that the Ramsey–Good result is entirely consistent with the complete rejection of (B) in favour of (C). To see this, note that the Ramsey–Good result uses (C), not (B), to show that W is better than any immediate bet: for it shows that W is better *on average* across the 0.6 probable 'h-series' and 0.4 probable 't-series', and, since your device has already been made, these numbers are knowledge-relative probabilities, not chances. True, the proof also assumes that after you get the extra information you will bet in line with the single-case probabilities; but this too need only assume (C), since, once you know the single-case probabilities, then acting on them is a special case of conformity to (C).

I know it is hard to get one's head around the idea that the single-case probabilities are a better guide to action than knowledge-relative probabilities because allowing yourself so to be guided will maximize your *knowledge-relative* expected gain. Once more, I can only ask readers to bear with me. All will become clear in due course.

4 The Many-Minds Interpretation of Quantum Mechanics

In this section I want to explain how the philosophy of quantum mechanics gives us reason to adopt a view of reality which makes the rejection of (A) and (B) quite natural.

Within quantum mechanics any physical system, such as a moving electron, is characterized by a mathematical device called a state vector, or wave function. This function does not specify exact values for the position or velocity of the electron. Instead it specifies the probabilities that the electron will turn up with any of a number of different positions or velocities when the quantities are measured.

Quantum mechanics also contains an equation, called Schrödinger's equation, which specifies how the wave function of an electron will evolve smoothly and deterministically over time. This is analogous to the way Newton's laws of motion determine the evolution of a body's position and velocity over time. Except that, where Newton's laws deal with actual positions and velocities, the Schrödinger equation describes the evolution of *probabilities* of positions and velocities.

So quantum mechanics, as normally understood, needs to appeal to another kind of process, in order to turn probabilities into actualities. This second process is commonly known as the 'collapse of the wave function', and is supposed to occur when a measurement is made. So, for example, if the electron collides with a sensitive plate, and registers in a particular position, the probability for that position instantaneously jumps to one, and for all other positions to zero.

However, if you stop to think about it, this scarcely makes sense. What qualifies the collision with the plate as a 'measurement'? After all, the joint system of plate plus electron can itself be viewed as a large collection of microscopic particles. And as such the joint system will be characterized by a probabilistic wave function, which will then evolve smoothly in accord with Schrödinger's equation. From this perspective, there will then be no collapse into an actual position after all, but simply probabilities of the electron being in different places on the plate once more.

In practice, most physicists assume that a wave-collapsing measurement occurs whenever a big enough physical system is involved. But how big is big enough? It seems arbitrary to draw the line at any particular point. And even we did know where to draw it, we wouldn't have any principled physical explanation of why it should be drawn there.

This is the moral of 'Schrödinger's cat'. Imagine that some unfortunate cat is put in a chamber which will fill with poison if the electron registers on the left half of the plate, but not if the electron registers on the right half. Until the wave function collapses, reality remains undecided between the two possibilities, alive or dead. So when does reality decide? When the electron hits the plate? When the poison kills the cat? Or only when a human enters the room and sees if the cat is alive or dead? Nothing in quantum mechanics seems to tell us when or why the collapse occurs.

Some philosophers hold that quantum mechanics is incomplete, and that in addition to the quantities recognized by quantum mechanics there are various further 'hidden variables'. Hidden variables can avoid the problem of Schrödinger's cat, by implying that it is fixed from the start whether the cat will be alive or dead. However any hidden variable theory which is consistent with the experimental data (in particular with non-local correlations) will be in tension with special relativity, since it will require the transmission of influences across spacelike intervals.

There is another way. Suppose we take quantum mechanics to be complete, but deny that the wave function ever collapses. That is, reality never does decide between the live and dead options for Schrödinger's cat. The electron keeps positive probabilities both of being on the left and of being on the right of the plate, the cat keeps positive probabilities both of being alive and of being dead, and your brain keeps positive probabilities both of seeing the cat alive and seeing it dead.

At first sight this might seem to contradict our experience. When we look, we either see a live cat or a dead cat, not some combination of both. But we need to ask: what exactly *would* it be like to have a brain whose wave function evolved into a superposition of seeing a live cat and seeing a dead cat? There is no obvious reason to suppose that it would involve some kind of fuzzy experience, like seeing a superimposed photo of a live and dead cat. Instead, perhaps it would be like being two people, one of whom sees a dead cat, and the other a live cat.

This is the 'many minds' theory of quantum mechanics. According to this theory, when an intelligent being interacts with a complex quantum system, its brain acquires a corresponding complexity, each element of which then underpins a separate centre of consciousness. One aspect of your brain sees a live cat, another a dead cat.

Of course, if these two consciousnesses are both present in reality, we need some account of why there is no direct evidence for this. But the many-minds theory can explain this. There are possible experimental circumstances which would demonstrate that your brain is in a superposition of both live cat and dead cat perceptions. But with a system as complex as a human brain, these experiments are far too difficult to carry out. And this is why there is no direct evidence for the duality of your brain. Even though both elements are present in reality, it is too hard to arrange the precise experimental circumstances which would allow this to manifest itself.

The mathematical underpinnings of the many-minds theory were laid out by Hugh Everett (1957) nearly forty years ago. Everett's ideas have been characterized by a number of writers as a 'many worlds' theory. But this is not the best way to read Everett's suggestion. The idea that the world splits in quantum measurements creates as many problems as it solves. Apart from anything else, it still ascribes a special status to measurements. A better thought is that there is just one world, characterized by an evolving wave function, in which the only things that split are the minds involved in that wave function.

It is important to realize that there is nothing inherently dualistic about this many-minds theory. If you think that the minds are physical systems, as I do, then you can carry on thinking this on the Everett view of reality. The resulting position will maintain that reality is exhausted by the evolving wave function of the universe, but will point out in addition (as does conventional physicalism about the mind) that certain subsystems of this physical reality have the kind of complexity that constitutes mental experience.

Where the Everett view differs from conventional thought is simply in holding that there are many more physical systems with this kind of complexity than is normally supposed. When your brain interacts with a chancy set-up, like Schrödinger's cat, for example, it evolves into a number of consciousness-underpinning physical systems, rather than just one. The later systems will share memories with the earlier system (of walking over to the cat-box, opening it, etc.), but will have divergent memories thereafter (seeing it alive versus seeing it dead). An amoeba splitting into two provides a simple partial analogy. And in mental terms we can think of the earlier self as having a number of successors, none of whom is identical with the earlier self, but all of which are connected to it. (Derek Parfit's account of personal survival fits very well with the many-minds view. See Parfit, 1984.)

So reality contains a set of branching perspectives. In reality, all outcomes occur in any chancy situation. But a given conscious perspective only ever registers one such outcome. For any continuing conscious individual, therefore, the world seems to evolve normally. Cats turn out to be either alive or dead, coins land either heads or tails, and so on. But from a God's-eye point of view all the outcomes occur, since all the different perspectives are equally present in reality. Note that the entities that branch over time, or 'split', are systems-with-a-certain-perspective-on-reality, not reality itself, which can be seen as the evolving sum of those perspectives.

These remarks only scratch the surface of the many-minds interpretation. I have been largely following Michael Lockwood's elaboration of Everett's ideas (Lockwood, 1989). A variant many-minds theory has been developed by David Albert and Barry Loewer (1988, 1991); their version, however, requires a commitment to dualism, for what seem to me bad reasons (see Papineau, 1995). For further discussion of the many-minds interpretations approach, and of the differences between the Lockwood and Albert–Loewer approaches, see Lockwood *et al.* (1996).

5 Probabilities and Many Minds

I don't know how seriously we should take the many-minds theory. My aim in this essay is only to establish the hypothetical claim: *if* you accept the many-minds view, *then* the puzzles raised in Sections 2 and 3 go away.

First, however, I need to say something general about the many-minds view and probabilities. Consider the example we started with. You are faced with a quantum-mechanical device, with a chance of 0.8 for H and 0.2 for T. You can bet either way, at evens. So you back H.

On the many-minds view, once you discover the result (i.e. you interact with the quantum-mechanical device after it has been 'spun') you split into two successors, one who sees H and wins £1, and one who sees T and loses £1. The former outcome has a probability of 0.8, the latter a probability of 0.2.

The initial issue here is whether the many-minds theory is still entitled to view these numbers as *probabilities*. It is true that the quantum-mechanical formalism still imposes a 0.8–0.2 measure on the two outcomes. But in what sense can this be viewed as a *probability* measure, if both outcomes are sure to occur in reality? Isn't probability a measure of which outcome is most likely to *win* the competition to become real? And doesn't the many-minds view deny that there is any winner in this sense?

I have addressed this issue in another paper (Papineau, 1995). I argue there that the many-minds view is no less entitled than conventional thought to regard the relevant numbers as probabilities. Probability is a rather puzzling notion within the many-minds view. But it is just as puzzling, and for just the same reasons, within conventional thinking.

It is true that, according to the many-minds views, all alternative outcomes with non-zero probability will occur, whereas conventional thought says that just one will. But I argue that, while this is a real difference (indeed it is a restatement of the difference between the many-minds and conventional views), it is not a difference that matters to anything else we do or think with probability. So it is a weak reason for denying the many-minds theory the notion of probability: it does nothing to show that many-minds theory cannot treat the relevant measure as a probability in every other respect.

To see this, note that probability enters into our reasoning in two ways. (1) We infer probabilities from observed frequencies. (2) We use probabilities to inform our choices.

Let me take these in turn. The logic by which we infer probabilities from observed frequencies is not well understood. In practice, our normal strategy is to assume that the probability is close to the observed frequency, and to hope that we are not the victim of an unlucky sample. The many-minds theorist can recommend any thinker should do just the same. As to the justification for this strategy, the many-minds theory can observe that conventional thought offers no agreed rationale. Moreover, the alternatives on offer (Fisherian, Neyman-Pearsonian, Bayesian) are equally available within the many-minds approach.

Now take the relevance of probability to choice. Consider our original example once more. You might doubt whether the many-minds theory can explain why you should bet on H. If you are inevitably going to have a successor whose coin shows T and so loses £1, alongside the successor who sees H and so wins £1, then what's so good about betting on H? Wouldn't you achieve just the same pair of results (namely, both winning and losing £1) by betting on T?

But the many-minds theorist can simply say that it is a *primitive fact about rational choice* that the best action is the one that maximizes the probabilistically expected gain, that is, the weighted average of gains weighted by the chance of each outcome. Since H has a chance of 0.8 and T only 0.2, the expected gain of backing H is greater than that of backing T, which is why we should bet on H.

You might feel inclined to object to the many-minds theory plucking this 'primitive fact about rational choice' from thin air. But before you do, note that this primitive fact is nothing but principle (B) from Section 2 once more. And remember that, however we turned it in Section 2, we couldn't find any justification for principle (B) within conventional thought either. Along with Peirce and Putnam, we were forced to accept it as a 'primitive fact about rational choice'. It would scarcely be reasonable to deny this primitive fact about probability to the many-minds theory, while allowing it to conventional thought.

6 Puzzles Dissolved

I have just pointed out that the many-minds theory is *no worse* than conventional thought at explaining uncertain choice. I now want to show how the many-minds theory is *better* than conventional thought on this issue.

In Section 2 I argued that the really puzzling thing about principle (B) isn't just that it has to be taken as primitive. Rather it is that it is in tension with the further principle (A), according to which the best action *isn't* the one that will *probably* gain, but the one that *actually* will. This tension led me to observe that we would be better off if we could jettison (A), and explain all our choices by (B) alone.

In Section 3 I made the same points about the knowledge-relative principle (C) in relation to principle (B). Principle (C) is in tension with (B), since (B) says the best action maximizes single-case expectation, not knowledge-relative expectation. So I suggested that perhaps we should jettison (B) along with (A), and explain everything by (C) alone.

At that stage it seemed to make little sense to jettison (B) and (A). Surely it is advisable to bet with the single-case odds, and even better to get what you want. However, from the many-minds point of view it makes perfect sense to jettison (B) and (A).

My simple initial example illustrated the tension between (A) and (B). Given a 0.8 chance of H, then betting on H at evens is the best$_B$ option. But this option isn't best$_A$ (it doesn't actually gain anything) if you get outcome T.

However, note that the whole notion of the best$_A$ option, and hence the resulting tension, is premised on the assumption that the device will *either* display H, *or* T, but not both. After all, the best$_A$ option is H *if* the device displays H, and T *if* it displays T. On the many-minds view, however, the device will in due course display both results: H relative to the probability 0.8 successor, and T relative to the probability 0.2 successor. So the notion of the best$_A$ option disappears, and we are left with the single idea that the best option is simply the option which maximizes your gain over the two outcomes, weighing them by their chances—that is, the best$_B$ option. There is no further worry that this won't really be best, if you get the unlucky outcome rather than the more probable one, for we are no longer supposing that you will get just one of these.

Similarly with the more complicated example which illustrated the tension between (B) and (C). Given a 0.6 probability that your device is H-biased, you prefer the best$_C$ option of backing H. But what if your device is T-biased? Then backing H won't be best$_B$.

Again, this worry is premised on the thought that the device is either H-biased or T-biased but not both. After all, the best$_B$ option is H *if* the device is H-biased, and T *if* it is T-biased. On the many-minds view, however, the device is in a superposition of both biases: if you have a look, you will split into two sucessors, the 0.6 probability successor who sees 'h-series', and the 0.4 probability successor who sees 't-series'. So the notion of the best$_B$ option disappears, and the only sense left in which a choice can be best is the best$_C$ sense of maximizing gain over the two types of bias, weighed by their respective knowledge-relative probabilities. The thought that this choice won't really be best, if the actual bias is the less probable one, dissolves along with supposition that the device definitely has one bias rather than the other.

7 *The Source of the Puzzles*

On the conventional view of the world, the single-case probabilities (the chances) relevant to any choice themselves evolve over time. These probabilities are naturally thought of as the probabilities fixed at any time by all the facts that are determinate at that time. Consider once more the outcome H on a 'spin' from a device from the machine, to be performed at noon, say. On the conventional view, at any time before the machine manufactures the device, when the device's bias is not yet fixed, the chance of H is 0.66 (0.6 × 0.9 + 0.4 × 0.3). Once the device has been made, with an H-bias or a T-bias, the chance of H is either 0.9 or 0.3, depending on which bias the device actually has. And just after noon, and from then on, the chance of H is either 0 or 1.

In practice, however, any agent acts on the basis of his or her current knowledge-relative probabilities. These need not be equal to the putative single-case chances at the time of the decision, nor need they correspond to the putative eventual unique outcome. These potential divergences are the source of the puzzles we faced earlier. We feel that, if the current single-case probabilities, or the eventually realized outcome, diverge from the agent's knowledge-relative probabilities, then the agent's deliberations will be based on less than ideal information. In such cases, we feel, the knowledge-relative probabilities somehow *misestimate* the actuality of the relevant outcomes. And because of this, it strikes us that decisions based on merely knowledge-relative probabilities can go wrong, in the sense of failing to select those actions which are actually most appropriate to agents getting what they want. This was why we had such trouble explaining the worth of decisions based on knowledge-relative probabilities. Such decisions don't seem apt to select actions which will *actually* give agents what they want, nor do they have any other non-question-begging relation to actions with this latter virtue.

From the many-minds perspective, however, there is no sense in which knowledge-relative probabilities are in danger of misestimating the actuality of outcomes. Consider the choice faced by an agent who is asked to bet on H or T from a device made by the machine. If the agent doesn't yet know what bias this device has, the agent will attach a 'knowledge-relative probability' of 0.66 to H, and bet accordingly. Suppose the agent now examines the device, to ascertain the bias. The agent will now split into two successors, each with a probability measure corresponding to the chance of the bias observed: the 0.6 probable successor who observes 'h-series', and the 0.4 probable successor who observes 't-series'. So the overall probability of H is *still* 0.66, since the probability of H across both the 'h-series' and the 't-series' branches is the probability of H on each (0.9 and 0.3 respectively), weighted by the probability of each branch (0.6 versus 0.4): $(0.9 \times 0.6) + (0.4 \times 0.3) = 0.66$.

Moreover, the probability of H will remain 0.66 *even after the* device has 'spun' and produced a result. After the spin, reality will contain four branches, one with H and one with T for each of the two biases. The 'h-series' branch, which has probability 0.6, will have an H-continuation with probability 0.9, *and* a T-continuation with probability 0.1. Similarly, the 't-series' branch, which has 0.4 probability, will have two continuations, H with probability 0.7 *and* T with probability 0.3. So the overall probability of H, across all branches, will be the probability of H on each branch weighted by the probability of that branch, which is still 0.66, just as before: $(1 \times 0.9 \times 0.6) + (0 \times 0.1 \times 0.6) + (1 \times 0.3 \times 0.4) + (0 \times 0.7 \times 0.4) = 0.66$.

So, on the many-minds picture, there is no question of the future turning out to undermine the knowledge-relative probabilities on which an agent acts. Since the future will come to contain branches corresponding to all the possibilities left open by what the agent knows, the probability of desired outcomes, averaged across all those branches, each weighted by its probability, will remain constant over time. If the agent is right at time t_0 in holding that p is the probability of outcome O relative to known circumstances C, then the later unfolding of reality will never show that p in fact misestimated O's future actuality. O's degree of actuality, averaged across all actual branches in the agent's future, will remain p, if it was p in the first place. And this is why there is no difficulty, on the many-minds view, of squaring the worth of choices based on knowledge-relative probabilities with the more basic prudential aim of actually maximizing what you want. For once we realize that the actual future contains all possible outcomes, to a degree corresponding to their probabilities, then we can see that the best$_C$ option is indeed the choice which actually maximizes what you want, on weighted average over all future branches.

On the many-minds view, all that happens, as the future unfolds, is that reality evolves into a branching structure, not that the probabilities of future outcomes change. In particular, as occasions for the acquisition of information arise, agents will split into successors, each of whom experiences different results. From the perspective of each, it will seem that reality has resolved itself in a certain dimension, and condemned certain prior possibilities to non-actuality: you examine the device, and it shows itself to be '*h*-series', say, and *not* '*t*-series'; the device spins, and you see that the outcome is *H*, say, and *not T*. However, this apparent sloughing off of possibilities is an illusion, fostered by the mistaken belief that your own branch of reality is the only one. From the objective perspective of the whole of reality, all branches are there, and outcomes retain the same probability that they always had.

The many-minds picture does not deny that it is rational for agents to delay acting until they have acquired relevant information about the future. It would still be worth finding out the bias, or even the actual result, before betting, if anybody were generous enough to leave the bet open that long. The many-minds view agrees with conventional thought that, other things being equal, it is better to get more information before acting. But from the many-minds point of view the advantage of waiting-and-seeing isn't that you will then be able to bet in line with the *uniquely real* single-case odds (0.9 or 0.3, 1 or 0), as opposed to the *various possible* single-case odds your limited information doesn't decide between. Rather it is that you will better be able to maximize your expected gain *over all the possibilities* if you can delay acting until after you 'branch', and thereby allow your successors each to choose the option that will maximize the expected gain within their own specific future.

So, for example, if you can turn the device over before betting, your '*H*-bias successor' will choose *H*, with expected gain of £0.80, and your '*T*-bias successor' will choose T, with expected gain of £0.40, and the weighted average over your two successors is thus £0.64, rather than the £0.32 offered by backing *H* immediately. The point is that your successors will do better overall if they are allowed to choose different options according to their individual circumstances, rather than your picking one option on behalf of all. Even more obviously, if you can wait to see the final result before betting, then your 'H successors' can bet on H, and your 'T successors' can bet on T, guaranteeing a gain of £1.

This is just the Ramsey–Good result again. But note how it now makes much more sense than it did in Section 3. At that stage it seemed odd to *justify* waiting-and-seeing in terms of its maximizing *knowledge-relative* expectation. (Isn't waiting-and-seeing better simply because it allows you to choose according to whichever of the possible single-case probabilities is *real*?) But from the many-minds point of view all the possibilities are real, and the point of waiting-and-seeing is indeed that it maximizes expected gain across all possibilities weighted by their knowledge-relative probabilities.

This now makes it clear why the many-minds perspective has no need, indeed no room, for any standard for assessing choices apart from principle (C). Any agent will do best for itself and its successors if it acts so as to maximize probabilistically expected gain across all the possibilities in its future with non-zero knowledge-relative probability—that is, if it conforms to principle (C). The only sense in which limited knowledge can be bad is that sometimes the best action is to *defer action*. Agents sometimes do best$_C$ by first 'splitting', and then allowing their successors to choose individually—but then these successors simply choose according to principle (C) in their turn.

So far in this section I have presented the initial knowledge-relative probabilities of our agent (0.66 for H, 0.34 for T) as impartial branch-independent quantities which do not change over time. But of course, relative to some yet earlier self, these quantities themselves will be updated probabilities for H and T, adopted by one particular successor among others, as a result of this successor 'renormalizing' when its branch resolves itself in some specific way along some chancy dimension.

I have been able to ignore this point because the probabilities that matter to any given agent are always the probabilities relative to the knowledge it has already acquired. I have been concerned to show that a proper appreciation of the rationality of choices made under probabilistic uncertainty requires that we view these initial knowledge-relative probabilities as stable over time from an objective point of view, even though they 'factor' into different components as the relevant agent 'splits' into multiple successors. (The initial knowledge-relative probabilities are stable over time in the sense that their weighted average *over all the agent's successors at any time* will always equal their initial value. In general, if R is the outcome of interest, and K_i ($i = 1, \ldots, n$) are the possible results of an agent's acquiring more information, then the agent's original probability for R, $Pr(R)$, will factor according to the equation $Pr(R) = \Sigma_i \ Pr(R/K_i)P(K_i)$. This weighted average will always yield the same value, if summed across all successors at any given time.)[4]

It is consistent with this central point that any given agent's initial knowledge-relative probabilities will themselves be the upshot of earlier factorings. Just as any given agent will have many successors, among whom its probabilities factor, so will that agent be one among many successors, and so its probabilities will be the upshot of earlier factorings.

In this essay I have tried to show how the many-minds theory makes better sense of decisions made under probabilistic uncertainty than conventional thought. Let me conclude by briefly noting that my remarks also point to two further ways in which the many-minds theory promises a philosophical advantage. First, it offers an obvious explanation for probabilistic *conditionalization*, in that it simply falls out of the metaphysics and our basic principle (C) that agents ought to set their new probabilities for R equal their old $Pr(R/K_i)$ when they discover K_i. Conventional approaches to probability and decision have difficulty accounting for conditionalization.

---

[4] We should of course allow that some 'successors' might be dead; these successors can be thought of as acquiring just this unfortunate information.

Secondly, the many-minds view implies that the overall objective probability of any given result *does not change over time*, since all 'branches' exist and the weighted sum of any Pr(R) over all branches remains constant. It is a demerit in conventional thought that it takes a fundamental physical quantity like objective probability to evolve asymmetrically over time, characteristically changing from intermediate values to a permanent value of either 1 or 0 as time progresses from past to future. However, these are topics for two further papers.[5]

REFERENCES

Albert, D. and Loewer, B. (1988), 'Interpreting the Many Worlds Interpretation', *Synthese*, 77.

—— —— (1991), 'The Measurement Problem: Some "Solutions" ', *Synthese*, 86.

Everett, H. (1957), ' "Relative State" Formulation of Quantum Mechanics', *Review of Modern Physics*, 29.

Good, I. J. (1967), 'On the Principle of Total Evidence', *British Journal for the Philosophy of Science*, 18.

Lockwood, M. (1989), *Mind, Brain and Quantum* (Oxford: Basil Blackwell).

—— with Brown, H., Butterfield, J., Deutsch, D., Loewer, B., Papineau, D., and Saunders, S. (1996), 'Symposium on "Many-Minds" Interpretations of Quantum Mechanics', *British Journal for the Philosophy of Science*, 47.

Parfit, D. (1984), *Reasons and Persons* (Oxford: Oxford Unversity Press).

Papineau, D. (1995), 'Probabilities and the Many-Minds Interpretation of Quantum Mechanics', *Analysis*, 55.

Peirce, C. S. (1924), 'The Doctrine of Chances', in M. R. Cohen (ed.), *Chance, Love and Logic* (New York: Harcourt).

[5] I would like to thank Helen Beebee, Scott Sturgeon, and the members of the King's College London Philosophy Department for help with the ideas in this essay.

Putnam, H. (1987), *The Many Faces of Realism* (La Salle: Open Court).

Ramsey, F. P. (1990), 'Weight or the Value of Knowledge', *British Journal for the Philosophy of Science*, 41.

INDEX